# CONSTRUCTION MANUAL:

# FINISH CARPENTRY

## BY T. W. LOVE

# CRAFTSMAN
### Craftsman Book Company of America
542 Stevens Avenue   Solana Beach,  California 92075

Library of Congress Cataloging in Publication Data

Love, T        W
      Construction manual.

      1. Carpentry--Handbooks, manuals, etc. 2. Wood-
work--Handbooks, manuals, etc. I. Title. II.   Title:
Finish Carpentry.
TH5604.L59          694'.6          74-12339
ISBN  0-910460-08-6

# CONTENTS

# Chapter 1

# CORNICES AND RAKES

In most cases the cornice or rake is the first exterior trim to be installed on a frame house. This is because the cornice or rake is more conveniently installed before the roof covering is placed. The cornice of a building is where the lower edge of the roof meets the wall line. This section is also referred to as the eaves and is built up of several plain or moulded members. The rake is the point where the wall and the gable roof extension meet. See figure 1-1.

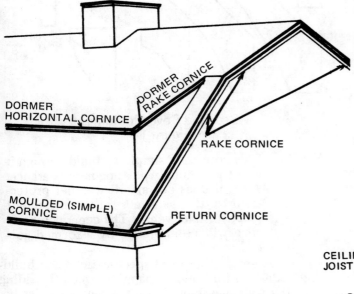

Position And Kinds Of Cornice
Figure 1-1

The design and types of cornices depend in most cases upon the architectural style of the building. Because of this, there is no standard type of cornice that may be used as a model. Cornices may be classified into two main divisions. The open cornice consists of exposed rafter tails and the closed type has the rafter tails enclosed. These two main divisions may be further subdivided into many sizes and shapes according to the cost, number of members, and decorative features.

In some cases the cornice is continuous around the building. It may also extend along two sides of the building and be returned a short distance around the ends of the building. This is called a return cornice (figure 1-1). The cornice may also

be extended up the slope of the roof at the intersection of the wall and the roof line. This section is called the rake cornice (figure 1-1). A cornice is also required on the dormer as in figure 1-1 and is called the dormer horizontal cornice and the dormer rake cornice.

A cornice provides a means of decorating the section where the roof and walls of a building meet. The cornice is often used to carry out the roof lines so that they are in keeping with the general style of the building. A projecting cornice protects the wall of the building by shedding water away from the wall surface and by providing a surface upon which gutters may be installed to carry the drainage to a downspout.

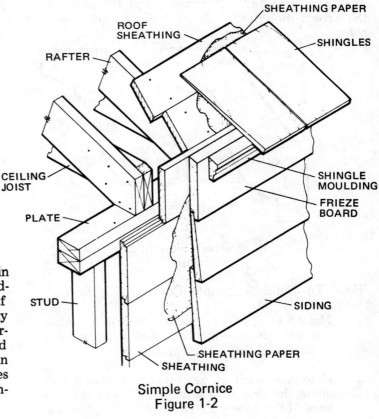

Simple Cornice
Figure 1-2

## The Simple Cornice

A roof with no rafter overhang usually has a simple cornice as shown in figure 1-2. This cornice consists of a single strip called a frieze. The frieze is beveled on the upper edge to fit close under the overhang of the eaves and rabbeted on the lower edge to overlap the upper edge of the top course of siding. A crown or shingle moulding is used to give the eave line a finished appearance. This moulding is a narrow strip of wood shaped into a depressed or extended surface. It is used for decorating flat surfaces and for internal and external corners. Although there are a large number of mouldings, only the common types will be considered here. These mouldings are standardized as to shape and dimensions and each has an identifying number which makes possible the perfect matching of mouldings in repair work. It also simplifies the grouping of mouldings so as to carry out desirable architectural lines in cornice construction. Crown mouldings are manufactured in two general shapes. This type of moulding is generally used on a cornice at the fascia and roof line. One size is shown in figure 1-3. The dimensions are taken along the major and minor axes of the moulding. The numbers are symbols for the identification of the moulding when ordering standardized stock. Standard sizes of crown moulding along the major axis run from 1 5/8 inches to 4½ inches. Bed and cove mouldings are sometimes used instead of, or in combination with crown mouldings. Examples of several shapes and sizes are shown in figure 1-4. They are identified and dimensioned the same as the crown mouldings. Additional sizes are available.

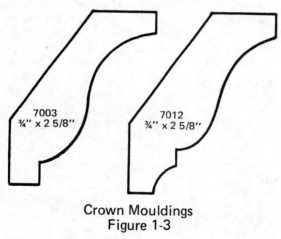

Crown Mouldings
Figure 1-3

## How To Build A Simple Cornice (Figure 1-2)

1. Make a templet with a piece of crown moulding and frieze about 6 inches long to show a section of the assembled members.

2. Hold the templet against the building and along the side of a rafter tail. Keep the top edge of the crown moulding flush with the top surface of the roof boards.

3. Mark the tail rafter of one end of the building at the back side of the crown moulding. This line will give the angle at which the rafter tail is to be cut.

4. Mark the bottom edge of the frieze on the building. This point will give the position in which the frieze is to be nailed.

5. Mark the tails of the rafters and the sheathing in the same manner at the other end of the building.

6. Snap a chalk line connecting these marks and cut the rafter tails accordingly.

7. Secure the frieze and crown moulding in position.

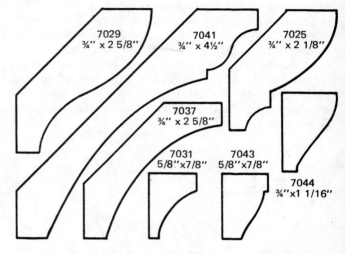

Bed And Cove Mouldings
Figure 1-4

*NOTE:* This cornice is simple to build though it is not particularly pleasing in appearance. Also, it does not afford weather protection to the sidewalls or a convenient place for inlet vents. The general appearance will be improved by a formed gutter.

Remember that most specifications and building codes call for building paper between the siding and the wall sheathing to form a vapor barrier between the interior and exterior of the structure. Building paper is applied horizontally beginning at the lower part of the wall and working upward with at least a 4 inch overlap. Before the cornice can be built, the top course of building paper must be in place over the sheathing. For open and closed cornices the paper must be fit around the rafters. The cornice and rake sections of the roof are often protected by a metal edging which forms a desirable drip edge at the rake and prevents rain from entering behind the shingles. See figure 1-5.

At the eave line, a similar metal edging may be used to advantage (figure 1-6). This edging, with the addition of a roll roof flashing will aid in resisting water entry from ice dams. They form a good drip edge and prevent or minimize the chance of rain being blown back under the shingles. This type of drip edge is desirable whether or not a gutter is used.

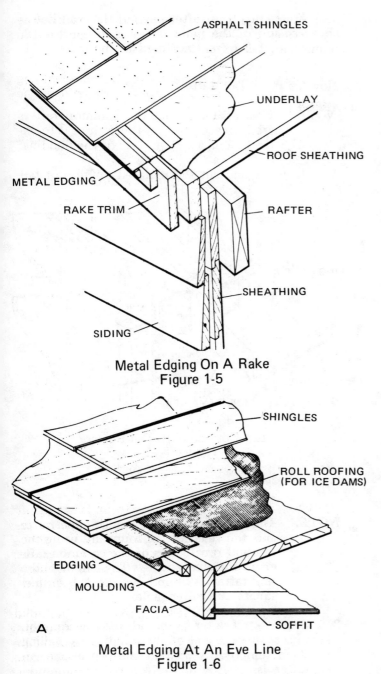

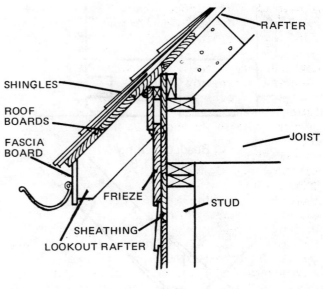

ASPHALT SHINGLES

UNDERLAY

ROOF SHEATHING

METAL EDGING

RAKE TRIM

RAFTER

SHEATHING

SIDING

Metal Edging On A Rake
Figure 1-5

SHINGLES

ROLL ROOFING
(FOR ICE DAMS)

EDGING

MOULDING

FACIA

SOFFIT

A

Metal Edging At An Eve Line
Figure 1-6

RAFTER

SHINGLES
ROOF
BOARDS
FASCIA
BOARD

JOIST

FRIEZE

STUD

SHEATHING
LOOKOUT RAFTER

Open Cornice
Figure 1-7

## The Open Cornice

Figure 1-7 shows a section of an open cornice. The lookout rafters are made of dressed stock, generally the size of the common rafter. They should extend approximately the same distance above the plate that they project beyond the building line so that they may be firmly spiked to the sides of the common rafters. The part of the lookout rafter that is exposed to view is, in many cases, cut to some ornamental curve at the bottom and to a plumb cut at its end so as to provide a surface on which a hanging gutter may be attached. A fascia board is sometimes nailed to the plumb cut of the rafters to form a solid base for the gutter.

The lookout rafters sometimes extend beyond the building as much as 3 feet and are supported by being spiked to the sides of the common rafters. The roof boards nailed to the top of the exposed lookout rafters are generally dressed beaded ceiling stock of the same thickness as the rough roof boards of the upper roof surfaces. This provides a finished appearance to the under side of the cornice between the rafters. Beaded ceiling stock is manufactured in many thicknesses and widths but usually has a cross section appearance similar to figure 1-8.

A wide frieze board is placed as shown in figure 1-7. A narrower frieze board extends from the top of the wide frieze up to the bottom of the roof boards between the lookout rafters. A moulding may be placed at the joint of these two frieze boards. A moulding would also be placed between the upper frieze and the roof boards.

The lookout rafters are sometimes fastened to the common rafters in such a way as to form a sweep to the roof at the cornice. See figure 1-9. This is done where the bottom end of the lookout rafter would be too low if it were continued in the same plane as the common rafter of the building. It also gives the roof a pleasing appearance and adds a low broad effect to the building.

In climates where snow may accumulate during winter months the open cornice can present a serious problem. If the building is not adequately insulated the heat that escapes through the roof above the wall line in the winter months melts the snow. The water then drains from the roof surface until it reaches the section of the roof beyond the building line. This outer section of the roof is exposed on the underside to cold winds. This causes the draining water to freeze on this surface and in

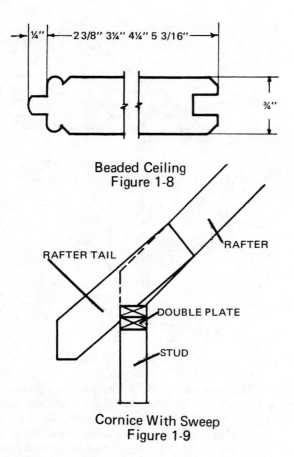

¼″ — 2 3/8″ 3¼″ 4¼″ 5 3/16″

¾″

Beaded Ceiling
Figure 1-8

RAFTER TAIL

RAFTER

DOUBLE PLATE

STUD

Cornice With Sweep
Figure 1-9

the hanging gutter. The accumulating ice at this section of the roof causes the water to back up underneath the shingles to a point above the building line where it seeps into the building. This decided disadvantage of the large overhanging open cornice together with the extra labor of installation and the costly upkeep have tended to make this type of open cornice obsolete in the northern part of the United States. When the roof is well insulated the heat of the building does not escape to such an extent as to melt the snow on the upper part of the roof and no serious difficulty will result.

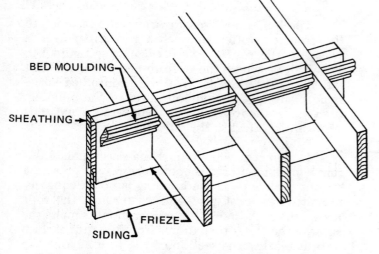

BED MOULDING

SHEATHING

FRIEZE

SIDING

Open Cornice Without Tail Rafters
Figure 1-10

Frequently the rafter beyond the wall line is an extension of the main rafter as in figure 1-10. Sometimes tail rafters are used as in figure 1-11.

### How To Place Tail Rafters

*NOTE:* It is assumed that the common rafters are in place and that the cornice is to extend along a straight side of the building.

1. Lay out and cut the required number of tail rafters (A, figure 1-11).

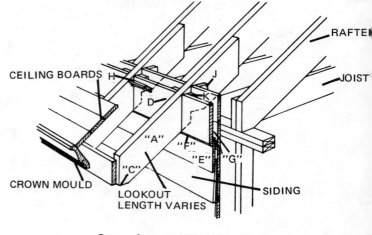

CEILING BOARDS H

RAFTER

JOIST

D

J

K

"A"

"F"

"E"

"G"

"C"

CROWN MOULD

LOOKOUT
LENGTH VARIES

SIDING

Open Cornice With Tail Rafters
Figure 1-11

*NOTE:* The plumb cut of the end of the rafter and the seat cut are found by using the rise and run figures of the common rafter on the steel square. The length of the tail rafter is found by using the steel square or a rafter table.

2. Secure a tail rafter to the sides of the common rafters at each end of the building by nailing them temporarily so that the top of the tail rafter is flush with the top of the common rafter.

3. Stretch and secure a chalk line from the top outermost edge of one tail rafter to a similar edge on the other tail rafter.

4. Check the position and elevation of the outermost edges of the tails so that they are in alignment with one another and in accordance with the dimensions given for the overhang.

5. Securely spike the tail rafters to the sides of the common rafters and to the plate.

6. Spike the intermediate tail rafters to the common rafters, keeping the ends in alignment with the chalk line.

*NOTE:* If the rafter tails extend beyond the building line 2 feet or more, they should be braced temporarily to the side of the building so that they will not sag when the roof boards and shingles are being placed. If the tail rafters are to have a sweep, nail them to the common rafters as shown in figure 1-9.

## How To Place The Frieze Boards

*NOTE:* In building an open cornice it is more convenient to place the frieze boards between the tail rafters before the fascia boards at the ends of the tails are nailed in place. In figure 1-11, a double frieze board (D and E) is used. To apply this type of frieze the order of procedure is as follows:

1. Cover the sheathing with building paper where the frieze board is to be nailed.

2. Snap a chalked line the full length of the wall to show the location of the bottom of the frieze board E. Allow the top of this frieze to be about ½ inch above the bottom edge of the rafter tails at the face of the sheathing.

3. Cut small furring blocks G of the same thickness as the top edge of the siding that is to be used. These blocks should be about 2 inches wide and about 6 inches long.

*NOTE:* These blocks are to be used to fur the frieze E, figure 1-11, out from the face of the sheathing so that siding may be slid behind the bottom edge of the frieze.

4. Nail the furring blocks to the sheathing at each stud location near the top of the frieze board.

5. Square the ends of enough frieze stock to reach to the ends of the cornice.

*NOTE:* If a return cornice is to be provided, be sure to miter the ends of the frieze at the ends of the cornice or wall.

6. Nail the frieze to the building, keeping the bottom edge in line with the chalk line. Nail only the top edge of the frieze, leaving the bottom edge loose. This edge should be nailed solidly after the siding has been put in place.

## How To Fit The Upper Frieze (D, Figure 1-11)

1. Cut blocks about ¾ inch x 3 inches x 5 inches and nail them to the sides of the tail rafters at the plate line. See J, figure 1-11. The outside edges of these blocks should be in line with the inside face of the sheathing.

2. Continue the sheathing up to the top of the rafters by nailing short pieces between the rafters and against these blocks.

3. Apply building paper over the surface of the sheathing where the frieze is to be placed.

4. Nail furring blocks K on the face of the sheathing. These blocks should be the same thickness as the frieze board E plus the block G to fur the frieze board D to a vertical line.

5. Nail the frieze boards D between the rafters and against the blocks K. These boards should be wide enough to extend from the top edge to the bottom edge of the tail rafter.

6. Nail and fit the cove moulding F at the bottom edge of the frieze D. Fit and nail a quarter round or bed moulding at H flush with the tops of the rafters.

## How To Place The Fascia

*NOTE:* In figure 1-11 the fascia board is shown at C.

1. Select straight dressed stock wide enough to reach from the bottom of the roof boards to about ½ inch below the level cut at the end of the tail rafter.

2. Square one end of a length of fascia board. Temporarily nail the board with 8d common nails to the plumb cuts of the tail rafters in the position as shown in figure 1-12. Allow the squared end to come half way on one tail rafter. The other end should extend beyond the end tail rafter far enough to allow for the return of the fascia up the rake. See B, figure 1-12.

3. Square additional lengths and secure them all along the building.

4. Sight along the bottom edge of the fascia to check it for straightness. If necessary straighten it by withdrawing the nails and bringing the fascia into alignment.

5. Nail the fascia board securely to the tail rafters when it is straight.

## How To Place The Crown Moulding

*NOTE:* In some cases a metal or wood gutter is used in place of the crown moulding. If a crown moulding is used it should be placed as follows:

1. Cut a piece of crown moulding about 6 inches long. Place it against the outside face of the

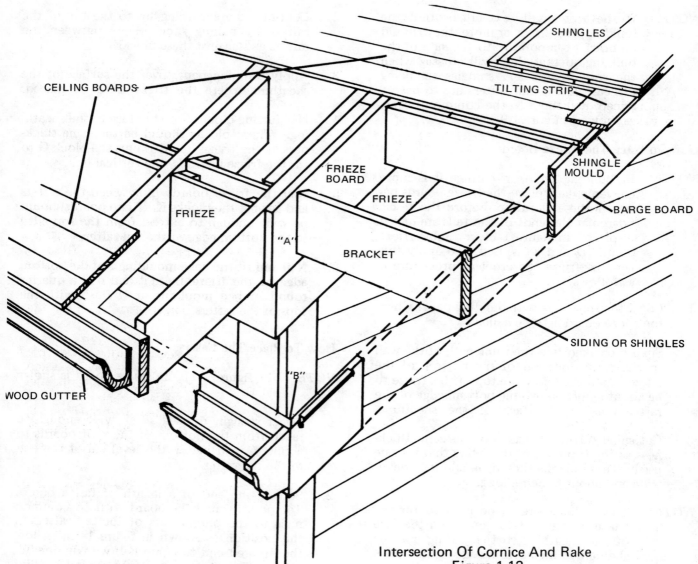

CEILING BOARDS

FRIEZE
BOARD

FRIEZE

"A"

FRIEZE

BRACKET

SHINGLES

TILTING STRIP

SHINGLE
MOULD

BARGE BOARD

SIDING OR SHINGLES

WOOD GUTTER

"B"

Intersection Of Cornice And Rake
Figure 1-12

fascia. Adjust it on the fascia so that the top edge of the crown moulding comes in line with the top of the roof board. See figure 1-11.

*NOTE:* Some carpenters prefer to have the top of the moulding about ½ inch above the roof board so as to form a tight fit between the top of the moulding and the first course of shingles.

2. Measure the distance between the bottom edge of the moulding and the bottom edge of the fascia.

3. Snap a chalked line along the full length of the fascia at this distance from the bottom edge.

4. Nail the bottom edge of the moulding at each rafter tail, keeping it lined up with the chalk line. The top edge may be nailed to the roof board. Set all the nails.

### How To Place Ceiling On An Open Cornice

*NOTE:* In placing a ceiling for an open cornice, be careful to use stock thick enough so that the shingle nails will not protrude through the boards and be exposed to view.

1. Lay the ceiling on the top of the rafters as subfloor is laid, using toe nailing only where the boards do not come together tightly. Face nail with 6d nails and be sure to have the beaded side down. Be sure that no loose knots come between the rafter tails.

2. Allow the boards to project beyond the end rafter the length of the rake overhang.

### How To Build The Rake Of An Open Cornice

1. Straighten the outside common rafter up the rake of the roof by temporarily nailing a stay

across the bottom edges of about four common rafters.

2. Apply the ceiling boards up the rake. Allow six or eight lengths of the boards to extend back to the second common rafter so as to support the overhang. These sections should be placed about every 2 feet up the rafter. The other ceiling boards should extend out from the first common rafter the width of the overhang.

3. Determine the distance the outside face of the bargeboard is to be from the sheathing. Mark this distance on the top of the ceiling boards near the ridge and at the eaves. See A and B, figure 1-13.

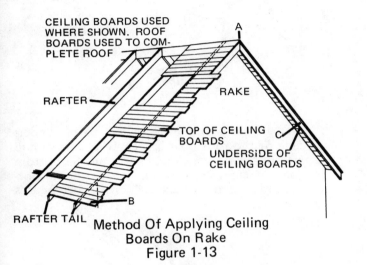

CEILING BOARDS USED WHERE SHOWN. ROOF BOARDS USED TO COMPLETE ROOF

RAFTER

RAKE

TOP OF CEILING BOARDS

UNDERSIDE OF CEILING BOARDS

RAFTER TAIL

Method Of Applying Ceiling
Boards On Rake
Figure 1-13

4. Snap a chalked line connecting these two points and saw off the ceiling boards along this line.

*NOTE:* The bargeboard is the outermost exposed rafter that extends up the rake of the roof. It is nailed to the underside of the roof ceiling boards and forms a surface upon which the crown or shingle moulding is nailed. In reality, it is the horizontal fascia returned up the rake.

5. Cut a plumb and 45 degree miter on the lower end of a length of bargeboard stock. Use the figures on the steel square that were used to lay out the plumb cut of the common rafter for the plumb cut of the bargeboard (figure 1-14).

*NOTE:* This cut is fitted to the miter cut of the horizontal fascia board. See B, figure 1-12.

6. Nail the bargeboard to the underside and outer edge of the ceiling boards. See C, figure 1-13.

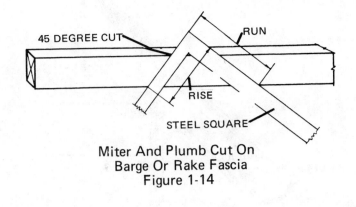

45 DEGREE CUT    RUN

RISE

STEEL SQUARE

Miter And Plumb Cut On
Barge Or Rake Fascia
Figure 1-14

7. Mark the length of bargeboard that is required to reach to the ridge of the roof. The top cut of the bargeboard, where it meets the bargeboard on the opposite side of the gable, is found by using the square as in finding the plumb cut of the common rafter.

8. Finish nailing the bargeboard to all of the roof boards.

9. Fit the crown or shingle moulding to the face of the bargeboard. The cuts at the lower and upper ends of the moulding are made parallel to the respective cuts of the bargeboard, or the moulding may be returned on itself. See B, figure 1-12. Keep the top edge of the shingle moulding flush with the top surface of the roof boards.

10. Nail the moulding to the bargeboard using nails that will not protrude through the bargeboard.

*NOTE:* In some cases a tilt strip is nailed from the top of the roof boards to the top edge of the shingle moulding and projects about 1 inch over the face of the moulding. A 5 inch board is sometimes used for this strip. See figure 1-12.

**How To Fit Cornice Brackets**

*NOTE:* Where the overhang is excessive at the rake, lookout rafters or brackets are built up the rake to support the overhang as shown in figure 1-12.

1. Use stock similar to that used for the tail rafters.

2. Lay out, square and cut the bracket stock using the same general curve as on the tail rafter. The brackets should be long enough to reach from the face of the frieze to the inside face of the bargeboard.

3. Nail the brackets in place, spacing them about 2 feet up the rake of the roof with the faces vertical.

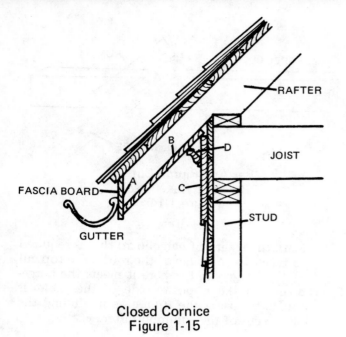

Closed Cornice
Figure 1-15

### How To Build A Closed Cornice

Figure 1-15 shows a closed cornice. This cornice is built on the extended common rafters. The fascia (A) is nailed to the plumb cut at the end of the rafter tail. The soffit (B) is fitted to the back of the fascia and nailed to the bottom edge of the rafter and extends up the rafter to the top edge of the frieze (C). A moulding (D) is fitted at the intersection to cover the joint. If this type of cornice is to be used, the rafter tails should be laid out and cut to accommodate the soffit, fascia and crown moulding before the rafters are nailed in place. When laying out the rafters, a templet should be made to mark the rafter tails so they may be cut to accommodate the cornice members. This may be done by nailing together a short section of soffit, fascia and crown moulding to represent a section of the finished cornice. The rafter tails should be cut according to this templet.

1. Nail the fascia board to the ends of the rafters. This procedure is similar to fitting the fascia board in the open cornice.

2. Fit the soffit to the back of the fascia and nail it to the underside of the rafters.

3. Fit and nail the frieze board to the building in the same way the lower frieze board was applied to the open cornice.

4. Fit and nail the moulding at the intersection of the soffit and frieze.

5. Fit and nail the crown moulding or gutter to the fascia as in fitting this member to the open cornice.

*NOTE:* The return up the gable rake of this type of cornice is composed of the same number and types of materials as are used on the horizontal cornice.

6. Allow the roof boards to project over the outside common rafter the combined distance of the thickness of the frieze board, the width of the soffit and the thickness of the fascia. See A, figure 1-16.

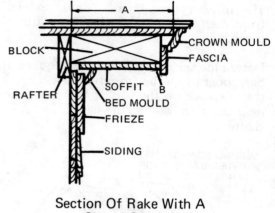

Section Of Rake With A
Closed Cornice
Figure 1-16

7. Nail blocks about every 4 feet to the underside of the roof boards. These blocks should be the proper thickness to bring the bottom face of the rake soffit in line with the bottom face of the horizontal soffit. See figures 1-16 and 1-17.

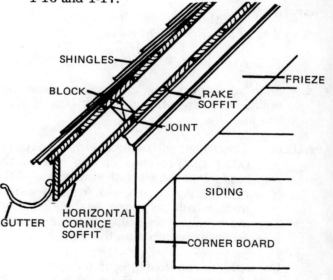

Section Showing Horizontal
And Rake Soffit Joint
Figure 1-17

8. Fit and nail the fascia, crown moulding, soffit and frieze up the rake as explained in the open cornice.

*NOTE:* Figure 1-17 shows how the rake cornice, soffit, fascia, crown mould and frieze intersect with these members of the horizontal cornice.

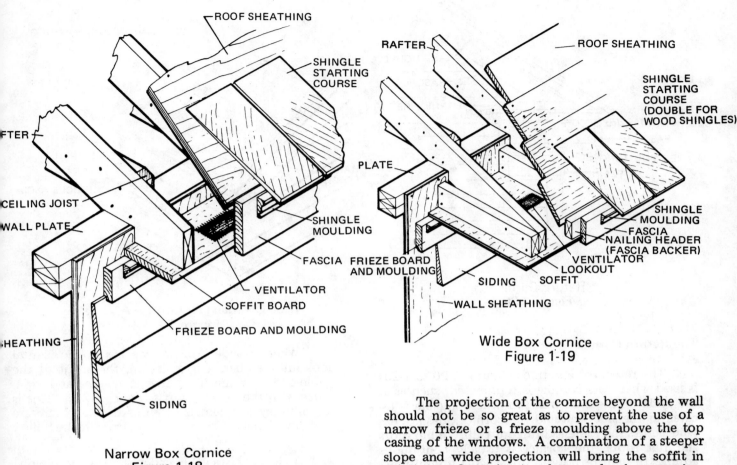

Narrow Box Cornice
Figure 1-18

Wide Box Cornice
Figure 1-19

## The Box Cornice

The box cornice is perhaps the most commonly used cornice design because it presents a more finished appearance and aids in protecting the sidewall from rain. In the narrow box cornice the rafter serves as a nailing surface for the soffit board as well as the fascia trim (figure 1-18). Depending on the roof slope and the size of the rafters, this extension may vary between 6 and 12 or more inches. The soffit provides a desirable area for inlet ventilators. A wide box cornice normally requires additional members for fastening the soffit. This is often supplied by lookout members which can be toenailed to the wall and face-nailed to the ends of the rafter extensions (figure 1-19). Soffit material is often lumber, plywood, paper-overlaid plywood, hardboard, medium-density fiberboard, or other sheet materials. Thicknesses should be based on the distance between supports, but 3/8 inch plywood and ½ inch fiberboard are often used for 16 inch rafter spacing. A nailing header at the ends of the joists will provide a nailing area for soffit and fascia trim. The nailing header is sometimes eliminated in moderate cornice extensions when a rabbeted fascia is used. Inlet ventilators, often narrow continuous slots, can be installed in the soffit areas. This type cornice is often used in a hip-roofed house.

The projection of the cornice beyond the wall should not be so great as to prevent the use of a narrow frieze or a frieze moulding above the top casing of the windows. A combination of a steeper slope and wide projection will bring the soffit in this type of cornice too low, and a box cornice, without the lookouts, should be used.

Prefabricated soffit systems are available in aluminum and fiberboard. These pre-cut sections save cutting and fitting time and have the advantage of ready made vents. Most soffit systems have complete supports, trim and brackets to give a finished appearance to the installation.

### How To Build A Wide Box Cornice (Figure 1-19)

1. Line up the tail plumb cuts and lower corners of the rafters by stretching a line and planing or sawing down any irregularities.

2. Lay out and cut the lookouts and nail them in place. Lookouts must be level with bottom edges and outer ends in perfect alignment. Each lookout should be first nailed to the rafter and then toenailed against the ledger.

3. Lay out, cut and rabbet the frieze and nail it in place just below the lookouts.

4. Lay out and cut the soffit and fit and nail it to the bottom edges of the lookouts.

5. Lay out, cut and bevel the fascia, and nail it to the ends of the rafters and lookouts.

6. Lay out, cut, bevel and nail on the mouldings.

13

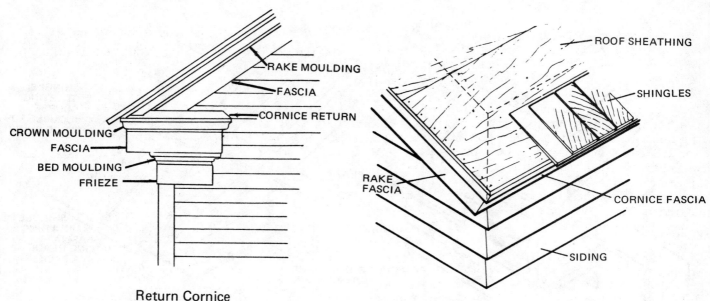

Return Cornice
Figure 1-20

Wide Overhang At Cornice And Rake
Figure 1-22

## The Return Cornice

The return of a cornice (figures 1-20 to 1-23) is used where the cornice is terminated, such as at the ends of the side walls, or where a gable is located at the side wall and the cornice does not extend across the gable as in figure 1-20. In hip roofs and flat roofs, the cornice is usually continuous around the entire house. In a gable house, however, it must be terminated or joined with the gable ends. The type of detail selected depends to a great extent on the type of cornice and the projection of the gable roof beyond the end wall.

When a wide box cornice has no horizontal lookout members (figure 1-17), the soffit of the gable-end overhang is at the same slope and coincides with the cornice soffit (figure 1-22). This is a simple system and is often used when there are wide overhangs at both sides and ends of the house.

A close rake (a gable end with little projection) may be used with a narrow box cornice or a close cornice. In this type, the frieze board of the gable end, into which the siding butts, joints the frieze board or fascia of the cornice (figure 1-23).

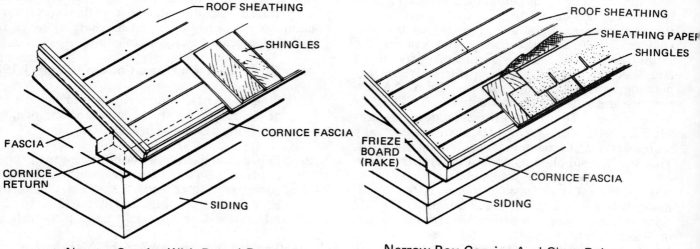

Narrow Cornice With Boxed Return
Figure 1-21

Narrow Box Cornice And Close Rake
Figure 1-23

A narrow box cornice often used in houses with Cape Cod or colonial details has a boxed return when the rake section has some projection (figure 1-21). The fascia board and shingle moulding of the cornice are carried around the corner of the rake projection.

While close rakes and cornices with little overhang are lower in cost, the extra material and labor required for good gable and cornice overhangs are usually justified. Better sidewall protection and lower paint maintenance costs are only two of the benefits derived from good roof extensions.

The principle of forming a return of any cornice or moulding is that its profile should be projected from one surface to another. This principle is followed in returning the individual cornice members around the corner of the building. Notice that the fascia and crown moulding project beyond the building line the same distance on the end of the building as they do on the side. The same general procedure is followed in forming the rake cornice which extends along the slope of the roof as shown in figure 1-1. In the colonial cornice, this return is snubbed as it returns around the corner of the building. This practice avoids a large overhang of the rake cornice.

In some cases where the open cornice returns up the rake, the frieze board extends from the horizontal frieze board up the rake of the roof. The return of the horizontal fascia extends beyond the end of the building up the rake of the roof. This board is sometimes increased in thickness and width and provides a surface upon which the horizontal crown moulding is extended up the rake to the peak of the roof. In this case it is called a bargeboard.

**The Rake Or Gable-End Finish**

The rake section is the extension of a gable roof beyond the end wall of the house. This detail might be classed as being a close rake with little projection or a boxed or open extension of the gable roof, varying from 6 inches to 2 feet or more. Sufficient projection of the roof at the gable is desirable to provide some protection to the sidewalls. This usually results in longer paint life.

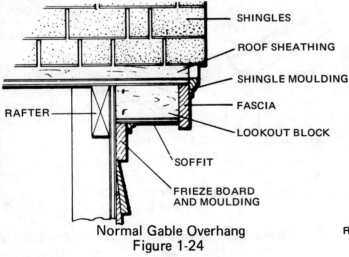

Normal Gable Overhang
Figure 1-24

When the rake extension is only 6 to 8 inches, the fascia and soffit can be nailed to a series of short lookout blocks as in figure 1-24. In addition, the fascia is further secured by nailing through the projecting roof sheathing. A frieze board and appropriate mouldings complete the construction.

In a moderate overhang of up to 20 inches, both the extending sheathing and a fly rafter aid in supporting the rake section (figure 1-25). The fly rafter extends from the ridge board to the nailing header which connects the ends of the rafters. The roof sheathing boards or the plywood should extend from inner rafters to the end of the gable projection to provide rigidity and strength.

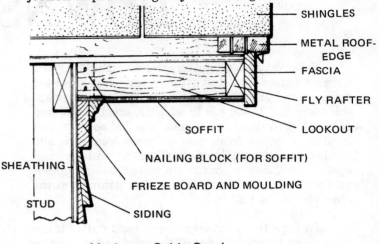

Moderate Gable Overhang
Figure 1-25

The roof sheathing is nailed to the fly rafter and to the lookout blocks which aid in supporting the rake section and also serve as a nailing area for the soffit. Additional nailing blocks against the sheathing are sometimes required for thinner soffit materials.

A close rake has no extension beyond the end wall other than the frieze board and mouldings. Some additional protection and overhang can be provided by using a 2 by 3 or 2 by 4 inch fascia block over the sheathing (figure 1-26). This member acts as a frieze board, as the siding can be butted against it. The fascia, often 1 by 6 inches, serves as a trim member. Metal roof edging is often used along the rake section as flashing.

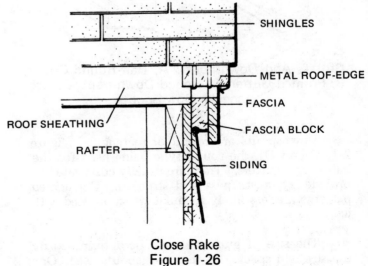

Close Rake
Figure 1-26

# Chapter 2

# GUTTERS AND DOWNSPOUTS

Several types of gutters are available to guide the rainwater to the downspouts and away from the foundation. Some houses have built-in gutters in the cornice. These are lined with sheet metal and connected to the downspouts. On flat roofs, water is often drained from one or more locations and carried through an inside wall to an underground drain. All downspouts connected to an underground drain should contain basket strainers at the junction of the gutter.

Perhaps the most commonly used gutter is the type hung from the edge of the roof or fastened to the edge of the cornice fascia. Metal gutters may be the halfround (figure 2-1, A) or the formed type (figure 2-1, B) and may be galvanized metal, copper, or aluminum. Some have a factory-applied enamel finish.

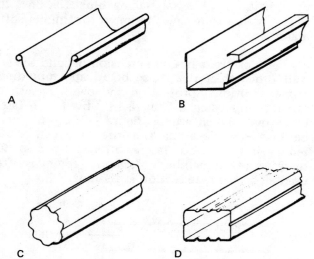

Gutters And Downspouts: A, Half-Round Gutter; B, Formed Gutter; C, Round Downspout; D, Rectangular Downspouts
Figure 2-1

Downspouts are round or rectangular (figure 2-1, C and D), the round type being used for the half-round gutters. They are usually corrugated to provide extra stiffness and strength. Corrugated patterns are less likely to burst when plugged with ice.

The size of gutters should be determined by the size and spacing of the downspouts used. One square inch of downspout is required for each 100 square feet of roof. When downspouts are spaced up to 40 feet apart, the gutter should have the same area as the downspout. For greater spacing, the width of the gutter should be increased.

On long runs of gutters, such as required around a hip-roof house, at least four downspouts are desirable. Gutters should be installed with a slight pitch toward the downspouts. Metal gutters are often suspended from the edge of the roof with hangers (figure 2-2). Hangers should be spaced 48 inches apart when made of galvanized steel and 30 inches apart when made of copper or aluminum. Formed gutters may be mounted on furring strips, but the gutter should be reinforced with wraparound hangers at 48-inch intervals. Gutter splices, downspout connections, and corner joints should be soldered or provided with watertight joints.

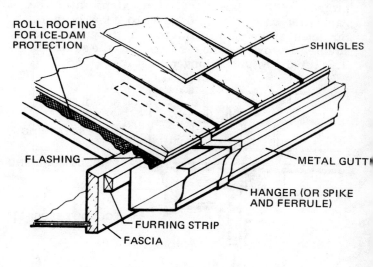

Formed Metal Gutter
Figure 2-2

Wood gutters are mounted on the fascia using furring blocks spaced 24 inches apart (figure 2-3). Rust-proof screws are commonly used to fasten the gutters to the blocks and fascia backing. The edge shingle should be located so that the drip is near the center of the gutter. The wood should be clear and free of knots and preferably treated, unless made of all heartwood from such species as redwood, western redcedar, and cypress. Continuous sections should be used wherever possible.

When splices are necessary, they should be square-cut butt joints fastened with dowels or a spline. Joints should be set in white lead or similar material. When untreated wood gutters are used, it is good practice to brush several generous coats of water repellent preservative on the interior.

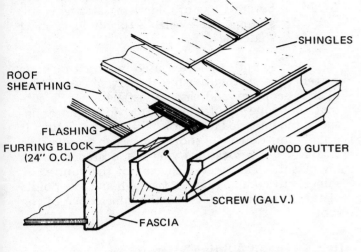

Wood Gutter On Fascia
Figure 2-3

If a hanging wood gutter such as shown in figure 2-3 is to be used, the fascia should be about 6 inches wide. This will provide firm support for the entire length of the gutter which has to be pitched to a low point to drain the water into the downspout or leader box. The gutter material is often shaped on the exposed surface to represent the contour of a crown moulding.

**How To Install A Wood Hanging Gutter**

*NOTE:* A wood hanging gutter is shown in figure 2-3. When this type of gutter is used, it replaces the crown moulding. It is fastened to the fascia but instead of being level it is pitched from a high point to a low point in order to drain the water which is shed from the roof surface.

1. Locate the high point of the gutter and mark this point on the fascia. See the position of the gutter in relation to the roof boards in figure 2-3.

*NOTE:* If there are to be two conductor pipe outlets in the gutter, the high point should be located midway between the outlets.

2. Locate the low point of the gutter and mark this point on the fascia at the outlets.

3. Snap a chalked line from the high point to the low point on the fascia.

4. Cut and fit the first length of gutter trough

and nail or screw it temporarily to the fascia. Use cadmium plated screws or copper nails.

5. Mark the locations and layouts of the joints required in the full length of the complete gutter.

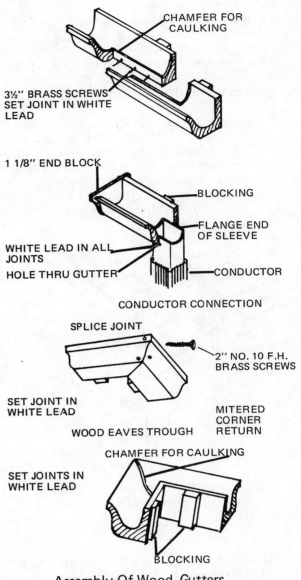

Assembly Of Wood Gutters
Figure 2-4

*NOTE:* Figure 2-4 shows the methods of making the splice joint, miter joint and conductor pipe outlet. The end block at the end of the gutter trough is also shown.

6. Fit the remaining lengths of gutter trough together by using the splice joint shown in figure 2-4.

*NOTE:* In making joints in this type of gutter, be sure the surfaces of the joint are square with the exception of a small bevel on the inside surface of the gutter trough. This bevel is later caulked with white lead and caulking.

7. Fit the miter joints and conductor outlets as shown in figure 2-4, using the same general procedure as in making the splice joint.

8. Assemble the complete gutter by heavily painting the joint surfaces with white lead and screwing or nailing them together.

9. Fasten the gutter to the fascia permanently, being sure the bottom of the gutter is parallel to the chalked line and that there are no low spots in which the water may lodge.

*NOTE:* In some cases small blocks of wood are nailed between the back of the gutter trough and the fascia so that if the gutter overflows the water will not run up under the shingles. See figure 2-3. Another method is to plane the outer edge of the gutter so that it is ½ inch lower than the back edge.

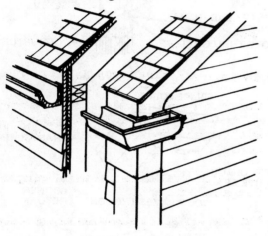

Simple Cornice With Gutter Return
Figure 2-5

Figure 2-5 shows a method of finishing the gutter at the rake so that it will represent a return of the cornice.

## How To Install A Metal Gutter

1. Lay out the high and low points on the fascia the same as in steps 1 to 3 for wood gutters.

2. Cut and fit the lengths of gutter. Use as few joints as possible.

3. Install the gutter with hangers spaced at 48 inches if the hangers are galvanized steel and 30 inches apart if they are aluminum or copper.

*NOTE:* Formed gutters may be mounted on a furring strip, but the gutter should be

reinforced with wrap-around hangers at 48 inch intervals. See figure 2-2.

4. Solder the gutter splices, downspout connections and corner joints.

*NOTE:* Several types of solderless watertight joint systems are available to eliminate most soldering.

A strip gutter is often used in place of a hung gutter. The strip gutter has the advantages of simplicity, economy and ease of installation. Be sure that the slope is sufficient to provide rapid drainage in the intended direction. Use of strip gutters is usually restricted to short runs such as over an entrance or to locations where appearance is less important. The uneven spacing of the courses of shingles to compensate for the high and low points of the gutter strip may mar the appearance of the roof.

## How To Install A Strip Gutter

*NOTE:* The strip should be at least 1 1/16 inch thick and 2 5/8 inches wide and should be of clear white pine.

The lower course of shingles should be laid before the strip gutter is installed but the courses above are laid after the gutter lining is nailed in place.

1. Locate the position of the high point of the gutter strip on the first course of shingles, above the building line. See figure 2-6.

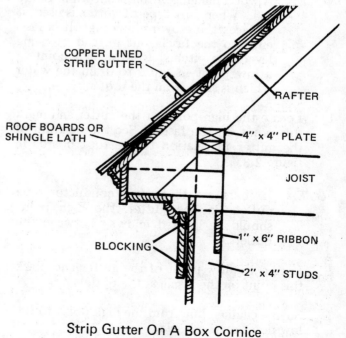

Strip Gutter On A Box Cornice
Figure 2-6

2. Locate the low point of the gutter strip in the same manner and on the same shingle course at the opposite end of the roof. Snap a chalked line connecting the high and low points.

*NOTE:* If the shingle spacing is 5 inches, the low point should be 5 inches lower than the high point. The gutter should have a drain of at least 1/8 to 1/4 inch per running foot.

3. Spike the gutter strip on top of the shingle course so that the bottom edge of the gutter strip will be on the chalk line. Drive and set the spikes through the edge of the gutter strip so that they will go through the shingles and into the rafters.

*NOTE:* Check over the surface of the gutter on which the metal gutter lining will be placed. See that the nail heads are set below the surface and that this surface is smooth.

4. Place the gutter metal on the finished gutter with the soldered joints up and the lap of the soldered seam toward the low point of the gutter.

5. Mark straight lines along the gutter tin according to the locations of the bends on the surfaces of the gutter. These lines are shown in figure 2-6 where the metal is formed over the gutter strip and on the roof surface.

6. Partly bend the metal along these lines with a straight edge to form the metal so that it will fit on the gutter strip and roof.

7. Place the tin in the gutter and temporarily nail the top edge to the roof. Break the tin down into the trough of the gutter, up the inside face, and over the edge of the gutter strip. Nail it about every 3 inches on the top of the gutter strip.

8. Continue the shingling starting with a double course as at the eaves.

Where appearance is a prime consideration a sunken or built-in gutter is often used. This gutter presents a straight appearance from the outside. The pitch required for the drainage of the gutter to the downspout is provided by sloping the bottom board from a high point to a low point. From the ground a box cornice with a correctly built sunken gutter looks like a box cornice without a gutter. Even the downspouts can be concealed within framing members so that nothing reveals the presence of a gutter.

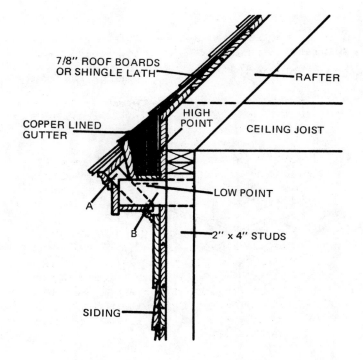

Box Cornice With A Sunken Gutter
Figure 2-7

**How To Make A Sunken Gutter In A Box Cornice.**

1. Cut the required number of lookout brackets (B, figure 2-7) to the correct length and width as determined by the size of the fascia and soffit.

2. Nail these brackets to the studs, lining them up with a chalk line.

3. Nail the soffit to the bottom of the brackets.

4. Nail the fascia in place as shown in figure 2-7.

5. Nail the crown moulding in place.

6. Nail the brackets A to the brackets B. They should rest against the back of the crown moulding.

*NOTE:* The top ends of these brackets should be lined up with a chalk line so they are in the same plane as the top edges of the rafters.

7. Place the frieze and bed moulding as shown.

*NOTE:* If this cornice is to be returned as shown in figure 2-8, and the return soffit is to be the same width as the cornice soffit continue as follows:

If this type of cornice return is to be used, it should be erected before the rake cornice is applied. The rake cornice is then fitted to the top of the return.

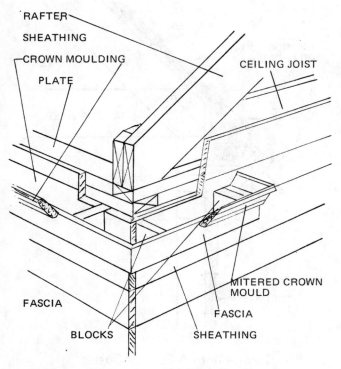

RAFTER
SHEATHING
CROWN MOULDING
PLATE
CEILING JOIST

FASCIA
BLOCKS
MITERED CROWN MOULD
FASCIA
SHEATHING

Return Of Box Cornice With Sunken Gutter
Figure 2-8

8. Cut the blocks (figure 2-8) to the proper length.

9. Nail these blocks in place as shown.

10. Square the end of the cornice soffit.

11. Cut and nail the return soffit in place to the edge of the blocks.

12. Miter and return the fascia around the end and back edge of the soffit to the building.

13. Miter and return the crown moulding around the fascia and back to the building. Miter and return the frieze and bed mould around the corner of the building.

*NOTE:* The return moulding and fascia should be temporarily nailed until after the siding is placed.

14. Lay out the high point of the gutter on the outer end of a bracket at the end of the building (figure 2-7).

15. Lay out the low point of the gutter on the outer end of a bracket at the opposite end of the building. See dotted line at B, figure 2-7.

16. Snap a chalked line between these points across the ends of the intermediate brackets.

17. Transfer these points in on the brackets and complete the layout for the gutter trough on each bracket.

18. Cut out these notches for the gutter.

19. Nail the three members of the gutter trough in place (figure 2-7).

20. Check the inside of the trough to see that it is straight and free from protruding nails.

21. Break the metal gutter lining over the top of the gutter, down the side and around the gutter trough in the same manner as for the strip gutter.

*NOTE:* This may require the services of a sheet metal craftsman.

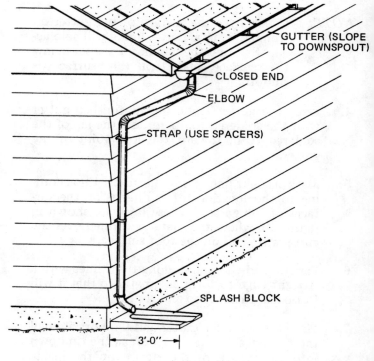

GUTTER (SLOPE TO DOWNSPOUT)
CLOSED END
ELBOW
STRAP (USE SPACERS)
SPLASH BLOCK
3'-0"

Downspout Installation
Figure 2-9

## Downspouts

Downspouts are fastened to the wall by straps or hooks (figure 2-9). Several patterns of these fasteners allow a space between the wall and downpout. One common type consists of a galvanized metal strap with a spike and spacer collar. After the spike is driven through the collar and into the siding and backing stud, the strap is fastened around the pipe. Downspouts should be fastened at the top and bottom. In addition, for long downspouts a strap or hook should be used for every 6 feet of length.

An elbow should be used at the bottom of the downspout, as well as a splash block, to carry the water away from the wall.

# Chapter 3
# WOOD SHINGLE ROOFING

At one time, the wood shingle was almost universally used for covering the roof of frame structures. During recent years wood shingles have been replaced to some extent by composition materials in the form of roll, strip and individual shingles.

Sheet materials such as roll roofing, galvanized iron, aluminum, copper, and tin are also used. Perhaps the most common covering for flat or low-pitched roofs is the built-up roof with a gravel topping or cap sheet. Plastic films, often backed with an asbestos sheet, are also being applied on low-slope roofs. While these materials are relatively new, it is likely that their use will increase, especially for roofs with unusual shapes. However, a well-built shingle roof has a natural attractiveness and durability that will undoubtedly be in demand for many years.

The pitch of the roof surface must be considered in selecting the roof material. In localities where there is excessive rain and snowfall, the shingled roof should have a pitch of at least 9 inches to the foot. The pitch of a shingled roof should never be less than 3 inches to the foot. The more readily the water can be drained from a wood shingled roof, the longer the roof will last. Table 3-1 gives minimum slope requirements for various shingle lengths and exposures. At standard exposures 4 bundles of shingles or shakes (1 square) will cover 100 square feet of roof. Standard exposures are: 24" shakes - 10", 16" shingles - 5", 18" shingles - 5½", 24" shingles - 7½".

Underlay or roofing felt is not required for wood shingles except for protection in ice-dam areas. Spaced roof boards under wood shingles are most common, although spaced or solid sheathing is optional.

The best shingles are sawed from cypress, western red cedar and redwood. In some sections of the country, eastern white cedar, white pine and the soft southern pines are used. The basic grades of shingles are grades No. 1, No. 2 and No. 3:

*Grade No. 1 shingles* are strictly clear edge grain and free from sapwood. They come in lengths of 16, 18 and 24 inches and in random widths of 3 or more inches. The butts or thickened ends come in thicknesses of 4/2, 5/2¼ and 5/2. This means that when 4 shingles are laid on top of one another, the butt ends in the first case measure a total of 2 inches in thickness or ½ inch each. In the second case it means that 5 butts will measure 2¼ inches in thickness. In the third case, 5 butts will measure 2 inches in thickness.

24 inch shingles are 4/2 inches at the butts.
18 inch shingles are 5/2¼ inches at the butts.
16 inch shingles are 5/2 inches at the butts.

*Grade No. 2 shingles* are strictly clear mixed edge and flat grain. These shingles are made in lengths of 16, 18 and 24 inches. They may not be under 3 inches wide and a small amount of sapwood is permitted. The butt thicknesses are the same as for the No. 1 shingles.

*Grade No. 3 shingles* must be clear for the bottom half of their length. None of the shingles may be narrower than 2½ inches. The butt thicknesses are the same as for the No. 1 shingles.

Wood shingles used for house roofs are No. 1 grade. Second grade shingles make good roofs for secondary buildings as well as excellent sidewalls for primary buildings. Third grade shingles are used for economy applications, sidewalls and under courses in double course applications. Shingles have a tendency to curl and hold moisture if the grain is flat or slash grain. No shingle having slash grain should be wider than 10 inches and it should be laid with the annual rings pointing down. See

| Shingle Length Inches | Shingle Thickness (Green) | MAXIMUM EXPOSURE | |
|---|---|---|---|
| | | Slope Less Than 4 in 12 | Slope 5 in 12 and Over |
| 16 | 5 butts in 2 inches | 3¾" | 5" |
| 18 | 5 butts in 2¼ inches | 4¼" | 5½" |
| 24 | 4 butts in 2 inches | 5¾" | 7½" |

As recommended by the Red Cedar Shingle and Handsplit Shake Bureau.
Minimum slope for main roofs---4 in 12.
Minimum slope for porch roofs---3 in 12.

Recommended Exposure For Wood Shingles
Table 3-1

figure 3-2. Badly crossgrained shingles should not be used. The color of the shingle is no defect in any grade unless it is discolored by the presence of excess sap or decay.

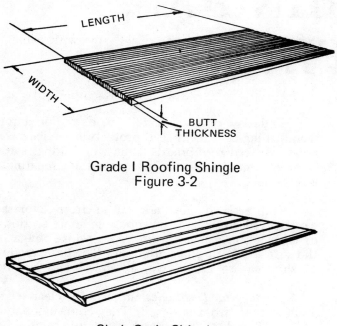

Grade I Roofing Shingle
Figure 3-2

Slash Grain Shingle
Figure 3-3

The shingle nail is an important factor in the durability of a shingled roof. The common wire nail should not be used because of its poor resistance to rust and its poor holding ability. The best nails to use are zinc-coated or galvanized nails. The length of the nail to be used is determined by the thickness of the shingles. If they measure 5 butts to 2 inches they should be nailed with 3d nails. Thicker shingles should be fastened with 4d nails. The 3d nails have flat heads 5/16 inch in diameter and are 1¼ inches long. The 4d nails have flat heads 5/16 inch in diameter and are 1½ inches long. There are about 382 of the latter size to the pound. Each shingle should receive 2 nails about ¾ inch from the outside edge and about 1½ inches above the butt line for the next course. A threaded ring shank nail should be used on plywood sheathing less than ½ inch thick.

Wood shakes are applied much the same as wood shingles. Because shakes are much thicker (longer shakes have the thicker butts), long galvanized nails are used. To create a rustic appearance, the butts are often laid unevenly. Because shakes are longer than shingles, they have a greater exposure. Exposure distance is usually 7½ inches for 18 inch shakes, 10 inches for 24 inch shakes, and 13 inches for 32 inch shakes. Shakes are not smooth on both faces, and because wind-driven snow might enter, it is essential to use an underlay between each course. An 18 inch-wide layer of 30 pound asphalt felt should be used between each course with the bottom edge positioned above the

butt edge of the shakes a distance equal to double the weather exposure. A 36 inch wide starting strip of the asphalt felt is used at the eave line. Solid sheathing should be used when wood shakes are used for roofs in areas where wind-driven snow is experienced.

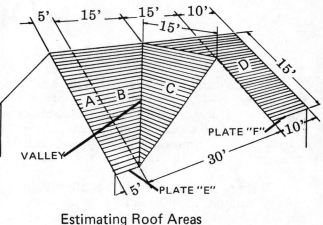

Estimating Roof Areas
Figure 3-4

**Estimating Shingle Requirements**

Figure 3-4 shows one side of a roof which is to be shingled. To find the total area of this side of the main roof and gable it is most convenient to divide the roof surface into squares, rectangles and triangles. The left side of the front section of the roof is composed of rectangle A and triangle B. The area of A is found by multiplying the length of the main common rafter including the overhang by the length of the plate E. The area of triangle B is found by multiplying the length of the main roof common rafter by the length of the ridge above the triangle and dividing by 2. There would be a corresponding triangle on the other side of the gable.

The area of the triangle C is found by multiplying the length of the gable ridge by the length of the gable common rafter and dividing by 2. The other side of the gable roof would have the same area.

The section D is found by multiplying the length of the plate F by the length of the main common rafter.

Section A:  5' times 15'  =  75  S.F.
Section B:  15' times 15' ÷2=  112½ S.F.
Section same as B on other
   side of gable  =  112½ S.F.
Section C:  15' times 15' ÷2=  112½ S.F.
Section same as C on other
   side of gable  =  112½ S.F.
Section D:  10' times 15'  =  150  S.F.
                                675  S.F.

If there are no roof projections on the opposite side of the ridge, the area for this side may be found by multiplying the length of the ridge by the length of the common rafter. In this case the total length of the ridge is 45 feet. 45 feet times 15 feet = 675 square feet.

Straight side of roof = 675 S.F.
Gable side of roof = 675 S.F.
1350 total S.F.

Allowances must be made if there is to be an overhang at the rake of the roof at the gables.

You can also estimate the roof area from the ground area. Be sure to include the overhang. Compute the ground area in square feet. If the pitch of the roof is 5" in 12", add 10% to the total. If it is 6" in 12" roof add 12%; if 12" in 12" add 42%; if 18" in 12" add 80% to the square foot total. Divide the total by 100. The answer is the number of shingle squares needed to cover the roof. Add one square for every 100 linear feet of hips and valley and add 33% if the roof pitch is less than 5" in 12" to compensate for reduced exposure. Exposure should be limited to a maximum of 3¾" for pitches between 5" in 12" and 3" in 12".

Shingles are bought by the square or in bundles. Four bundles make a square or enough to cover 100 square feet at standard exposures. Table 3-5 gives more precise coverage figures for accurate estimating. Approximately two and one-half pounds of 3d nails are required for every 100 square feet of roof area. Flashing for valleys and strip gutters should be at least 16 inches wide. The length is determined by the number of linear feet in the valley or gutter, allowing about one foot extra on each end to allow for lap and pockets.

Flashing is needed for every course of shingles that intersects the side of the dormer. Shingle or shake hip and ridge units will cover 16 2/3 linear feet of hip or ridge.

**How To Lay Wood Shingles.**

*NOTE:* Assume that a straight roof with gable ends is to be shingled.

1. Nail a shingle at one end of the roof to the roof boards and the crown mouldings of the rake and horizontal cornice. See figure 3-6.

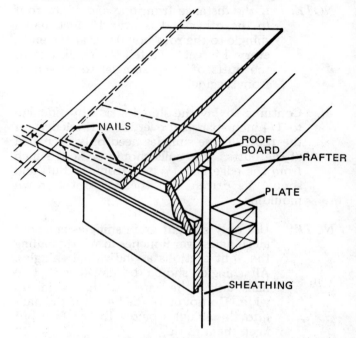

Position Of Shingles On Crown Moulding
Figure 3-6

| LENGTH AND THICKNESS | 16" x 5/2" | 18" x 5/2¼" | 24" x 4/2" | |
|---|---|---|---|---|
| 3½" | 70 | -- | -- | |
| 4" | 80 | 72½" | -- | |
| 4½" | 90 | 81½ | -- | Maximum Exposure Recommended For Roofs. |
| 5" | 100 | 90½ | -- | |
| 5½" | 110 | 100 | -- | |
| 6" | 120 | 109 | 80 | |
| 6½" | 130 | 118 | 86½ | |
| 7" | 140 | 127 | 93 | |
| 7½" | 150 | 136 | 100 | |
| 8" | 160 | 145½ | 106½ | |
| 8½" | 170 | 154½ | 113 | |
| 9" | 180 | 163½ | 120 | Maximum Exposure Recommended For Single Coursing On Sidewalls. |
| 9½" | 190 | 172½ | 126½ | |
| 10 | 200 | 181½ | 133 | |
| 10½" | 210 | 191 | 140 | |
| 11" | 220 | 200 | 146½ | |
| 11½" | 230 | 209 | 153 | |
| 12" | 240 | 218 | 160 | |
| 12½" | -- | 227 | 166½ | |
| 13" | -- | 236 | 173 | |
| 13½" | -- | 245½ | 180 | Maximum Exposure Recommended For Double Coursing On Sidewalls. |
| 14" | -- | 254½ | 186½ | |
| 14½" | -- | -- | 193 | |
| 15" | -- | -- | 200 | |
| 15½" | -- | -- | 206½ | |
| 16" | -- | -- | 213 | |

Approximate coverage of one square (4 bundles) of shingles based on following weather exposures

Shingle Coverage
Table 3-5

The shingle butt should project 1¼ inch below the horizontal mouldings. The edge of the shingle should project 1 inch over the rake crown moulding. Place the nails in the shingle as shown, keeping them at least 1¼ inch from the edges and from the butt of the shingle.

2. Nail a shingle in the same manner at the other end of the roof.

3. Stretch and fasten a chalk line from the butt of one shingle to the butt of the other.

*NOTE:* If the distance from one end of the roof to the other end is over 14 feet, nail a shingle to the roof boards, as at the ends, every 14 feet. Fasten the chalk line to the butts of these shingles to prevent it from sagging.

4. Continue to lay the shingles side by side 1/8 to 1/4 inch apart and over the entire length of the roof. These shingles need only be nailed at the butts. The nails should be kept 1 inch from the edge and 1¼ inch from the butt and should be driven into the horizontal crown moulding.

*NOTE:* Use only straight grain shingles and split all shingles over 9 inches in width, nailing the split sections as individual shingles. All shingles should be nailed with two nails unless they are less than 4 inches wide. Do not drive the heads of the nails into the shingles below the surface but keep them flush.

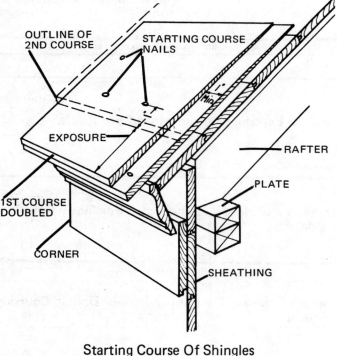

Starting Course Of Shingles
Figure 3-7

5. Lay another course of shingles on top of the first course (figure 3-7). Nail the end shingles to the rake moulding in the same manner as the first course. Be sure to keep the nails far enough above the butts so that they will be covered by at least 1 inch of the succeeding course. The nails should not be closer than 1 inch to the edge of the shingle.

6. Space a shingle on each end of the building on the rake crown moulding as shown at A, figure 3-8. This space is the width of the shingle course or the exposed length of the shingle. Snap a chalk line between the butts of these two shingles.

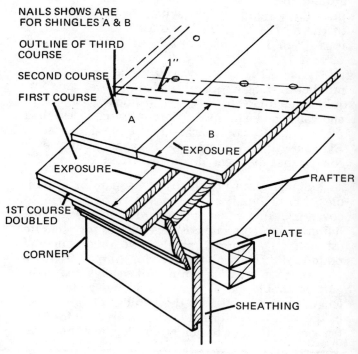

Second Course Of Shingles
Figure 3-8

*NOTE:* Another method in place of the chalk line is to use a straight edge from the butt of one shingle to that of the one on the opposite end of the roof. Generally a piece of lumber the width of the shingle course is used.

7. Nail the second course of shingles in the same manner as the starting course with the butts along the chalk line.

*NOTE:* Some carpenters prefer to nail three shingles up the rake moulding at each end of the roof, spacing them up the rake according to the width of the courses. A chalked line is then snapped between the butts of each pair of shingles. This marks three guide lines across the roof for the succeeding courses.

8. Break all side joints of the second course of shingles 1½ inches away from the side joints of the starting course. No joint should come directly over another on any three consecutive courses. See figure 3-9.

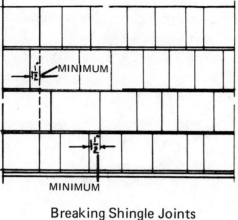

Breaking Shingle Joints
Figure 3-9

9. Continue laying the courses of shingles up the roof in the same manner as described for the second course. Normally only the first course is doubled. Subsequent courses are laid in a single layer.

*NOTE:* Stack vents and roof ventilators are provided with flashing collars which are lapped by the shingles on the upper side. The lower edge of the collar laps the shingles. Sides are nailed to the shingles and caulked with a roofing mastic.

**How To Build A "Shingle Scaffold".**

On roofs with a pitch over 9 in 12 it is difficult to maintain a firm footing and it will be necessary to use a "shingle scaffold" about every 6 feet up the roof.

1. Select a 2 x 4 free of knots or fractures and about 12 feet long. Lay it parallel to the shingle line on the roof with one end even with the end of the roof.

2. Place three 4 or 5 inch wide shingles on the face of the 2 x 4, one about 4 inches from each end and one in the middle. Place the butts of the shingles on the 2 x 4 as shown in figure 3-10. Be sure that the butts extend at least 1½ inches across the 2 x 4 and that they center on the joints of the shingle course above. See A, figure 3-10. Nail each shingle to the 2 x 4 in this position with about five shingle nails as shown.

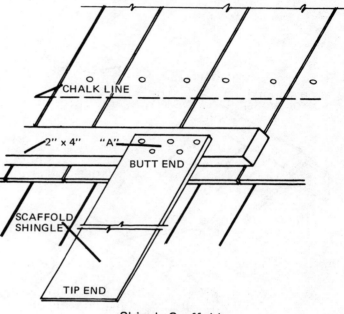

Shingle Scaffold
Figure 3-10

3. Nail a shingle in a similar fashion to additional 2 x 4's every 6 feet. Use enough pieces to cover the entire length of the roof. See figure 3-11.

4. Turn the 2 x 4 over so that the shingles take the position they would if being nailed to the course marked by the chalk line in figure 3-10. Adjust the 2 x 4 so that the top edge comes about ¼ inch below the chalk line (figure 3-11).

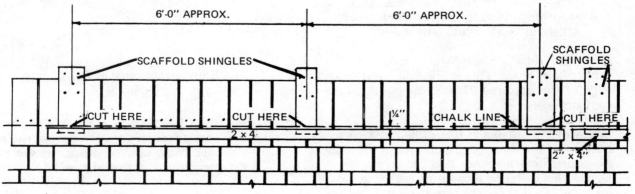

Method Of Applying Shingle Scaffold
Figure 3-11

5. Nail the scaffold shingles to the roof. Keep the nails in a similar position to those of the other shingles but drive at least five nails into each of these shingles.

*NOTE:* When the scaffold is of no further use to the carpenter, the scaffold shingles should be cut off on a line with the shingle course (figure 3-11) and the 2 x 4 should be removed from the roof.

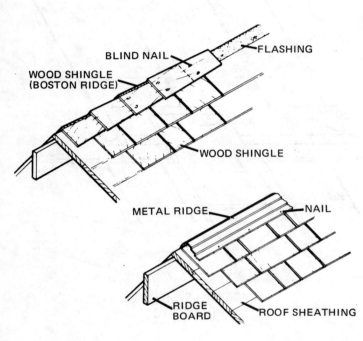

Methods Of Covering A Ridge
Figure 3-12

**How To Space The Shingle Course At The Ridge.**

*NOTE:* Figure 3-12 shows two methods of covering the ridge of the roof. Often pre-manufactured hip and ridge units are used. These units require longer nails. Be sure the nails used penetrate into the sheathing. The spacing of the final courses should be approximately equal.

1. Place the ridge covering in position on the ridge of the roof. This will locate the bottom edge of the covering. Mark this point on the roof surface.

2. Space off the distance from this mark to the bottom of a course of shingles when the shingle courses reach about 3 feet from the ridge. Divide this distance into equal spaces as close as possible to the exposure distance you are using. Use this new exposure dimension to complete shingling to the ridge.

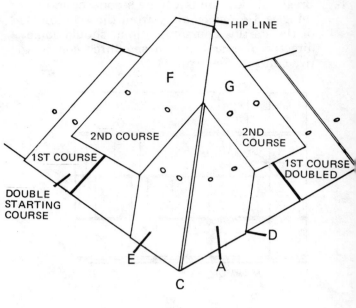

Woven Hip
Figure 3-13

**How To Shingle A Woven Hip.**

*NOTE:* Figure 3-13 shows a woven hip in which the shingles are placed over the top of the hip as the shingle courses progress up the roof. The shingles that overlap the hip are cut to a special shape so that they fit against the edges of the regular courses of shingles. A cut shingle is shown at A, figure 3-13.

1. Nail about six shingles together, keeping the butt ends and one edge of each shingle flush as shown at A and B, figure 3-14A.

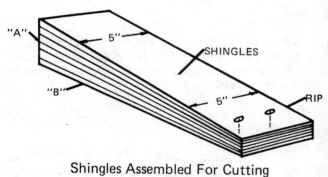

Shingles Assembled For Cutting
Figure 3-14A

2. Mark the top shingle at the butt and tip ends 5 inches from the flush edge of the shingle. Connect these points with a straight line and rip along this line. See figure 3-14A.

3. Lay a steel square across the top shingle so that the distance BC, figure 3-14B will represent the run of the common rafter and the

26

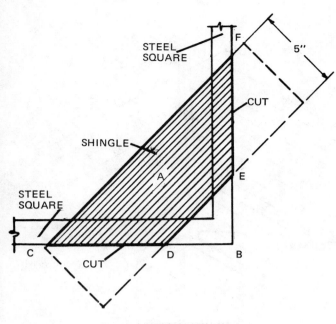

Layout Of Hip Shingle
Figure 3-14B

distance BF will represent the rise of the common rafter. Mark the shingle along the outside edges of the square.

4. Adjust the square so that its edges are parallel to the marks on the shingle and so the distance BE, figure 3-14B is equal to the width of the shingle course.

5. Mark the shingle along the outside edges of the square and cut the shingles as shown in figure 3-14B.

6. Lay the doubled first course of shingles up to the hip. Cut the tops of these shingles off roughly along the hip line.

7. Nail one of the special cut shingles in the proper position on top of the double course as at A, figure 3-13. Allow the edge of the cut shingle to project over the hip so that it may be shaved off on a line with the opposite side of the roof so that the cut shingle E, figure 3-13 may overlap it.

8. Nail the cut shingle E in the same manner. Shave the edge of this shingle even with the edge of shingle A.

9. Start the second course of shingles by nailing the shingle G, figure 3-13 against the top cut of shingle A. Cut off the top end of shingle F where it overlaps the top of the hip. Continue the regular courses of shingles on both sides of the hip.

10. Nail the succeeding hip shingles over the top of the hip as the shingling progresses up the roof. Be sure to alternate the lap of the hip shingles as shown in figure 3-15.

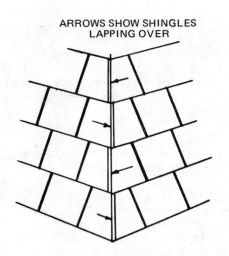

Lap Of Hip Shingles
Figure 3-15

**How To Shingle A Boston Hip.**

*NOTE:* Figure 3-16 shows a Boston hip. Specially manufactured hip and ridge shingles will save time here. If these units are not available, standard shingles can be used.

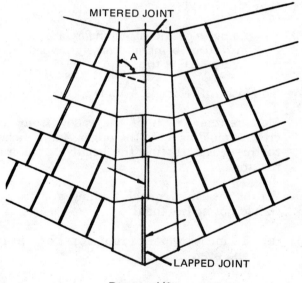

Boston Hip
Figure 3-16

Ridge flashing should be used under a Boston hip in wood shingle or shake roofs to prevent water entry. The flashing should extend about 3 inches on each side of the ridge and be nailed in place only at the outer edges.

1. Apply the straight courses of shingles on both sides of the hip.

2. Cut the tops of these shingles off roughly where they project over the edge of the hip.

*NOTE:* In many cases, special hip shingles are cut. This prevents the top of the shingles from lapping over the hip. See layout of the hip shingle in figure 3-17. They may be random widths. Lay off the diagonal cut as shown, using the rise and run of the common rafter. Cut along this line and apply the shingles on each side of the hip.

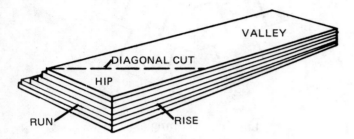

Method Of Cutting Hip Or Valley Shingles
Figure 3-17

3. Lay out and cut the top hip shingles as shown in figure 3-14A.

4. Apply these over the top of the regular shingle courses as shown in figure 3-16. Note how they are lapped.

*NOTE:* Sometimes the hip shingles are mitered instead of being alternately lapped. See figure 3-16 at top.

**How To Flash And Shingle A Valley.**

1. Measure the length of the valley from the crown moulding up to the ridge. Add 6 inches to this length to find the length of material required.

2. Widths of sheet metal flashing for valleys should not be less than:

   (a) 12 inches wide for roof slopes of 7 in 12 and over.

   (b) 18 inches wide for 4 in 12 to 7 in 12 roof slopes.

   (c) 24 inches wide for slopes less than 4 in 12.

   Several types of pre-formed valley flashing are available to speed and simplify flashing valleys. On the material selected mark a center line the entire length of the flashing.

3. Mark the shingle guide lines so that there is about a 5 inch gutter opening at the bottom and a 4 inch space between the lines at the top. See figure 3-18.

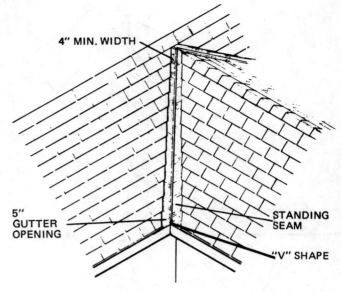

Valley Flashing
Figure 3-18

4. Cut the bottom of the valley flashing in a V shape so that it will overlap the top of the crown moulding.

5. Bend the flashing with a straightedge along the center line, in a "V" shape so that it will lie flat on the roof on each side of the valley.

   *CAUTION:* Be sure the soldered joint is face up and that the seams are turned so that the lap is facing down toward the crown moulding. If tin flashing is used, be sure it is painted with two coats of red lead on each side.

6. Nail the flashing in place. Place the nails ½ inch from the edge of the flashing and about 3 feet apart.

7. Bend the top edges over the ridge.

8. Place a cut valley shingle at each side of the valley with the smooth edge along the shingle guide line on the flashing and the point of the shingle about 4 inches below the crown moulding. Valley shingles are cut as shown in figure 3-17.

9. Place a regular shingle (B, figure 3-19) against the valley shingle with the butt 1¼ inch below the crown moulding and nail it in place. Finish this course.

10. Place another valley shingle on top of the first valley shingle, this time keeping the point of the shingle at the same height as the butt of the square shingle B.

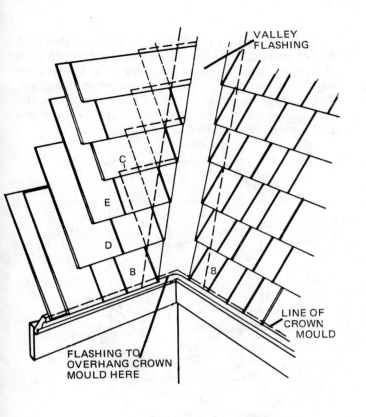

VALLEY FLASHING

C

E

D

B

B

FLASHING TO OVERHANG CROWN MOULD HERE

LINE OF CROWN MOULD

Valley Shingles And Flashing In Place
Figure 3-19

11. Continue this double course of shingles, placing the regular shingle against the valley shingle.

12. Cut off the tip of the bottom valley shingle in line with the butt of shingle B, figure 3-19.

13. Repeat steps 8-12 on the other side of the valley.

14. Continue the regular courses of shingles as shown at D and E.

*NOTE:* If a closed shingle valley is desired, the simplest and most satisfactory way is to bring the opposing cut valley shingles together at the center of the flashing and to lap them.

When adjacent roof slopes vary, such as a low-slope porch roof intersecting a steeper main roof, a 1 inch crimped standing seam should be used (figure 3-18). This will keep heavy rains on the steeper slopes from overrunning the valley and being forced under the shingles on the adjoining slope. Nails for the shingles should be kept back as far as possible to eliminate holes in the flashing. A ribbon of asphalt-roofing mastic is often used under the edge of the shin-

gles. It is wise to use the wider valley flashings supplemented by a width of 15 or 30 pound asphalt felt where snow and ice dams may cause melting snow water to back under shingles.

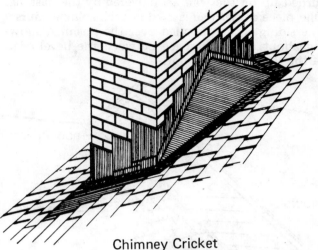

Chimney Cricket
Figure 3-20

**How To Flash At Intersections.**

*NOTE:* Figure 3-20 shows the method of flashing a chimney. If the masonry is not in place, cut the flashing long enough so that it will extend up the wall of the chimney at least 6 inches.

1. Build the cricket or saddle at the top of the chimney hole so that it will divert the water to the side of the chimney. The saddle should extend 2 inches over each side of the masonry.

2. Cut and bend the flashing to the pitch of the roof as shown in figure 3-20 and insert one piece of flashing in every shingle course. Nail the flashing to the roof surface. Keep the nails back 3 inches from the bend in the flashing.

3. Flash the top of the cricket and other abutting chimney surfaces as shown in figure 3-20. The flashing should extend 6 inches up under the shingles after they are applied.

*NOTE:* Flashings against dormer sides may be cut to 5 inches by 7 inches and inserted in every course in the same manner as in flashing the side of the chimney. Do not nail the flashing to the roof surface, but only to the side of the dormer.

Joints between the flashing and masonry surface should be caulked to provide a watertight connection.

When shingles on a roof intersect a vertical wall, shingle flashing is used at the junction. These tin or galvanized-metal shingles are bent at a 90 degree angle and extend up the side of the wall over the sheathing a minimum of 4 inches (figure 3-21). When roofing felt is used under the shingle, it is turned up on the wall and covered by the flashing. One piece of flashing is used at each shingle course. The siding is then applied over the flashing, allowing about a 2 inch space between the bevel edge of the siding and the roof.

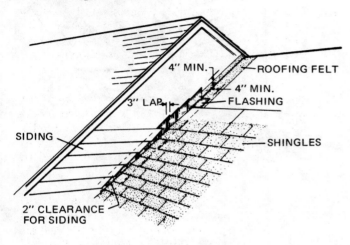

Flashing At A Wood Wall
Figure 3-21

If the roof intersects a brick wall, the same type of metal shingle flashing is used at the end of each shingle course. In addition, counterflashing or brick flashing is used to cover the shingle flashing (figure 3-22). This counterflashing is often preformed in sections and is inserted in open mortar joints. Unless soldered together, each section should overlap the next a minimum of 3 inches with the joint caulked. In laying up the brick wall, the mortar is usually raked out for a depth of about 1 inch at flashing locations. Lead wedges driven into the joint above the flashing hold it in place. The joint is then caulked to provide a watertight connection.

Around small chimneys, chimney flashing often consists of simple counterflashing on each side. For single-flue chimneys, the shingle flashing on the high side should be carried up under the shingles. The vertical distance at top of the flashing and the upturned edge should be about 4 inches above the roof boards (figure 3-23).

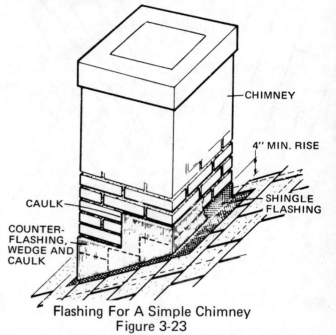

Flashing For A Simple Chimney
Figure 3-23

**How To Re-Roof With Wood Shingles.**

Wood shingles may be applied directly over an old roof of wood or asphalt shingles but not over slate, tile or asbestos roofing. Application on an existing roof saves the time of removing the old covering and results in a roof with a better insulation value than a single layer shingle roof.

A shingler's or lather's hatchet will make removal and application easier. See figure 3-24.

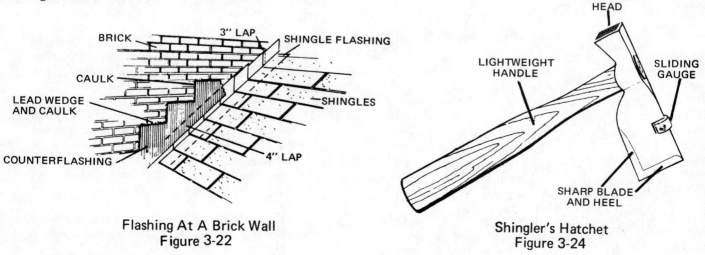

Flashing At A Brick Wall
Figure 3-22

Shingler's Hatchet
Figure 3-24

1. Remove the first and second course of shingles at the eaves to expose about 6" of the sheathing. Be careful to disturb the upper courses as little as possible.

2. Cut back old shingles from the gable ends to expose about 6 inches of roof sheathing.

3. Apply a 2 x 6 over the exposed sheathing along the gable ends and eaves.

4. Remove the old ridge covering and replace it with bevel siding, overlaping the butt edges at the peak. The thin edge of the siding should be downward. Nail with 5d box nails of aluminum or with a zinc coating. Make sure the nails penetrate to the sheathing below.

5. Place a 1 x 6 on each side of the valley to separate the old metal from the new.

6. Reflash as at the eaves, valleys, hips and intersections.

7. Apply the new shingles right over the old shingles with 5d rust resistant nails.

## Shingle Lath.

Shingle lath, sometimes called roof board, is usually strips of wood 1 inch by 3 inches or 1 inch by 4 inches nominal size. Hemlock is most frequently used for this purpose in these sizes. Other materials such as pine, spruce, and fir generally come dressed two sides and two edges to ¾ inch x 2 5/8 inches and ¾ inch x 3 5/8 inches. They come in standard lengths. Only clear straight stock should be used, as the chief function of these parts is to brace the roof rafters and to form a solid and true base upon which to nail the wood shingles. For most purposes, plywood sheathing has replaced roof boards though occasionally plans may call for more traditional building practice.

Roof boards are laid on the rafters in about the same way as sheathing is laid on side wall studs. There is a difference of opinion as to whether solid roof boards or shingle lath spaced a few inches apart are best. The solid roof boards make the roof somewhat more rigid and provide better insulation and fire resistance than the spaced shingle lath. It is sometimes claimed that shingles over lath are less subject to decay than those over solid roof boards because of the better ventilation they receive. However, this is open to question. The material cost and labor are less for shingle lath than for solid roof boards.

If matched boards are laid tight, twenty per cent should be added to the total roof surface to find the amount of roof boards. No deductions for small openings such as chimneys need be considered. If shingle lath are to be used and if they are to be spaced a distance equal to the shingle exposure minus the width of a lath, one half of the roof area should then be deducted to determine the number of board feet required.

## How To Lay Shingle Lath.

*NOTE:* Assume that shingle lath ¾ inch x 2 5/8 inches is to be used:

1. Nail the first board to the top of the rafters and nail through the edge of the moulding into this board (figure 3-24). The first board may have to be wider than 2 5/8 inches so it can be nailed to the rafters.

2. Space the boards about 3 inches apart or space them the same distance apart from center to center as the shingle exposure. This distance for an 18 inch shingle is 5½ inches as shown in figure 3-24. Fasten each board to each rafter with two 8d nails.

*NOTE:* This spacing will vary as the length of the shingle and the width of the shingle lath vary. The lower edge of the shingle lath should come directly under the butt of a shingle course to provide a solid nailing surface for the preceding course.

3. Continue in the same manner, keeping the shingle lath parallel to one another over the entire roof surface.

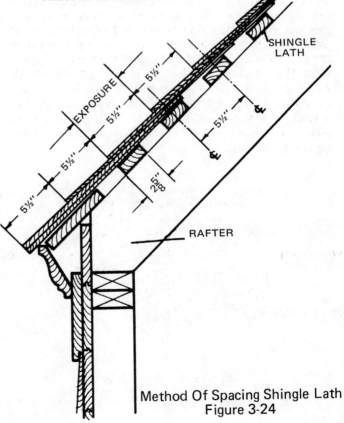

Method Of Spacing Shingle Lath
Figure 3-24

1.  To find the face cut use the steel square the same as in laying out a rafter. Use the unit of run of the rafter and the diagonal length per foot of the rafter. Mark and cut on the run side of the square.

    *Example:* On a roof with a rise of 8 inches and a run of 12 inches, the figures would be 12 and 14 3/8, the latter being the diagonal of 8 on 12. Cut along 12.

2.  To find the edge cut use the rise and the diagonal length per foot of rafter. Mark and cut on the rise.

    *Example:* On a roof with a rise of 8 inches and a run of 12 inches, the figures would be 8 and 14 3/8. Cut on 8.

*NOTE:*   These cuts would also be used for the roof boards meeting over the hips.

**How To Make Valley And Hip Cuts On Shingle Lath Or Roof Boards.**

*NOTE:*   The cut for the roof boards or shingle lath that run into the valley of the roof is composed of the face cut and the edge cut. See figure 3-25.

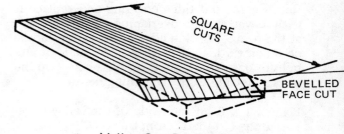

Valley Cut On Roof Board
Figure 3-25

# Chapter 4

# COMPOSITION ROOFING

The carpenter may be asked to apply several types of roofing materials other than wood shingles. Roll roofing, asphalt shingles, strip shingles, asbestos shingles and even canvas and built-up roofing are applied by carpenters rather than roofers in many communities. Such materials as tile, slate, and sheet metal roofing are generally applied by specialists.

Before composition roofing is applied, the roof surface should be carefully prepared to prevent damage to the roofing. The material should be applied in such a way that the wind cannot get between it and the roof sheathing. If this happens it might seriously damage the roofing. Expansion and contraction of this type of roofing material often causes difficulty but some precautions may be taken to help overcome this.

## How To Prepare The Roof.

1. Composition roofing should be applied over 1 inch lumber laid solid or over plywood. Board sheathing should be laid in a diagonal pattern to prevent racking during high winds. Only seasoned wood containing a maximum of 12% moisture should be used. If plywood is used it should be standard sheathing grade and the face grain should be perpendicular to the rafters. In damp climates exterior glueline plywood should be used. When rafters are spaced 16 inches on centers 5/16 inch plywood may be used. Do not use sheathing boards wider than 6 inches. Use only dry straight sound stock free from large knots. Break the joints on the rafters, staggering them over the surface. If any holes or weak spots are found, cover them with tin patches.

2. Double face nail the sheathing on each rafter with 8d nails. Slant the nails so as to draw boards together and set the heads of the nails below the surface. If board sheathing wider than 6 inches must be used, three nails should be used at each support point.

3. After the roof has been covered, inspect the surface to see that there are no projecting nails and that the joints do not form sharp edges which would cut the roofing material.

4. Clean the roof surface of chips and other material.

5. Cover the entire roof surface with a good grade of water proofed building paper or builders felt. If there is a valley in the roof, the valley strips should be laid before the other roofing material is applied. Maintain a 4 inch lap as indicated in figure 4-1.

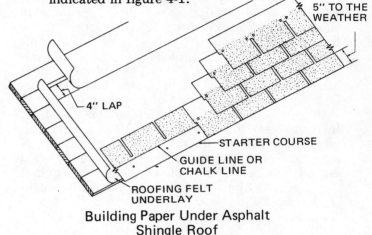

Building Paper Under Asphalt
Shingle Roof
Figure 4-1

| TYPE OF ROOFING | Shingle per Square | Nails Per Shingle | Length of Nails | Nails per Square | Pounds Per Square (Approx.) 12 ga. by 7/16" head | 11 ga. by 7/16" head |
|---|---|---|---|---|---|---|
| Roll Roofing on new deck | -- | -- | 1" | 252** | .73 | 1.12 |
| Roll Roofing over old roofing | -- | -- | 1¾" | 252** | 1.13 | 1.78 |
| 19" Selvage over old shingle | -- | -- | 1¾" | 181 | .83 | 1.07 |
| 3 Tab Sq. Butt on new deck | 80 | 4 | 1¼" | 336 | 1.22 | 1.44 |
| 3 Tab Sq. Butt reroofing | 80 | 4 | 1¾" | 504 | 2.38 | 3.01 |
| Hex Strip on new deck | 86 | 4 | 1¼" | 361 | 1.28 | 1.68 |
| Hex Strip reroofing | 86 | 4 | 1¾" | 361 | 1.65 | 2.03 |
| Giant American | 226 | 2 | 1¼" | 479 | 1.79 | 2.27 |
| Giant Dutch Lap | 113 | 2 | 1¼" | 236 | 1.07 | 1.39 |
| Individual Hex | 82 | 2 | 1¾" | 172 | .79 | 1.03 |

(*) Length of nail should always be sufficient to penetrate at least ¾" into sound wood. Nails should show little, if any, below underside of deck.

(**) This is the number of nails required when spaced 2" apart.

Nail Requirements For Asphalt Roofing
Table 4-2

6. Careful consideration should be given to selecting the correct nails for the type of material to be applied. See table 4-2.

Anything that projects through the roof surface should receive special attention. Vent stacks and conduit should be secure and flashed or equipped with a jack. Drains should be leveled so that they will drain the roof properly. If air conditioning equipment or any type of roof structure is to be installed it should be in place and secure.

## Roll Roofing

Roll type roofing suitable for single-layer roofing comes in many weights and surface coverings. Rolls of this material are generally 36 inches wide and contain enough material to cover approximately 100 square feet of roof surface. The rolls weigh from 85 to 95 pounds per square, depending upon the number of plies of felt in the material but is generally called 90 pound roofing. The surface covering may be smooth or may be coated with sand, colored crushed flint or small pebbles. In most cases the rolls are coated as a solid pattern but it may be obtained with the coated surface marked to represent the individual or strip asphalt shingle. Each roll contains the required number of flat head nails and cement to thoroughly nail and seal the joints.

Roll roofing may be laid upon a comparatively flat roof, even if the fall of the roof is as little as ½ inch to the foot providing the roof surface is flat and smooth. This however is not good practice where the total fall of the roof does not exceed 6 inches because the roll roofing will buckle after it is laid. These buckles cause high and low spots on the roof surface which in turn provide pockets in which the water collects. When the pitch of the roof is less than 2 inches in 12, double coverage of a 19 inch exposure selvage roll should be used. All nails should be concealed and at least a 3 inch lap should be maintained. Roll roofing will expand in summer and contract in winter, thus working itself loose from the roof surface and becoming subject to tearing. The exposed edges of the roofing at the bottom edge and the rake are often the first points to fail in roll roofing because the wind will get under the edges and tear the material. Roll roofing is often used on temporary buildings. If it is used on a permanent structure, it must be applied very carefully as the roofing material itself will withstand the elements over the period of only from 5 to 15 years. Poor application will cause a much earlier failure.

## How To Lay The Valley Strip

The valley strip must be laid before the roof is covered.

1. Use a full width strip long enough to reach from the ridge down to and overlap the crown moulding.

2. Place it in the valley so that an equal amount lies on each side.

3. Push the material down into the valley with a 2 x 4 about 8 feet long. Nail the edges of the material about every 2 feet while it is being held down. See figure 4-3.

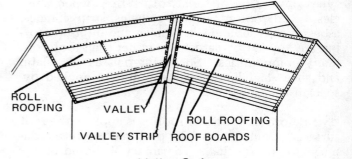

ROLL ROOFING    VALLEY
VALLEY STRIP    ROLL ROOFING    ROOF BOARDS

Valley Strip
Figure 4-3

*NOTE:* Sometimes the valley is doubled. In this case the upper layer of material should be about 6 inches narrower than the lower strip. This is to taper off the double thickness at the edges so that a ridge will not show when the other covering overlaps the valley strip. When a double layer valley is used the mineral surface of the bottom layer should be down. A strip of lap cement should be applied to the outside two inches of each edge of the top side. A full width roll is then centered over the full length of the first strip and pressed into the cement.

## How To Flash A Chimney Or Wall

*NOTE:* In laying good grades of roll roofing, the chimney and all other intersections with the roof surface should be flashed with metal the same as a wood shingle roof. However, if roll roofing is used for this purpose, there should be a cant strip of wood placed at all intersecting surfaces. See figure 4-4.

1. Cut the roofing material so that it will fold up 4 inches against the chimney surface.

2. Cut and install the flashing cant strip. Nail it in position and set the nails. Round off any sharp edges that might damage the roofing material. See figure 4-4.

3. Build a cricket or saddle at the top side of the chimney and cover it with flashing and roofing material. Cement all joints on the upper and lower surfaces.

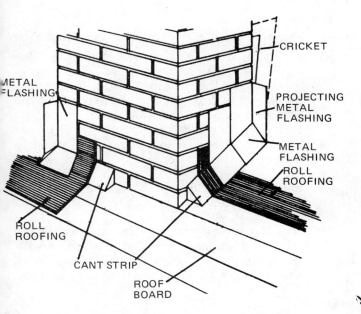

Method Of Flashing Chimney With Roll
Roofing And Metal Flashing
Figure 4-4

## How To Apply Roll Roofing Parallel To The Rafters

*NOTE:* On steep roofs the roll roofing is sometimes put on parallel to the rafters. In
this position the material is less apt to
sag and form wrinkles.

1. Cut lengths of material long enough to reach
from the ridge to the crown moulding, allowing about a 4 inch lap at the ridge and a 1 inch
lap at the eaves.

2. Starting from the end of the roof, measure
along the roof boards 34 inches at the ridge
and at the eaves. Mark these points and snap
a chalked line connecting them.

*NOTE:* This allows for a 2 inch lap over the end
of the roof boards. If there is a valley or
any projection on the roof surface, it is
advisable to start at the end of the roof
to lay the material. However, if the roof
surface is unobstructed, it is sometimes
advisable to start in the middle of the
roof so that the pieces of roofing at each
end of the roof will be of equal width.

3. Align the first strip with the chalked line,
smooth its surface, and nail it temporarily 1
inch from the ridge.

4. Start at a point half way up to the ridge to
turn the roofing material over the edge of the
roof boards at the rake.

*NOTE:* There are several methods of securing the
material over the edges of the roof boards

at the rake. This is a point where the
wind might tear the roofing so it should
be well fastened. The more common
methods are shown in figure 4-5.

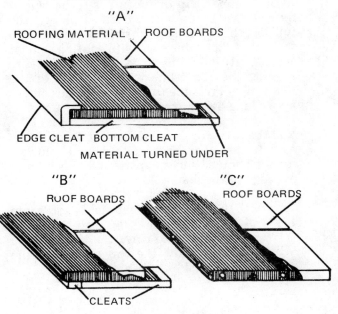

Methods Of Fastening Roof Material
Figure 4-5

If the method A, figure 4-5 is used, the
nailing strip will help hold the material
in a flat position with no wrinkles, providing it is nailed from the center to the
top and from the center to the bottom.
This method of nailing should be used
regardless of the method of fastening the
material.

A convenient scaffold may be made by
using a ladder placed up the slope of the
roof and provided with a hook so that
it may be hooked over the ridge of the
roof. An improvised ladder may be made
of 2 x 4's and 2½" x ¾" rungs nailed to
the 2 x 4's.

5. Place the ladder so that the edge of the material which lies along the chalked line may be
nailed. Nail this edge about every 2 feet if the
next strip is to overlap it.

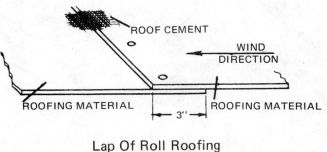

Lap Of Roll Roofing
Figure 4-6

*NOTE:* The laps should be made so they face away from the prevailing wind. See figure 4-6.

6.  If the second strip of roofing is to be lapped by the first strip, snap a chalked line on the full length of the second strip 3 inches from the edge. Paint this edge with roofing cement and slip it under the edge of the first strip, aligning the chalk line with the edge of the first strip. Press the top strip into the cement by walking over the cemented area.

7.  Nail the joints of the roofing material with the nails furnished in each roll. They should be spaced about 3 inches apart and 1 inch from the edge of the material.

    *Caution:* If the roofing material is soft from the heat of the sun, care should be taken not to drive the heads of the nails below the top surface of the material but flush with it.

8.  After each seam is nailed it should be coated with roofing cement as shown in figure 4-6. If flint coated material is used, this painting is not necessary, but the individual nail heads should be covered with a daub of cement.

*NOTE:* If joints are to be made in the strips, they should be parallel to the ridge and lapped 4 inches, cemented and nailed like the other joints in the material.

### How To Lay Roll Roofing Parallel To The Ridge

1.  Prepare the roof surface as previously explained.

2.  Lay the valley strip as previously explained.

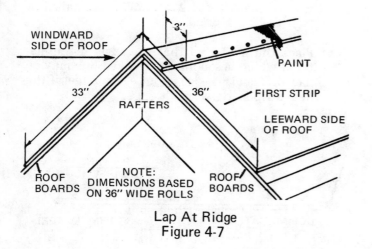

Lap At Ridge
Figure 4-7

3.  The first strip should be started at the ridge and lapped at the ridge with the wind. See figure 4-7. If the first strip is laid on the leeward side of the roof the bottom edge should be 36 inches from the top of the ridge. If the first strip is laid on the windward side the bottom edge should be approximately 33 inches from the ridge. Assume that the first strip is to be on the leeward side.

4.  Snap a chalked line parallel to the ridge and 36 inches from it.

5.  Nail the top edge of the first strip along the ridge so that the bottom edge is in line with the chalked line. Space the nails about 2 feet apart. Allow a 1 inch overlap at the eaves and gable ends.

6.  Roll the second strip into position as shown in figure 4-8.

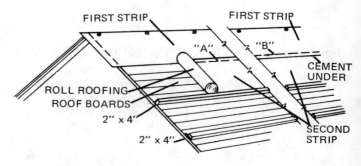

Application Of First And Second Strips
Figure 4-8

7.  Snap a chalked line 3 inches from the top edge of the second strip. Cover this border with cement, being careful not to cover the chalked line.

*NOTE:* If the distance from the ridge to the eaves is such that the last strip will be narrower than the others, use a wider lap than 3 inches to make the exposed width of each strip the same.

8.  Slip the second strip under the first and line up the chalked line with the bottom edge of the first strip. Nail the first strip at the bottom edge, beginning at the center and working toward the ends. Nail as explained for roofing parallel to the rafters.

9.  If joints are to be made in the strips, they should be made so that they lap with the wind. They should be squared, painted and nailed the same as the other seams. See figure 4-3.

10. Continue laying the strips down the roof until the eaves are reached. Fasten the material at the ends and bottom edge as previously described.

11. Lay the top strip on the other side of the roof in the manner shown in figure 4-7.

12. Complete this side of the roof.

*NOTE:* Spiked 2 x 4's have been used in figure 4-8 to hold the roofing roll in the correct place as it is moved across the roof. On roofs with less than a 9 in 12 pitch this may not be necessary.

## How To Apply Hip And Ridge Flashing For Roll Roofing

*NOTE:* Roll flashing for hips and ridges is usually applied after all other roofing is laid.

1. Cut 12 inch wide strips to the desired length. Allow a 1 inch overlap at the gable ends.

2. Apply a 2 inch wide strip of cement to the under side of each outside edge of the strip.

3. Center the strip over the hip or ridge and press the strip down firmly.

4. Nail the overlap down at the eaves and trim the strip off neatly at the ridge ends.

5. Nail around the entire perimeter of the strip at three inch intervals and 1 inch from the edge.

## Asphalt Shingles

Asphalt shingles come in many different weights and sizes. The usual minimum recommended weight for asphalt shingles is 235 pounds for square-butt strip shingles. This may change in later years, as 210 pounds (weight per square) was considered a minimum several years ago. Strip shingles with a 300 pound weight per square are available, as are lock-type and other shingles weighing 250 pounds and more. Asphalt shingles are also available with seal-type tabs for wind resistance. Many contractors apply a small spot of asphalt roof cement under each tab after installation of regular asphalt shingles to provide similar protection.

The square-butt strip shingle is 12 by 36 inches, has three tabs, and is usually laid with 5 inches exposed to the weather. See figure 4-9. There are 27 strips in a bundle, and three bundles will cover 100 square feet. Bundles should be piled flat for storage so that strips will not curl when the bundles are opened for use.

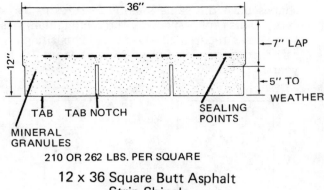

12 x 36 Square Butt Asphalt
Strip Shingle
Figure 4-9

Underlay may or may not be required under asphalt shingles depending on the slope and coverage. If underlayment is required it should be 15 pound saturated felt. See table 4-10.

| | MINIMUM ROOF SLOPE | |
|---|---|---|
| Underlayment | Double Coverage [1] Shingle | Triple Coverage [1] Shingles |
| Not required | 7 in 12 | [2] 4 in 12 |
| Single | [2] 4 in 12 | [3] 3 in 12 |
| Double | 2 in 12 | 2 in 12 |

1  Double coverage for a 12" x 36" shingle is usually an exposure of about 5" and about 4" for triple coverage.
2  May be 3 in 12 for porch roofs.
3  May be 2 in 12 for porch roofs.
(Headlap for single coverage of underlayment should be 2" and for double coverage 19".)

Underlayment For Asphalt Shingles
Table 4-10

Interlocking strip shingles are made in many shapes, but the hexagon is the one most commonly used because of the ease in which the edges of the shingles may be locked. See figure 4-11. Individual manufacturers have applied their own distinctive shapes and locking features to this type of shingle.

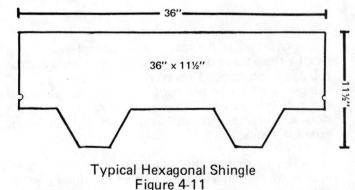

Typical Hexagonal Shingle
Figure 4-11

The individual asphalt shingle is in most cases very similar in composition and weight to the strip shingle. The rectangular shapes often represent as closely as possible the appearance of the wood shingle. See figure 4-12. The hexagonal and angular

37

shapes have the same locking features as the strip type. This type, especially the rectangular ones are sometimes tapered at the butt. This shingle gives satisfactory service for periods of from 10 to 15 years.

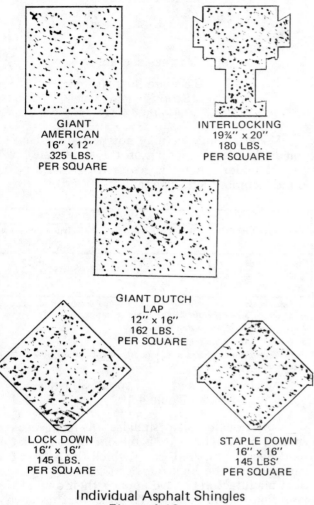

GIANT
AMERICAN
16″ x 12″
325 LBS.
PER SQUARE

INTERLOCKING
19¾″ x 20″
180 LBS.
PER SQUARE

GIANT DUTCH
LAP
12″ x 16″
162 LBS.
PER SQUARE

LOCK DOWN
16″ x 16″
145 LBS.
PER SQUARE

STAPLE DOWN
16″ x 16″
145 LBS'
PER SQUARE

Individual Asphalt Shingles
Figure 4-12

Strip and individual asphalt shingles are subject to the same ravages of the sun and wind as the roll type material. However, because this type of shingle is nailed to the roof in smaller sheets than the roll type, there is more allowance for expansion and contraction and as a result, the buckling effect is avoided.

The tearing of this shingle by the wind is prevented by the interlocking devices provided on the better types of these shingles. With this shingle water may be driven by the wind up underneath and over the top of the shingles and onto the sheathing. To prevent this, a water proofed covering should be applied to the entire surface of the roof before the shingles are laid unless the shingle is stiff enough to form a tight bond between it and the shingle to which it is nailed.

If neither of these precautions are taken, the shingles should be cemented to each other as they are nailed.

An asphalt shingle roof can be protected from ice dams by adding an initial layer of 45 pound or heavier roll roofing, 36 inches wide, and insuring good ventilation and insulation within the attic space.

A course of wood shingles or a metal edging should be used along the eave line before application of the asphalt shingles. The first course of asphalt shingles is doubled; or, if desired, a starter course may be used under the first asphalt shingle course. This first course should extend downward beyond the wood shingles (or edging) about ½ inch to prevent the water from backing up under the shingles. A ½ inch projection should be used at the rake.

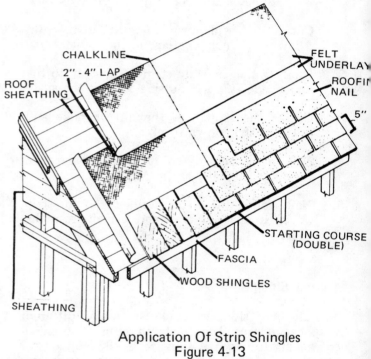

CHALKLINE
2″ - 4″ LAP
ROOF
SHEATHING
FELT
UNDERLAY
ROOFIN
NAIL
5″
STARTING COURSE
(DOUBLE)
FASCIA
WOOD SHINGLES
SHEATHING

Application Of Strip Shingles
Figure 4-13

**How To Lay Strip Asphalt Shingles**

1. Start at the eaves and lay a single layer of wood shingles as in laying a shingle roof. See figure 4-13.

2. Lay the strip shingles, if they are not the slotted type, over the course of wooden shingles.

*NOTE:* If no starter course is used and the shingles are of the slotted type, the strips should be laid upside down, that is the slotted edge of the shingle should point towards the ridge. This is to avoid having the slots in the composition shingles come over the joints in the first course of wooden shingles.

*Caution:* Be sure to nail the strip shingles at the rake. All nails should be driven into these shingles above the exposed area of the shingle.

3. Start the second layer of strip shingles by using a part of a strip at the rake edge of the roof.

*NOTE:* Follow the specifications of the shingle manufacturer in regard to the exposure of the shingle.

Each shingle strip should be fastened securely according to the manufacturer's directions. The use of six nails for each 12 by 36 inch strip is considered good practice in areas of high winds. A sealed tab or the use of asphalt sealer will also aid in preventing wind damage during storms. Some contractors use four nails for each strip when tabs are sealed. When a nail penetrates a crack or knothole, it should be removed, the hole sealed, and the nail replaced in sound wood; otherwise, it will gradually work out and cause a hump in the shingle above it.

4. Continue the second layer by using full length strips to the opposite end of the roof. Cut the last shingle to fit over the rake.

5. Start the third course of shingles by using a full strip at the starting end of the roof. Snap a line, if necessary to keep the courses straight.

6. Start every other course with a cut shingle.

*NOTE:* If there is a valley in the roof, the valley strip should be painted with roofers dope where the strip shingles overlap the valley roofing.

*NOTE:* If strip shingles are to be used to cover the ridge, they should be cut into 12 inch sections so that they may be nailed over the ridge. (Figure 4-14). Another method is to cut a continuous strip of roll roofing about 10 inches wide and nail it over the ridge, spacing the nails 3 inches apart. Be sure to make the laps with the wind and cement them thoroughly. Lap at least 5 inches on each shingle.

If the individual type of composition shingle is used, the same general procedure should be followed. Where special locking features are provided on the shingles the directions of the manufacturer of the shingle should be observed.

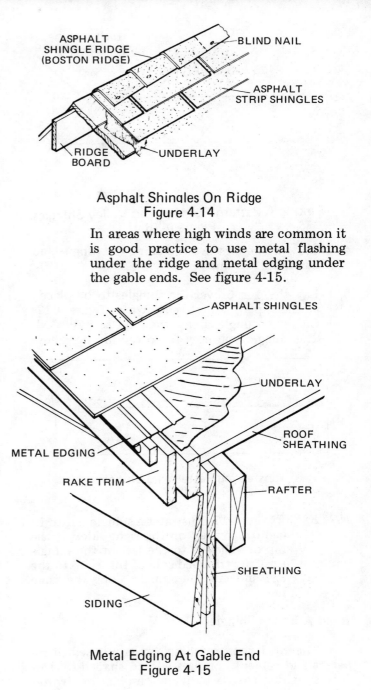

Asphalt Shingles On Ridge
Figure 4-14

In areas where high winds are common it is good practice to use metal flashing under the ridge and metal edging under the gable ends. See figure 4-15.

Metal Edging At Gable End
Figure 4-15

**How To Lay Asphalt Shingles At Hips And Valleys**

*NOTE:* One side of a hip or valley shingle must be cut at an angle to obtain a line which will match the line of the hip or valley rafter.

1. Select a piece of 1 x 6 about 3 feet long.

2. Determine the pitch of the rafter where the hip or valley occurs. For example a roof which rises 9 inches for each 12 inches of horizontal distance ("run") is a 9 in 12 pitch roof.

3. Set the run dimension on the square body and the rise dimension on the tongue across one edge of the 1 x 6 as shown in figure 4-16.

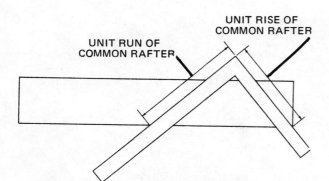

Marking A Pattern For Hip And Valley Shingles
Figure 4-16

4. Draw a line on the 1 x 6 along the tongue and cut along this line.

5. Lay the 1 x 6 over the shingles to be placed at the hip or valley as shown in figure 4-17. Cut the shingle along the line as indicated. The shingle will now fit to the hip or valley.

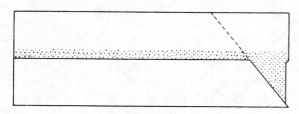

Transferring Pattern To Shingle
Figure 4-17

*NOTE:* Figure 4-17 illustrates a shingle cut to fit a hip or valley on the right side. If the hip or valley is to the left of the shingle turn the trimmed side of the 1 x 6 to the left and cut the shingle along the same line.

### Rigid Asbestos Shingles

The rigid type of shingle is composed of asbestos and cement compressed and shaped to sizes corresponding to the individual asphalt and wood shingles. The angular shapes have special locking features. The rectangular shapes are sometimes tapered at the butt and come in random widths. The outer surfaces and edges are left rough to present a rustic weathered appearance. The weight of this type shingle ranges from 650 to 800 lbs. per square but does not, in most cases, require a heavy roof frame to support them. The life of this type roof is from 15 to 40 years.

Asbestos shingles present many advantages as a roof covering in terms of appearance and durability. Water may be driven up underneath them and they should be laid upon saturated felt which covers the entire roof. The felt should be of the quality specified by the manufacturer because this type shingle is brittle and subject to cracking. If the felt is soft it furnishes a cushion for the shingles, thus reducing broken shingles.

### How To Lay Asbestos Shingles

1. Use the best materials for flashing such as copper, zinc or heavy galvanized iron painted on both sides. The nails should be copper or zinc coated and long enough to go through the shingles and three quarters of the way into the roof boards.

2. Lay the shingles about ¼ inch apart and follow the general procedure as outlined for wood shingles.

*NOTE:* Several different shapes of shingles are on the market and it is impossible to state any definite procedure here that would apply to all. However, the specifications of the manufacturer should be followed.

Special cutting machines may be procured from the manufacturers for cutting the shingles for the hips and valleys.

3. In laying the valley shingles on the valley strip, roofers' cement should be applied to the underside of shingles where they come in contact with the metal.

4. Protect the roof surface when the shingles are laid by providing scaffolds upon which the workmen may walk without putting a load on the shingles. The mason and plumber should have their roof jobs finished before this type of shingles is laid.

### How To Lay Canvas Roofing

Canvas is still used occasionally to cover flat roof surfaces or porch decks. The material should be close woven cotton duck weighing from 12 to 18 ounces per lineal yard of 27 inch width.

This type of covering is used where the deck surface is to be walked upon, or where rainfall is an annoyance such as on a tin roof.

*NOTE:* The life of a canvas deck is dependent to a great extent upon the roofing material directly underneath it. Use clear dry tongue and grooved soft pine, spruce or cypress flooring.

1. Toenail and prepare the surface as for composition roofing. If there are any high spots, such as ridges where the boards join together, plane them down so the roof surface is smooth.

*NOTE:* Any sharp edges that are covered by the canvas will quickly wear through if the roof surface is to be walked upon.

2. Lay the material across the roof surface. Do not try to stretch it but smooth the wrinkles and tack it temporarily in place with copper tacks.

3. Work from the center of each strip toward the ends, laying the successive strips with a 3 inch lap.

4. Cover the surface of the deck, allowing the material to run up the sides of the building at least 6 inches.

5. When the surface is covered and free of wrinkles, nail the seams with copper tacks ¼ inch from the edge of the material and ¾ inch apart.

6. Prepare the canvas surface by applying a coat of raw linseed oil until the canvas is saturated.

*NOTE:* Some mechanics prefer to cover the entire surface with calcined plaster of paris or whiting while the oil is still wet. If this procedure is followed, care must be taken to brush the excess plaster of paris off before it hardens. This process hardens the threads of the canvas which counteracts shrinkage and fills the surface to a smooth finish, giving a better wearing surface. The canvas should then be given two coats of paint.

## Built-Up Roofing

Built-up roofing is usually installed by roofers that specialize in this type of work. Smaller jobs or repair work are often done by non-specialists and anyone working in residential or light commercial construction should have an understanding of how built-up roofing is applied.

Built-up roofing consists of several layers of tar-rag-felt, asphalt-rag-felt, or asphalt-asbestos-felt set in a hot binder of melted pitch or asphalt. A final layer of binder is spread on top and sprinkled with a layer of gravel, crushed stone, or slag. Built-up roofing is confined to roofs which are no steeper than about 4 in 12. On steeper roofs the binder tends to work down and clog gutters and drains. Pitch binder should not be used on a roof with any rise. Asphalt binder may be used on up to about 4 in 12 pitch. For built-up roofing, roof sheathing should be tight-laid and, preferably, doubled. A built-up roof may have 3, 4, or 5 layers of roofer's felt, each mopped down with tar or asphalt, with the final surface coated with asphalt and covered with gravel embedded in asphalt or tar, or covered with a cap sheet. For convenience, it is customary to refer to built-up roofs as 10, 15, or 20 year roofs, depending upon the method of application.

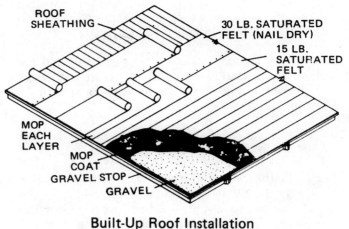

Built-Up Roof Installation
Figure 4-18

For example, a 15 year roof over a wood deck (figure 4-18) may have a base layer of 30 pound saturated roofer's felt laid dry, with edges lapped and held down with roofing nails. All nailing should be done with either roofing nails having 3/8 inch heads driven through 1 inch diameter tin caps or special roofing nails having 1 inch diameter heads. The dry sheet is intended to prevent tar or asphalt from entering the rafter spaces. Three layers of 15 pound saturated felt follow, each of which is mopped on with hot tar rather than being nailed. The final coat of tar or asphalt may be covered with roofing gravel or a cap sheet of roll roofing.

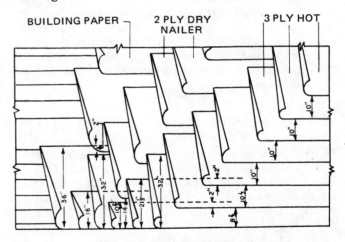

Laying A Five-Ply Built-Up Roof
Figure 4-19

## How To Apply Built-Up Roofing

Built-up roofing, like shingling, is started at the eaves, so that strips will overlap in the direction of the watershed. Figure 4-19 shows the manner of laying 32 inch material to obtain 5 ply coverage at all points on the roof. Nailing must be in accordance with a predetermined schedule designed to distribute the nails in successive plys evenly among the nails already driven.

1. Lay the building paper with a 2 inch overlap as shown. Spot-nail it down just enough to keep it from blowing away.

2. Cut a 16 inch strip of saturated felt and lay it along the eaves. Nail it down with nails placed 1 inch from the back edge, spaced 12 inches on centers.

3. Nail a full-width (32 inch) strip over the first strip, in the same nailing schedule.

4. Nail the next full-width strip with the outer edge 14 inches from the outer edges of the first two, to obtain a 2 inch overlap over the edge of the first strip laid. Continue laying full-width strips with the same exposure (14 inches) until the opposite edge of the roof is reached. Finish off with a half-strip along this edge. This completes 2 plys laid without hot mopping.

5. The next 3 ply start with one-third of a strip, covered by two-thirds of a strip and then by a full strip, as shown. To obtain a 2 inch overlap of the outer edge of the second full strip over the inner edge of the first strip laid, the outer edge of the second full strip must be 8 2/3 inches from the outer edges of the first three strips laid. To maintain the same overlap, the outer edge of the third full strip must be 10 1/3 inches from the outer edge of the second full strip. Subsequent strips may be laid with an exposure of 10 inches. Finish off at the opposite edge of the roof with a full strip, two-thirds of a strip, and one-third of a strip, to maintain 3 plys throughout. See figure 4-19.

The binder is melted and maintained at proper temperature in a pressure fuel kettle. The kettle must be set up and kept level. If it is not level it will heat unevenly, and this creates a hazard. The first duty of the kettle man is to inspect the kettle, especially to ensure that it is perfectly dry. Any accumulation of water inside will turn to steam when the kettle gets hot. This may cause the hot binder to bubble over, which creates a very serious fire hazard.

The kettle man must maintain the binder at a steady temperature, as indicated by the temperature gauge on the kettle. Correct temperature is designated in binder manufacturer's specifications; for asphalt it is about 400° F. The best way to keep an even temperature is to add material as melted material is drawn off. Pieces must not be thrown into the melted mass, but placed on the surface, pushed under slowly and then released.

When mopping the felt with hot binder, care should be taken to see that the binder is the right temperature. Binder which is too hot will burn the felt and the layer it makes will be too thin. A layer which is too thin will eventually crack, and the felt may separate from the binder. Binder which is too cold goes on too thick so that more material is used than necessary.

The felt should be laid over the hot binder as quickly as possible after the binder is placed. If the interval between mopping and felt-laying is too long, the binder will cool to the point where it will not bond well with the felt. The man laying felt should stay within three feet of the area being mopped. Immediately after the felt is applied air bubbles should be worked out with a broom and the felt should be pressed solidly into the hot binder.

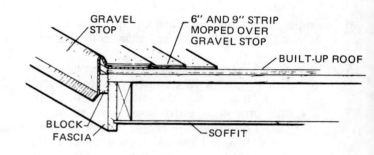

Gravel Stop On A Built-Up Roof
Figure 4-20

The cornice or eave line of projecting roofs is usually finished with metal edging or flashing, which acts as a drip. A metal gravel strip is used in conjuction with the flashing at the eaves when the roof is covered with gravel (figure 4-20). Where built-up roofing is finished against another wall, the roofing is turned up on the wall sheathing over a cant strip and is often also flashed with metal (figure 4-21). This flashing is generally extended up about 4 inches above the bottom of the siding.

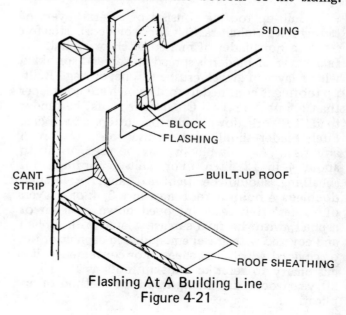

Flashing At A Building Line
Figure 4-21

## Reroofing Over A Built-Up Roof

Repairing or replacing a built-up roof which has failed presents unique problems. Assuming that mere patching will not solve the problem, there are two possible answers: Badly deteriorated roofs must be stripped down to the sheathing and reroofed completely. Roofs which are sound but have a leaking roof covering may be merely recovered after some surface preparation has been done.

Several factors determine whether the existing roof must be removed. The most important considerations are the condition of the roof sheathing and the adhesion of the original roofing to the sheathing. If the sheathing has parted to form fissures in the roof, the sheathing must be repaired in most cases before the new roofing is applied. Repair of the underlying sheathing usually requires removal of the existing roof. Check for deflection of the surface of the roof or evidence of standing water. Any variation in the normal pitch of the roof is an indication that the sheathing or supporting members are not sound. Replacement of the roof covering under these conditions will not solve the problem more than temporarily. "Blisters" in the roof surface (a separation of one layer of felt from the layer below) are the result of air or water trapped between the layers. Small blisters an inch or two in diameter are not as serious as large blisters a foot or more across which indicate a complete break in the bond of the roof. Do not reroof over large blisters. Blisters tend to expand and contract as they are heated and cooled and will cause failure of new roofing laid over them.

Check the flashing for signs of shifting, deterioration or poor installation. Drains, vents and conduit projecting from the roof may have to be replaced or repaired before a sound roof can be laid. Finally, determine whether the roof can support a new covering. Many roofs have been covered and recovered several times. Each new roof covering adds 200 to 600 pounds to the weight of each 100 square feet of roof. A roof that has been recovered several times may not be able to support the new weight with an acceptable margin of safety.

## How To Re-Cover A Built-Up Roof

Most reroofing jobs can be done over the existing built-up roof. This has the advantage of improving the insulating value of the roof and saving the time and expense of removing the old roof and hauling away the debris.

1. Remove any gravel or foreign substance that is on the roof. Power equipment will be helpful here. The roof surface must be free of sharp or irregular shapes that will puncture the new roof.

2. Cut off or flatten out any wrinkles or irregularities in the roof. Cut "X" shaped slits over the full diameter of blisters. Make sure the cut edges then lie flat against the sheathing material. Nail any loose ends or flaps to the sheathing with roofing nails.

3. Inspect areas that have been flashed to determine the condition of flashing and cant strips. Where walls and chimneys meet the roof line, a cant strip should be in place to avoid sharp changes of direction in the roofing. If no cant strip was placed on the original roof, one should be installed before the new roof is applied. Occasionally large cracks will form at valleys and walls. If this has happened, cut the old roof back several inches on each side of the crack, and place metal flashing over the area where the crack existed.

4. Where flashing is defective or has separated from the built-up material, cut the old roof back for several inches and replace the flashing if necessary.

5. Make sure that the new roof will not cause a high point around drains. A build-up of roofing material around the drain may cause water to collect on the new roof. If it appears that a drainage problem may exist, cut off the old roof for several feet around drainage points. Lift off the mouth of the drain and place a layer of 15 lb. felt under the drain before replacing it. This will ensure a watertight roof even if the drain mouth and the new roof material become separated.

6. Inspect the roof for regular pitch. If low spots exist, they can be filled with hot asphalt and felt providing the roof is sound underneath. Don't try to reroof over deteriorating sheathing or rafters that have failed.

7. Inspect the flashing around pipes and vents. Rusted or broken roof jacks should be replaced. Cut the roof back 6 inches beyond the edge of jacks and flashing and replace as necessary.

8. Finally, sweep the roof clean and make a final inspection for any nails or sharp objects protruding from the roof. When a smooth, even surface is present, apply the new roof as described for new construction.

*NOTE:* Built-up roofing can be applied over asphalt shingles using the same procedure outlined above. Replace any missing shingles before reroofing so that the finished surface is even. Don't try to apply built-up roofing over asbestos or wood shingles or tile. If the existing roof is so badly deteriorated that it must be removed, make sure the sheathing is smooth and tight before applying the new roof.

# Chapter 5

# WINDOWS AND FRAMES

Most windows arrive at the job as a complete unit with the frame assembled, sash fitted, exterior casing in place and weatherstripping installed. However, some contractors prefer to have the window and door frames built on the job. This procedure provides work for the carpenters during inclement weather. It might save time when waiting for masonry work to be finished or it may avoid waiting for the frames to be delivered from the mill. Occasionally a frame and sash must be custom made to fit an existing non-standard opening. For these reasons, carpenters should have a basic knowledge of the construction of a few of the more commonly used frames. However, it is usually more desirable that the entire window unit be manufactured by the mill because of the quality of workmanship and the special features which are impossible for the carpenter to equal unless he has special machinery.

The frame is made up of four basic parts: the head, the jamb (two), and the sill. Good construction around the window frame is essential to good building. Where openings are provided, studding must be cut away and its equivalent strength replaced by doubling the studs on each side of the opening to form trimmers and inserting a header at the top. At the bottom of the opening, the bottom header or rough sill is inserted.

The installation of finish outside window frames is usually going on simultaneously with the roof covering. These frames may be ordered ready-made and delivered to the site either assembled or K.D. (meaning "knocked down"), or in parts to be assembled at the site.

Wood window frames should be made from a clear grade of all-heartwood stock of a decay-resistant wood species or from wood which is given a preservative treatment. Species commonly used include ponderosa and other pines, the cedars, cypress, redwood, and the spruces.

The materials used in the building of window frames should be of standard size. They may be obtained from any lumber mill in case the carpenter wishes to build the frames on the job. However, many mills have ready cut members which may be assembled by the carpenter to make stan-dard size frames. A knowledge of the sizes and shapes is essential to the carpenter who has the responsibility of ordering frames, especially when they are built at the mill.

Rough opening sizes for exterior door and window frames vary slightly between manufacturers, but the following allowances should be made for the stiles and rails, thickness of jambs, and thickness and slope of the sill:

*Double-Hung Window (Single Unit)*

Rough opening width = glass width plus 6 inches.

Rough opening height = total glass height plus 10 inches.

For example, the following tabulation illustrates several glass and rough opening sizes for double-hung windows:

| Window glass size (each sash) Width    Height | Rough frame opening Width    Height |
|---|---|
| 24" x 16" | 30" x 42" |
| 28" x 20" | 34" x 50" |
| 32" x 24" | 38" x 58" |
| 36" x 24" | 42" x 58" |

*Casement Window (One Pair - Two Sash)*

Rough opening width = total glass width plus 11¼ inches

Rough opening height = total glass height plus 6 3/8 inches

## Insulating Window Openings

Window frames and glass surfaces are the chief causes of heat loss through outside walls. This is especially true if the side walls are well insulated. Therefore, it is important that both the window frame and the sash be well constructed and that provision be made in the frame for metal weather strips or storm sash or both in order to provide the maximum insulation. The proper flashing around the frame is also an important measure to insure a leakproof wall. These features are often more easily obtained by the use of modern precut window frames.

A window frame should be so constructed that it will prevent rain and cold air from entering the building and heat from filtering out of the building. It should also provide a means by which the sash may be conveniently opened. The sash may be hung on balances or may swing on pivots or hinges. The type of construction between the sash and the frame requires consideration because the joint must be loose enough for the free movement of the sash and at the same time prevent the passage of water and air.

There are two general methods of avoiding the passage of water and air through the joints where the sash and frame meet.

A. Storm windows are perhaps the best means of providing insulation at the window openings because they not only prevent the wind and rain from entering between the sash edges and the frame but they also provide a double thickness of glass with a dead air space between the storm sash and the regular sash. This dead air space acts as a good insulator to prevent heat loss and helps to avoid condensation of moisture on the glass surfaces in cold weather.

B. Metal weather stripping of the sash and window frames does much to prevent air leakage into the building. The disadvantage of using only storm sash as a means of insulation is that they are generally taken off for the summer months and during this time the sash and frame lack protection against the entrance of wind and rain around the edges. The disadvantage of using only metal weather strips is that there is only a single thickness of glass and there is no insulation as with the storm sash. However, the strips prevent the leakage of air and water both in winter and in summer.

To avoid this leakage at the window frame the year around and to provide adequate insulation, a combination of weather strips and storm sash should be used in cold climates. In this case, frames should be so constructed that they provide space for weather strips and storm sash.

Window frames and sash are often the first members of the exterior trim to rot. The material of which they are constructed should be thoroughly painted on all surfaces after they are fitted, or some other means should be taken to treat the wood against rot.

## Flashing Window Frames

Before the window frame is set into the opening, the edges of the opening should be flashed so that the joint between the back of the window casing and the sheathing will be weather-tight. This flashing is generally heavy building paper or felt and should be about 6 inches wide. Building papers are manufactured of different materials and in various thicknesses. The chief function of a building paper is to prevent moisture or air from passing through to the sheathing. Most building papers come in rolls 36 inches wide and contain 200 to 500 square feet. Some papers are coated with rosin or a light coating of creosote and pitch. Some of the felts are soft so when they are forced against the sheathing by the trim they form a flexible covering which is not torn by the shrinkage of the sheathing. The hard glazed and tarred papers have a tendency to shrink, thus forming large holes where the nails go through and allowing air to filter into the building.

After the frame is in place the drip cap should be flashed with a light metal flashing. Sometimes heavy canvas is used for this purpose. This material provides a tight fit when the siding is placed against the drip cap.

In the prefabricated window frame, the jambs, sill, casings and other members are accurately machined and matched together to insure a weather tight joint. In many cases the lumber is treated with a chemical preservative and moisture repellant to insure long life of the frame. The frames are so constructed that screens and storm sash may be readily installed. The necessary hardware is fitted accurately to the frame. The sash are often fitted to their respective frames at the factory, thus saving labor at the job and assuring satisfactory operation of the sash.

There are many types and styles of standard size frames manufactured today that may be ordered complete with sash fixtures and interior trim, either knocked down or in assembled form. Prefabricated frames should be ordered far enough in advance of the time they are needed on the job to allow the mill ample time to build them. This may prevent delay in enclosing the structure.

## Single Hung Frames

Single hung frames are made to hold a single sash. The sash may be fastened permanently in place or it may swing in or out from either the side or the head jamb.

Stationary window frames are often made of plain plank stock. Regular frame members may be used as shown in the sectional view of a stationary window frame in place. See figure 5-1. The sill in this case is a pine plank 1 5/8" x 5 5/8" machined to receive a check strip and sash on the inside edge of the sill, and rabbeted to receive a storm sash or screen on the outside. The side and head jamb members are 1 5/8" x 5 5/8" stock rabbeted to receive the sash on the inside and the storm sash on the outside.

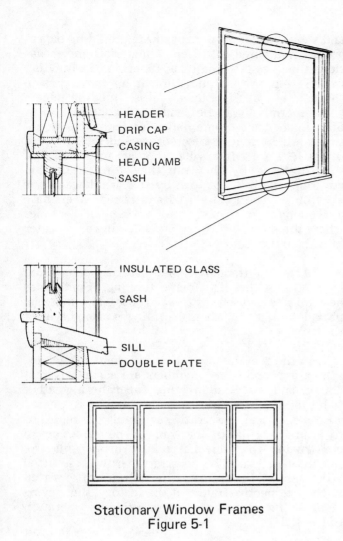

Stationary Window Frames
Figure 5-1

Stationary windows used alone or in combination with double-hung or casement windows usually consist of a wood sash with a large single light of insulated glass. They are designed to provide light, as well as for attractive appearance, and are fastened permanently into the frame. Because of their size, (sometimes 6 to 8 feet wide) 1¾ inch thick sash may be used to provide strength. The thickness may be required because of the thickness of the insulating glass.

**How To Cut Stationary Window Frames**

1. Select a piece of pine stock for the sill. It should be 2 inches longer than the width of the required frame.

2. Select material for the side and head jambs of the frame. The head jamb should be the same length as the sill. The side jambs should be about 6 inches longer than the height of the frame.

3. Mark the height of the sash that is to be used in the finished frame on the inside edge of each side jamb (figure 5-2). These points

mark the inside lines of the head and sill dado joints. Allow about 3 inches on each end of the jamb to provide for the dado joints and the horns.

4. Lay out the dadoes 1 5/8 inch wide and 3/8 inch deep for the head jamb. These dadoes are square across the jamb.

5. Lay out the points for the dadoes of the same size for the sill on the inside edges of the side jambs. Be sure to lay out one right hand jamb and one left jamb.

6. Mark the sill dadoes across the face of the jambs using the sliding T bevel set at about 8 to 12 degrees. This angle will provide for the pitch of the sill. See figure 5-2.

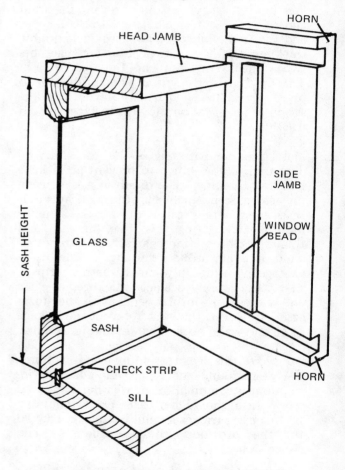

Construction Of A Stationary Window Frame
Figure 5-2

7. Cut the four dadoes on the two side jambs 3/8 inch deep and as shown in figure 5-2.

8. Cut the head jamb and sill 7/8 inch longer than the outside width of the sash. This extra length is added to allow the head jamb and sill to be set into the dado joints which are 3/8 inch deep. The additional 1/8 inch permits the completed frame opening to be

left 1/8 inch oversize since the sash come considerably larger than necessary. This saves extra planing in fitting the sash into the frame.

## How To Assemble The Stationary Window Frame

1. Set the head jamb and sill into the dadoes of the right hand side jamb. Nail through the jambs into the head and sill, keeping the inside edges of the three pieces flush.

2. Set the sill and head jambs into the dadoes of the left hand side jamb and nail as explained in step 1.

3. Square and brace the frame as shown in figure 5-3.

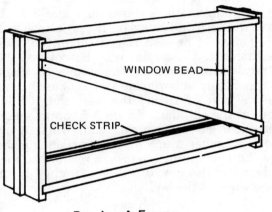

Bracing A Frame
Figure 5-3

4. Nail strips to the outside of the side jambs to hold the frame in place in the wall.

*NOTE:* Sill and jamb stock may be procured from the mill already rabbeted so as to provide a tight joint between the sash and the frame. If plain jambs and sills are used, a stop head should be nailed around on the inside of the jambs and sill to provide a recess into which the sash may be fitted. Another method is to rabbet the sill so that a check strip may be inserted into the sill and the bottom rail of the sash rabbeted to fit over the strip. See figure 5-2.

If casings are applied to the outside of the jamb, they should be kept back 1/2 inch from the face of the jambs to provide a recess for storm windows or screens.

## How To Flash A Window Frame

1. Cut strips of metal or paper flashing as long as the drip cap. They should be wide enough to extend from a point 3 inches up the wall down to the drip cap and then out on the drip cap to a point beyond the outside edge of the siding.

2. Mark a line for the bend of the flashing.

3. Place a straight piece of board on this line and bend the metal up.

4. Place the metal on the drip cap. Press it down firmly and nail it to the sheathing with shingle nails.

*NOTE:* It is only necessary to nail the metal to the building enough to hold it in place since the siding will be placed over it.

5. Nail the flashing to the top of the drip cap with 1/2 inch brads spaced about 6 inches apart.

## How To Install Stationary Window Frames In A Masonry Wall

1. Cut off the top horns of the frame.

2. Brace the frames in position on the masonry wall so that the mason may lay the concrete blocks against the side jambs, and use the frame merely as a form.

*NOTE:* It is not necessary to plumb and level the frame until after the joist sill plate and joists have been placed on the finished masonry wall. The head jamb may then be nailed flush with the outside edge of the sill plate.

3. Check the frame for squareness and insert wooden wedges between the outside edges of the jambs at the sill line and the ends of the concrete blocks.

4. Plumb the frame both ways and drive the wedges tight so as to hold the frame in position.

*NOTE:* The mason may then fill the openings between the outside of the jambs and sill surfaces and the ends of the concrete blocks with mortar. If these openings are small, caulking compound will give a satisfactory job.

Some types of stationary windows may be used without a sash. The glass is set directly into rabbeted frame members and held in place with stops. As with all window-sash units, back puttying and face puttying of the glass (with or without a stop) will assure moisture-resistance.

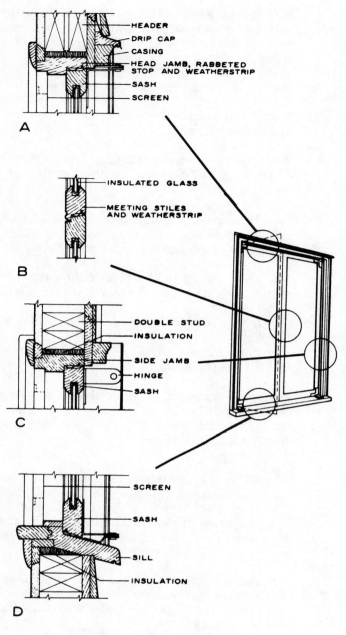

Typical Casement Window
Figure 5-4

Weatherstripping is also provided for this type of window, and units are usually received from the factory entirely assembled with hardware in place. Closing hardware consists of a rotary operator and sash lock. As in the double-hung units, casement sash can be used in a number of ways -- as a pair or in combinations of two or more pairs. Style variations are achieved by divided lights. Snap-in muntins provide a small, multiple-pane appearance for traditional styling.

Metal sash are sometimes used but, because of low insulating value, should be installed carefully to prevent condensation and frosting on the interior surfaces during cold weather. A full storm-window unit is sometimes necessary to eliminate this problem in cold climates.

Casement frames may be made to house single or double sash as shown in figure 5-4. In this case, the sash are hung on hinges attached to the side jambs. The sash rails meet in the middle of the frame and the joint may be covered with an astragal strip. Casement frames may be adapted to inswinging or outswinging sash by merely changing the method of fitting the sash and the interior stool at the sill line. Figure 5-5 shows a casement frame for an outswinging sash while figure 5-6 shows a similar frame for an inswinging sash. Notice the location of the sash in relation to the jamb and sill and also how this type of frame fits into the framework of the building.

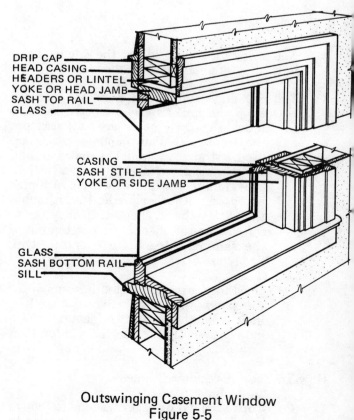

Outswinging Casement Window
Figure 5-5

## Casement Windows

Casement windows consist of side-hinged sash, usually designed to swing outward (figure 5-4) because this type can be made more weathertight than the inswinging style. Screens are located inside these out-swinging windows and winter protection is obtained with a storm sash or by using insulated glass in the sash. One advantage of the casement window over the double-hung type is that the entire window area can be opened for ventilation.

Sills for this type of frame are generally pine, cypress or redwood 1¾" x 7 5/8". They are machined to receive either an outswinging or an inswinging sash. The side and head sections (figures 5-5 and 5-6) show the jambs and how they are machined to receive either the outswinging or inswinging sash. The outside casing on the head section is generally the same as on the side section. This member is 1 3/32" x 4½" and of the same material as the rest of the frame. The drip cap is generally 1 1/16" x 1 5/8" and machined to fit underneath the siding and on top of the head casing, thus forming a drip for the water coming off the side of the building.

## How To Build A Single Casement Frame

*NOTE:* Select stock for casement jambs. The side jambs are laid out in the same manner as those of the stationary window frame except that the side and head jambs of the casement frame are generally 25/32 inch or 1 1/16 inch thick.

1. Lay out the dadoes for the head jamb and sill on the side jambs, making one right hand jamb and one left. The slope of the sill should be from 12 to 15 degrees.

*NOTE:* The distance between the top of the sill cut and the bottom of the head jamb cut along the inside edge of the jamb should be equal to the height of the sash that is to be used in the frame. If necessary, allow for the rabbet cut in the jamb, sill and sash bottom rail (figure 5-5 and 5-6).

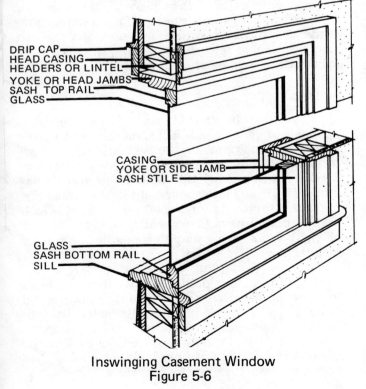

DRIP CAP
HEAD CASING
HEADERS OR LINTEL
YOKE OR HEAD JAMBS
SASH TOP RAIL
GLASS

CASING
YOKE OR SIDE JAMB
SASH STILE

GLASS
SASH BOTTOM RAIL
SILL

Inswinging Casement Window
Figure 5-6

2. Square and cut the head jamb to a length equal to the width of the sash plus an allowance for the head jamb to enter the dadoes in the side jambs.

3. Lay out and cut the sill as shown in figure 5-7. The distance A should be the same as the length of the head jamb. The distance B is the same as the width of the side jamb. The distance C is the width of the casing that is to be used on the window frame.

4. Nail the head jamb into the dadoes in the side jambs as shown in figure 5-7. Use three 8d common nails at each joint.

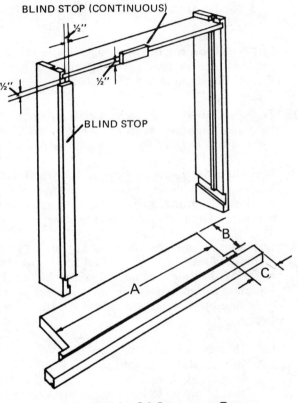

BLIND STOP (CONTINUOUS)

½"

½"

½"

BLIND STOP

B

A

C

Assembly Of Casement Frame
Figure 5-7

5. Nail the sill into the sill dadoes of the side jambs. Use three 8d nails.

6. Nail a blind stop on the outside edge of the side jambs as shown in figure 5-7. These blind stops butt onto the top side of the sill. They extend to ½ inch below the inside edge of the head jamb and project ½ inch over the inside edge of the side jamb. Use 6d common nails and space them about 14 inches apart.

7. Nail a strip of blind stop across the head jamb. Allow it to extend to the outside edges of the blind stops on the side jambs and keep it tight against the top of the side blind stops. This should provide a ½ inch margin across the head

jamb similar to the margin made in nailing the side blind stops to the side jambs. See figure 5-7.

8. Square the frame at the inside faces of the head and side jambs.

9. Brace the frame to hold it square by nailing a strip about ¾" x 1 5/8" to the inside edges of the head and side jamb. If the frames are being built on a bench, the jambs and sill may be temporarily toenailed to the top of the bench to hold them square until after the outside casing has been put on.

*NOTE:* The outside casings are cut and applied to the frame in about the same way as the blind stops.

10. Cut bevels on the bottom edge of the side casing material so that it fits against the top of the sill the same as the blind stop.

11. Cut the top edge of the side casing square and to a length which will bring it ½ inch above the bottom edge of the head blind stop.

12. Nail the side casing on top of the blind stop, keeping the edge ½ inch from the inside edge of the side blind stop. Use 8d casing nails and space them about 12 inches apart.

13. Cut and secure the head casing in a similar manner, allowing it to extend to the outside edges of the side casings. Be sure the cuts on the ends of the top casing are square and that they line up with the outside edges of the side casings.

*NOTE:* If only a drip cap is to be used on the top of the frame, it should be the same length as the head casing. If a bed moulding is to be used underneath the drip cap, the drip cap will necessarily have to be wider and longer. Assume that a moulding is to be used.

14. Cut the drip cap to length. It should extend over each end of the head casing the same amount that it extends over the face of the casing.

*Example:* Assume that the drip cap is to be 2½ inches wide and the head casing 1 1/6 inch thick. The drip cap, when nailed flush with the back of the head casing, would then project over the face of the casing 1 7/16 inch. Therefore in this case, the drip cap should also project over each end of the head casing 1 7/16 inch to provide for the return of the bed moulding.

15. Nail the drip cap with 6d nails.

16. Cut and miter the bed moulding across the head casing at the intersection of the drip cap and casing.

*NOTE:* In putting on the short bed moulding returns, cut a right and left miter on a piece of moulding about 6 inches long. Nail one mitered end to one end of the head casing and cut it off flush with the back of the head casing. Nail the remaining piece to the opposite end of the casing. Use 6d casing nails for the long piece of moulding and 1½ inch brads for the returns.

If a bed moulding is not going to be used on the head casing, the drip cap should be cut off flush with the outside edges of the casing.

The casement frame is installed in the wall opening in the same manner as a stationary window frame.

**Double Hung Window Frames**

The double-hung window is perhaps the most familiar window type. It consists of an upper and lower sash that slide vertically in separate grooves in the side jambs or in full width metal weatherstripping (figure 5-8). This type of window provides a maximum face opening for ventilation of one-half the total window area. Each sash is provided with springs, balances, or compression weatherstripping to hold it in place in any location. Compression weatherstripping, for example, prevents air infiltration, provides tension, and acts as a counterbalance; several types allow the sash to be removed for easy painting or repair.

Sash may be divided into a number of lights by small wood members called muntins. A ranch-type house may provide the best appearance with top and bottom sash divided into two horizontal lights. A colonial or Cape Code house usually has each sash divided into six or eight lights. Some manufacturers provide preassembled dividers which snap in place over a single light, dividing it into six or eight lights. This simplifies painting and other maintenance.

Hardware for double-hung windows includes the sash lifts that are fastened to the bottom rail, although they are sometimes eliminated by providing a finger groove in the rail. Other hardware consists of sash locks or fasteners located at the meeting rail. They not only lock the window, but draw the sash together to provide a "windtight" fit.

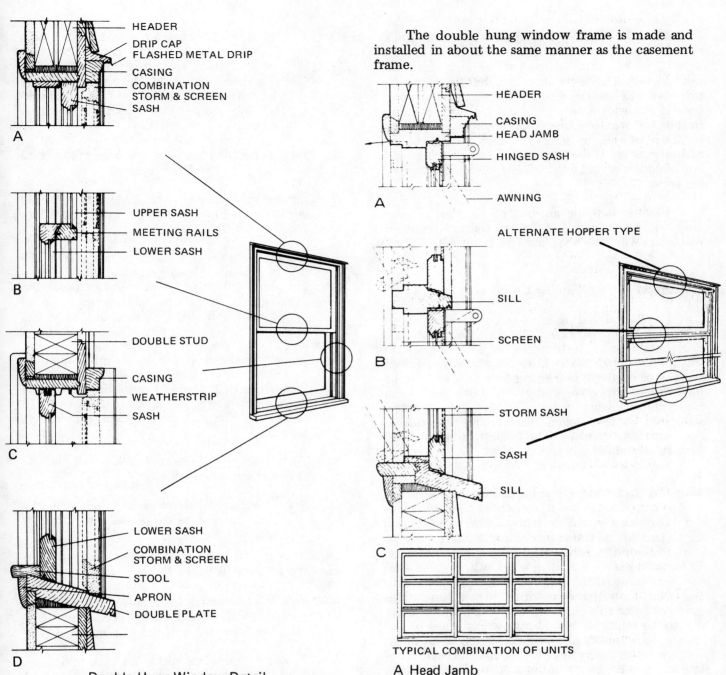

Double Hung Window Detail
Figure 5-8

**A**
- HEADER
- DRIP CAP
- FLASHED METAL DRIP
- CASING
- COMBINATION STORM & SCREEN
- SASH

**B**
- UPPER SASH
- MEETING RAILS
- LOWER SASH

**C**
- DOUBLE STUD
- CASING
- WEATHERSTRIP
- SASH

**D**
- LOWER SASH
- COMBINATION STORM & SCREEN
- STOOL
- APRON
- DOUBLE PLATE

The double hung window frame is made and installed in about the same manner as the casement frame.

**A**
- HEADER
- CASING
- HEAD JAMB
- HINGED SASH
- AWNING

**B**
- ALTERNATE HOPPER TYPE
- SILL
- SCREEN

**C**
- STORM SASH
- SASH
- SILL

TYPICAL COMBINATION OF UNITS

A Head Jamb
B Horizontal Mullion
C Sill

Awning Window
Figure 5-9

Double-hung windows can be arranged in a number of ways -- as a single unit, doubled (or mullion) type, or in groups of three or more. One or two double-hung windows on each side of a large stationary insulated window are often used to effect a window wall. Such large openings must be framed with headers large enough to carry roof-loads.

The jambs (sides and top of the frames) are made of nominal 1 inch lumber; the width provides for use with dry wall or plastered interior finish. Sills are made from nominal 2 inch lumber and sloped at about 3 in 12 for good drainage (figure 5-8D). Sash are normally 1 3/8 inches thick and wood combination storm and screen windows are usually 1 1/8 inches thick.

## Awning Windows

An awning window unit consists of a frame in which one or more operative sash are installed (figure 5-9). They often are made up for a large window wall and consist of three or more units in width and height.

Sash of the awning type are made to swing outward at the bottom. A similar unit, called the hopper type, is one in which the top of the sash swings inward. Both types provide protection from rain when open.

Jambs are usually 1 1/16 inches or more thick because they are rabbeted, while the sill is at least 1 5/16 inches thick when two or more sash are used in a complete frame. Each sash may also be provided with an individual frame, so that any combination in width and height can be used. Awning or hopper window units may consist of a combination of one or more fixed sash with the remainder being the operable type. Operable sash are provided with hinges, pivots, and sash supporting arms.

Weatherstripping and storm sash and screens are usually provided. The storm sash is eliminated when the windows are glazed with insulated glass.

## Horizontal Sliding Window Units

Horizontal sliding windows appear similar to casement sash. However, the sash (in pairs) slide horizontally in separate tracks or guides located on the sill and head jamb. Multiple window openings consist of two or more single units and may be used when a window wall effect is desired. As in most modern window units of all types, weatherstripping, water repellent preservative treatments, and sometimes hardware are included in these fully factory assembled units.

## How To Assemble Prefabricated Window Frames

The assembly of prefabricated frames is similar to that of the frame made on the job but due to the tight joints, certain precautions are necessary. It is customary to set the window frames so that the head jamb of the window will be on a line with the head jamb of the interior finished door. This may not be possible in every case, especially if there are to be window frames at stair landings or entrance door frames at levels below the main floor. In such cases the type of siding and the method of spacing the courses should be considered so that the top of the frame will come even with the bottom of a course of siding.

Most of the modern ready cut frames can be assembled without much trouble but there are occasions when the assembly requires a skilled mechanic. In some cases the manufacturer of the frame supplies specific instructions for assembling. These should be followed. The following instructions apply to prefabricated frames in general.

1. Assemble the side and head jambs first, being sure the edges at the intersections are perfectly flush. Next assemble the sill to the side jambs. Pull the joints in by using a block and hammer, giving the joints light taps until they are thoroughly seated.

*NOTE:* It is well to let the heads of the nails stick out about ½ inch beyond the face of the jambs so that if the frame is not assembled correctly, the nails may easily be withdrawn. After the frame is checked and squared the nails may be driven home.

2. Install the blind stop in the manner illustrated in figure 5-7. Use 6d casing nails.

3. Square the frame on two diagonally opposite corners and brace the frame in this position. See figure 5-3.

4. Install the two side casings, being sure the rabbeted joints fit perfectly and that the margin along the edge of the blind stop is the same the full length of the casing. Use 8d casing nails and space them about 14 inches apart.

5. Install the head casing in a similar manner.

6. Install the drip cap and moulding, using the same procedure as explained in steps 14 to 16 of the section on building single casement frames.

7. Temporarily tack the parting strip in place in the head and side jambs.

*NOTE:* The assembled frame is installed in the same manner as explained for stationary window frames.

## How To Install A Window Frame

*NOTE:* It is assumed that the rough opening in the wall is laid out in accordance with the dimensions of the window frame.

1. Procure the window rod that was used to mark the rough openings of the window frames. Cut a notch so that the head jamb of the window frame will fit into it. This notch should hold the jamb the required distance from the top of the floor.

2. Trim off the projecting sheathing at the top of the opening.

3. Cover the outside edges of the window opening with building paper as shown in figure 5-10. Note the way the paper is lapped at the corners. If the sheathing projects over the sides of the window opening, cut the sheathing off even with the face of the 2 x 4.

4. Cut the jamb horns off square so they rest on the 2 x 4 sill.

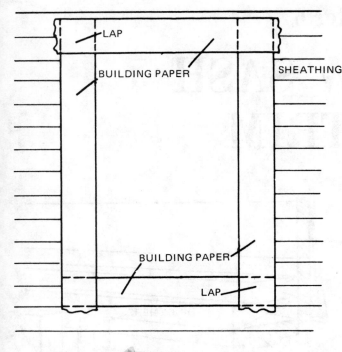

Building Paper On Window Opening
Figure 5-10

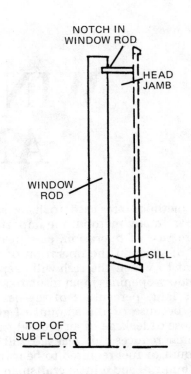

Window Rod Height
Figure 5-11

5. Place the frame into the opening and suspend the head jamb by placing it into the notch of the window rod as shown in figure 5-11.

6. Center the bottom of the frame in the opening at the sill. Temporarily nail the bottom end of one side casing into the sheathing.

7. Level the sill by holding the level first across the inside edge of the sill and then upright against the parting strip of the frame. Use a straight edge and level if the frame is large.

8. Set a nail in the bottom of the opposite side casing. When the sill is level, temporarily nail the casing to the sheathing.

9. Plumb the side casing by placing the spirit level into the recess of the casing and blind stop. Set a nail at the top of the casing and

when the casing is plumb, drive the nail partly into the sheathing.

10. Plumb the opposite side casing, check the sill for levelness again and if it is still level and both casings are plumb, drive the nails home.

11. Finish nailing the side and head casings, spacing the nails about 14 inches apart and opposite the nails that hold the casing to the blind stop. Set all nails.

*NOTE:* If the side jamb horns of the frame do not rest on the 2 x 4 sill they should be blocked so that the frame has a solid bearing on the rough opening. Care should be used in putting the wedges between the 2 x 4 and the bottom of the jamb so as not to disturb the levelness of the frame sill.

# Chapter 6

# WINDOW SASH AND TRIM

Several methods are used to hang sash in a window frame. In any method, the important considerations are ease of operation, ease of cleaning, conservation of space in the operation of the sash and the extent to which the sash will keep out the weather. Window openings in an insulated building account for a large percentage of the heat loss in cold weather because of the amount of glass area and also because of leakage of air around the edges. Anything which reduces this leakage will also reduce the amount of fuel required to heat the structure. A few minutes and a little craftsmanship will yield dividends in lower heating costs over the life of the window.

Basement and attic sash are generally fitted so that they may be hung on hinges. The sash should be fitted with about 1/8 inch clearance on all edges between the sash and the frame. This is to allow for the expansion of the wood members. This is especially important in the basement. The hinges may be applied to the top or side of the frame and let in the jamb as a butt hinge, or fastened to the surface of the sash and edge of the jamb as a surface hinge. Special hardware, such as extension hinges that hold the window open, and fasteners that lock the sash are often used.

In some cases, the single sash is fitted into the frame so that it may be permanently nailed in place. In this case, the sash should be fitted with about a 1/16 inch clearance, and the edges of the sash and the jamb and sill surfaces should be painted before the sash is permanently placed.

## How To Fit A Basement Sash

1. Test the frame with a steel square at two diagonally opposite corners for squareness.

2. Measure the width of the sash opening in the frame. Take this measurement by using an inside measuring steel tape or a small wooden rod.

3. Transfer this distance to the sash, allowing an equal amount on each side. Mark these points on the side stiles.

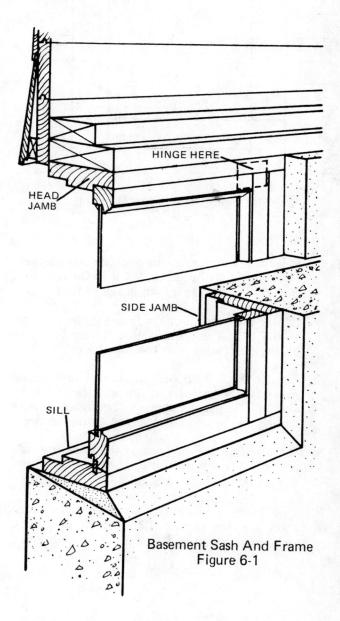

Basement Sash And Frame
Figure 6-1

4. Extend these points by drawing lines parallel to the edges of the stiles the full height of the sash.

5. Cut along these lines with a rip saw and plane the edges square and smooth. If only a small amount of stock is to be removed, use the plane only.

6. Measure the height of the sash opening on the inside of the frame.

7. Transfer this distance to the sash by measuring from the outside edge of the top rail and marking the distance on the bottom rail. The point on the bottom rail shows the height on the inside surface of the sash. Extend this point the length of the bottom rail.

8. Saw through the side stile with a fine crosscut saw, following the line on the bottom rail of the sash. Continue along the line with a rip saw until the opposite stile is reached. Finish the cut through this stile by using the crosscut saw.

9. Plane the surfaces smooth with a jack plane. Plane from the edges toward the center. Plane the top rail in the same manner.

10. Mark the size of the stop that is rabbeted in the sill on the outside of the bottom rail.

11. Set the rabbet plane and plane a rabbet along the outside edge of the rail so that the rail will fit over the stop in the sill.

12. Test the sash in the opening and refit it so there is an allowance of about 3/16 inch between the edges of the sash and the frame. Bevel the edges about 1/16 inch toward the outside and round the sharp edges about 1/8 inch.

## How To Hang A Sash With Hinges

1. Adjust the sash in the opening so that none of the edges of the sash touch the frame. Small wedges may be used to hold the sash in place.

2. Locate the position of the hinges on the sash and window jamb. Use a nail or a nail set to mark holes through the holes of the hinges into the sash and jamb. Be sure the holes are square with the surface of the sash and jamb.

3. Drive enough screws through the holes in the hinges to hold them firmly in place.

4. Remove the wedges and try the sash for clearance and swing. If the sash swings clear, place the remaining screws in the hinges.

NOTE: If the sash binds it is generally caused by the outer edge of the hinge side of the sash rubbing against the stop in the frame, or by lack of clearance at the edges. These conditions may be corrected by removing the sash and providing clearance at these points.

5. Secure the locking device to the sash when it is in a closed position. Swing the sash to its full open position and secure it with hardware to hold it temporarily open.

## How To Hang A Double Hung Sash

Double hung sash are generally fitted into a frame having two runways. The lower sash slides to the top or bottom of the frame on the inner runway. The upper sash slides in a similar manner in an outer runway.

The upper and lower sash are generally the same size so that when the windows are closed, the meeting rails of both sash are midway between the head jamb and sill. There are cases, however where the upper sash may take less than half of the height of the opening, the lower sash height taking up the remaining height. Then the meeting rails would meet above the center.

1. Remove the parting strips from the side jambs of the frame.

2. Fit the upper sash in the same general manner as the single basement sash except that neither the meeting nor the top rail of this sash should be made narrower. Cut and plane the horns only.

3. Measure the distance the parting strip projects beyond the face of the jamb when the strip is fully seated in the rabbet of the jamb. This distance is generally about 5/8 inch.

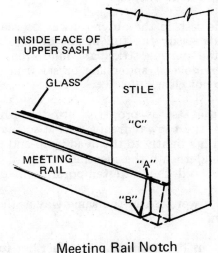

Meeting Rail Notch
Figure 6-2

4. Mark this distance on the meeting rail as shown at A, figure 6-2. Square from this point to the edge of the meeting rail as shown at B.

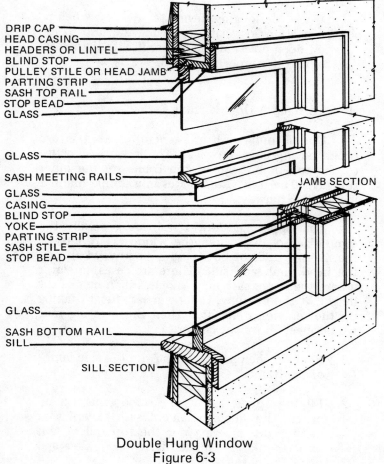

DRIP CAP
HEAD CASING
HEADERS OR LINTEL
BLIND STOP
PULLEY STILE OR HEAD JAMB
PARTING STRIP
SASH TOP RAIL
STOP BEAD
GLASS

GLASS

SASH MEETING RAILS

GLASS
CASING
BLIND STOP
YOKE
PARTING STRIP
SASH STILE
STOP BEAD

GLASS

SASH BOTTOM RAIL
SILL

JAMB SECTION

SILL SECTION

Double Hung Window
Figure 6-3

5. Cut out this piece with a fine crosscut saw. See the dotted line in figure 6-2.

6. Lay out and cut the other end of the meeting rail in the same manner.

7. Test the sash in the outer runway to see if it will slide easily the full height of the frame when the parting strips are in place. If it binds, remove it and plane or saw the edges that do not clear.

8. When the sash is properly fitted so that it slides in the runway freely, raise it so that the top rail fits tightly to the head jamb and place a nail underneath the meeting rail in the runway to hold the sash temporarily in place.

9. Fit the lower sash in the same way as the upper sash.

10. Place it in the frame and set a scriber to the distance the top of the meeting rail of the bottom sash is above the top of the meeting rail of the top sash.

11. Lower the top sash half way and scribe the bottom rail of the bottom sash to the sill with the scriber.

12. Set the sliding T bevel to the slope of the sill and mark the side rails with the bevel setting, placing the long point of the bevel at the scribe mark. Cut and plane the bottom rail, following the bevel cut.

### How To Fit And Hang A Casement Sash

The inswinging casement sash is fitted in exactly the same manner as the basement sash. The outswinging sash is fitted the same as the lower sash of the double hung window except that there is no meeting rail to be notched. These sash are hung in the same general way as the basement sash. The hinges may be placed on either side jamb and may be the butt type or the extended hinge type. Extension hinges are applied in the same general manner.

### How To Fit And Install Horizontal Sliding Sash

Horizontal sliding sash may be installed by placing runways at the sill of a large casement window frame. This requires a filler strip which is ploughed similar to the side jamb and is beveled to fit the sill.

Another form of sliding sash acts in a ploughed track in the sill and head jamb. These guide the sash past one another in a single casement frame. This method of operating the sash in the frame is often used where the sash are large and the double hung system could not be used. Sash up to 5 feet 8 inches wide by 5 feet 6 inches high may be used without counterweights. The sash, when closed, fall in the same plane as those of a hinged casement sash. When open, the right hand sash glides into an inner head and sill track so that the sash can pass each other. The sash may easily be removed for cleaning and for placing storm sash or screens. The operating equipment includes two steel guides attached to the bottom of each sash and two steel guide pins at the top plus the operating handle and lock.

There are several other methods of hanging sash in a frame. Some require a special frame and others may be adapted to a standard frame. However, it is advisable to hang the sash in a frame particularly designed for that type of hanging. In most cases the sash should be prefitted to the frame at the mill so as to avoid any looseness at the window opening. Sliding sash are fitted the same as casement sash except that the bottom rail is left square instead of being beveled or rabbeted. A parting strip is nailed on the side rail where it overlaps the side rail of the opposite sliding sash. In some cases, small brass rollers are inserted 3 inches from each end of the sash in the bottom rail so that the sash will roll along the surface of the runway more easily. Small metal round faced pins, metal weather strips or metal tracks are also used for this purpose. Be sure to insert the rollers in the center of the thickness of the bottom rail. Cut into the rail deep enough to allow enough clearance for the rollers to revolve. If a metal track is used, the male section of the track should be used on the sill and the female section on the bottom rail. This also applies to metal weather strips.

## How To Fit And Hang Storm Sash

Fit storm sash in the same manner as basement sash except for the bottom rail which is fitted like the bottom rail of a double hung sash. Be sure to allow 3/16 inch on all edges for paint and to avoid damage to the edges of the soft casing of the frames. Special hanger hinges are made for storm sash and screens. These may be applied to the top of the sash in the same manner as surface hinges. Several types of hardware are used to hold the sash open or closed. Directions for applying them are generally enclosed in the package with the hardware.

## Window Trim

Window side and head casings are generally of the same design as the door casings. The door trim consists of two sides and a head casing whereas the window trim includes these casings together with the sill trim. The description of the side and head trim for windows will therefore be omitted. Only the sill and stop bead will be considered.

The plain, moulded, back band and cabinet head styles of trim as described in this volume for doors are the same for windows. Figure 6-3 shows the window trim on a double hung window. It is fitted to the top of the stool in the same manner as the door trim is fitted to the floor. The edges of the casings are flush with the jamb instead of showing a margin 3/16 inch as in door casings.

The stool is generally 1 1/16" x 3½" and extends beyond the sides of the side casings as shown. It is rabbeted to fit the bevel of the sill and to provide a level top upon which the side casings may be fitted.

The stop bead, which is usually ½ inch thick and 1½ inch wide, forms one edge of the runway for the lower sash. It is applied to the head and side jambs. The joints at the two corners may be coped or mitered and the lower end butts against the stool.

The apron serves as an added support for the stool and a means of forming a trim at the bottom of the window opening. It is generally made up of 25/32 inch stock and dimensioned to correspond to the side casings of the window trim.

## How To Fit A Stool For A Double Hung Window

1. Select clear stool stock. Square off one end.

2. Round this end with a plane to correspond to the profile of the front edge of the stool. Take a fine cut and work across the end grain from the front edge of the stool.

3. Measure the distance the ends of the stool are to extend beyond the inside faces of the jambs and mark these points on the adjacent wall. The stool should extend beyond the outer edge of the side casing the same distance it will project beyond the stool in front.

*NOTE:* If the window is of the casement type 3/8 inch would be added to the stool to allow for a margin 3/16 inch on each side at the inside of the casings.

A templet may be made to hook over the jamb of the window frame. Notches may be made in the templet so that the location of the outer edge of the casing and the end of the stool may be quickly and accurately marked on the wall of both sides of all the window openings, thus avoiding successive measurements. See figure 6-4.

4. Cut the stool to the same length as the distance between the two marks on the wall and round off the second end.

5. Place the stool against the window jambs at the sill line. Keep the ends of the stool even with the stool marks on the wall.

6. Place the combination square blade against the inside face of the window jamb and on top of the window stool. Mark along the blade and on the top of the stool as at A, figure 6-5. Mark the other end in the same way.

7. Set the scriber to the distance between the square edge of the stool and the inside of the bottom sash rail (B, figure 6-5).

*NOTE:* Be sure the sash is down to the sill and that it is tight against the parting strip.

8. With one end of the scriber against the wall, scribe the top surface of the stool, making a mark as shown at C. Mark both ends of the stool in the same way.

9. Cut along the lines C with a rip saw. Use a crosscut saw to cut along line A. Cut out the other end in the same way.

10. Replace the stool on the sill and trim it so that it fits against the sash and the wall surface.

11. Move the lower sash up and down to see that it does not hit the stool edge. The distance between the sash and the stool should be no greater than 1/16 inch or a double thickness of sandpaper.

12. When the stool fits properly, nail it to the window sill, using 8d casing nails about 10 inches apart.

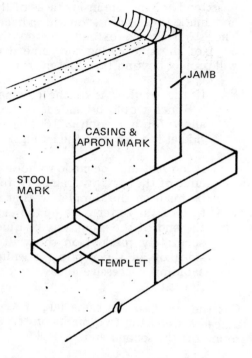

Templet For Sill Trim
Figure 6-4

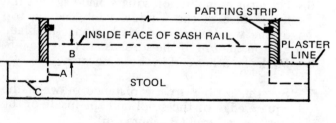

Stool Layout
Figure 6-5

### How To Fit The Sill Apron

1. Select the apron stock and cut it to length. This length should be the same as the distance between the two marks on the wall which represent the outside edges of the side casings (figure 6-4).

*NOTE:* If the apron is of a moulded type, return the profile on the ends.

2. Place the apron in position on the window sill and even with the marks made on the wall for the ends of the apron (figure 6-4).

3. Fit the apron to the bottom of the stool and nail it in place. Insert nails at the top of the apron into the sill and also at the bottom into the subsill of the rough window opening. Use 6d finishing nails spaced 14 inches apart.

*NOTE:* Be sure the stool is level both ways before nailing the apron and that the apron does not crowd it up as it is being nailed.

4. Fit the side and head casings in the same way as those of the door. However, the edges of the casings come flush with the inside surface of the window jambs. The nails in the side casings should not be driven into the removable pocket of the side jambs. The head casing is the same length as the apron.

### How To Fit The Stop Bead

1. Select the head stop bead material and cut it to fit in between the faces of the side jambs.

2. Fit it into place and nail it temporarily.

3. Cut the side stop beads so that they extend from the top of the stool to the underside of the window head jamb. Leave them 1/16 inch long and cope the top ends to fit against the head stop bead.

4. Adjust the side stop bead so that a double thickness of sandpaper will fit between the lower sash and the stop bead. Temporarily nail it in this position and move the lower sash to the top and bottom of the frame to see if the stop is the same distance from the sash the full height of the frame.

5. After the two side stops have been properly adjusted, nail them with 1½ inch brads spaced 10 inches. Nail the top stop to line up with the side stops.

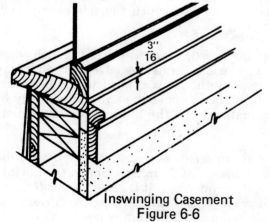

Inswinging Casement
Figure 6-6

## How To Fit The Stool Of A Casement Window

*NOTE:* An inswinging casement is shown in the sill section of figure 6-6. The only difference in fitting the casings and stool of this frame from that of the double hung frame is that the stool is butted against the inside edge of the window sill and a margin of 3/16 inches is left between the top of the sill and the top of the sill stool. The side and head casings also show a margin at the jamb rather than being flush as in the double hung frame.

1. Select the stool stock and cut it to length the same as for a double hung frame.

2. Form the returns on the ends.

3. Rip the stool to fit the edge of the sill. Allow the front edge and the ends to project over the face and ends of the apron the same distance as in the double hung frame.

4. Nail the stool to the sill temporarily. Fit the apron and nail it permanently in place. Nail the stool permanently by driving 8d finishing nails through the edge into the sill. It should also be nailed to the apron.

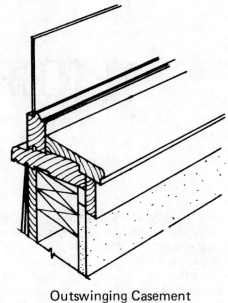

Outswinging Casement
Figure 6-7

5. Secure the head and side casings.

*NOTE:* An outswinging casement frame is shown in figure 6-7. This type frame is cased in the same way as the double hung frame except that an extra wide stool is provided.

# Chapter 7

# PREFABRICATED WINDOW UNITS

## Metal Window Units

A wide variety of assembled metal window units are available. Most come with frame, sash and trim assembled. Often they are glazed and have the appropriate screens, weatherstripping and hardware in place or on hand for quick assembly. Usually the entire unit can be nailed into the opening in a fraction of the time needed to fit and install a complete window using more traditional methods.

Modern assembled window units do not eliminate the value of craftsmanship, however. Several points should be observed before and during installation. Regardless of the type of window used, it should be of the size, combination, and type indicated or specified. Windows should be constructed to produce the results specified and to assure a neat appearance. Permanent joints should be formed by welding or by mechanical fastenings, as specified for each type window. Joints should be of sufficient strength to maintain the structural value of members connected. Welded joints should be solid, have excess metal removed, and be dressed smooth on exposed and contact surfaces. The dressing should be done so that no discoloration or roughness will show after finishing. Joints formed with mechanical fastenings should be closely fitted and made permanently watertight. Frames and sash, including ventilators, come assembled as a unit with hardware unattached.

Hardware should be of suitable design and should have sufficient strength to perform the function for which it is used. It should be attached securely to the windows with noncorrosive bolts or machine screws; sheet metal screws should not be used. Where fixed screens are specified, the hardware should be especially adapted to permit satisfactory operation of ventilators.

Aluminum windows in concrete or masonry walls should be set in prepared openings. Unless indicated or specified otherwise, all other windows should be built-in as the work progresses, or they should be installed without forcing into prepared openings. Windows should be set at the proper elevation, location, and reveal. They should be set plumb, square, level, and in alignment. They should also be braced, strutted, and stayed properly to prevent distortion and misalignment. Ventilators and operating parts should be protected against accumulation of cement, lime, and other building materials by keeping ventilators tightly closed and wired fast to the frame. Screws or bolts in sill members, joints at mullions, and contacts of windows with sills, built-in fins, or subframes should be bedded in mastic sealant of a type recommended by the window manufacturer. Windows should be installed in a manner that will prevent entrance of water.

Ample provision should be made for securing units to each other, to masonry, or to other adjoining or adjacent construction. Windows that are to be installed in direct contact with masonry must have head and jamb members designed to enter into masonry not less than 7/16 inch. Where windows are set in prepared masonry openings, the necessary anchorage or fins should be placed during wall construction. Anchors and fastenings should be built into, anchored, or bolted to the jambs of openings and should be fastened securely to the windows or frames and to the adjoining construction. Unless indicated otherwise, anchors should be spaced not more than 18 inches apart on jambs and sills. Anchors and fastenings should have sufficient strength to hold the member firmly in position.

After windows have been installed and upon completion of glazing and painting, all ventilators and hardware should be adjusted to operate smoothly and to be weathertight when ventilators are closed and locked. Hardware and parts should be lubricated as necessary. Adjustments and tests should be as follows:

A    Double-hung windows should have balance adjusted to proper tension, and guides waxed or lubricated.

B    Casements equipped with rotary operators should be adjusted so that the top of the ventilator makes contact with the frame approximately ½ inch in advance of the bottom.

C    Casements equipped with friction hinges or friction holders should be adjusted to proper tension.

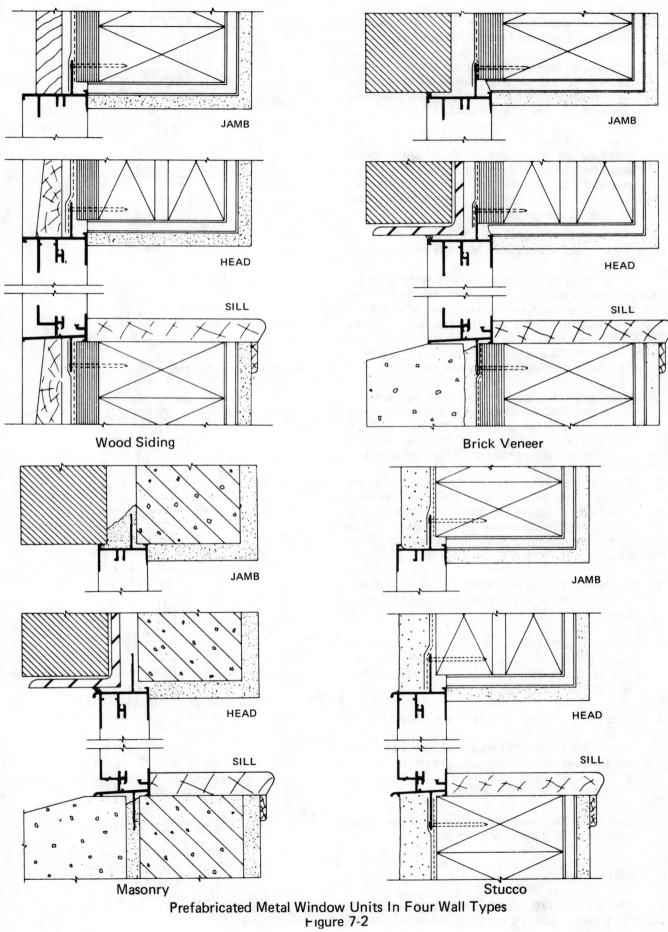

JAMB

HEAD

SILL

Wood Siding

JAMB

HEAD

SILL

Brick Veneer

JAMB

HEAD

SILL

Masonry

JAMB

HEAD

SILL

Stucco

Prefabricated Metal Window Units In Four Wall Types
Figure 7-2

D    Projected sash should have arms or slides lubricated and adjusted to proper tension.

E    Awning windows should have arms or ventilators adjusted so that the bottom edge of each ventilator makes continuous initial contact with frames when closed.

F    Where windows are weatherstripped, weatherstripping should make weathertight contact with the frames when ventilators are closed and locked. The weatherstripping should not cause binding of sash, or prevent closing and locking of the ventilator.

## How To Install Prefabricated Metal Windows

Window units are installed before the exterior finish is put in place. The jamb width and sill detail must be appropriate for the type of construction and exterior finish of the structure. Figure 7-1 illustrates jamb, head and sill details for masonry construction and frame construction with either brick veneer, stucco or wood siding exterior.

1.   Window units can be installed most easily from the outside. Make sure the rough opening is the correct size to fit the unit ordered and is square and plumb. Studs are usually doubled at the opening in frame construction.

2.   Place the window unit in the opening. Leave the shipping clips and any inserts in the window until it has been installed. These clips and inserts protect the window and keep all parts in place until the window is ready to be operated.

3.   Use wedge blocks or shims to adjust the height of the window in the opening and to level the unit.

4.   Nail through the blind stop to the stud to anchor the unit. Anchor clips are often used in masonry construction to secure the window to the opening frame.

5.   Remove the shims. Caulk as necessary.

6.   When interior and exterior wall finish has been applied, install the trim as appropriate.

7.   Install the operating hardware.

8.   Remove the inserts and clips and check the operation of the window.

## Wood Window Units

Though prefabricated metal window units have increased in popularity, wood windows are

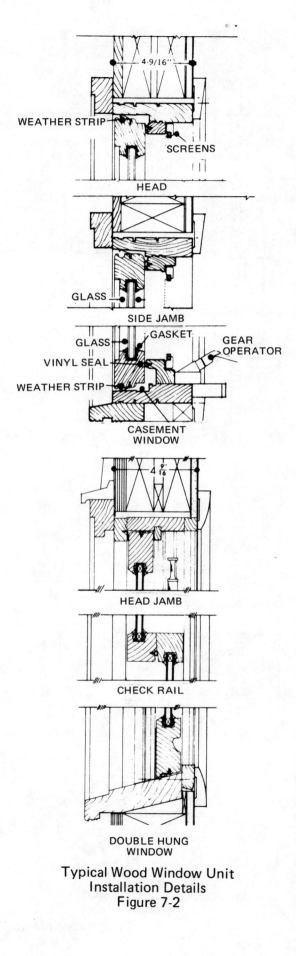

Typical Wood Window Unit
Installation Details
Figure 7-2

still used widely in most parts of the U.S. Wood windows offer superior insulating properties though they may require additional framing because they usually can not support as much weight as a metal window. The window will arrive on the job glazed, with frame, jambs, sill, sash and weatherstripping in place. Units can be ordered with storm sash and screens, also. Single hung, double hung, casement, sliding and awning types are available. The units should be treated with water-repellent preservative at the mill and only need finish painting once installed.

Prefabricated wood window units are easy to install. However, several points should be observed. Most window units have complete directions and these directions should be followed. As with most wood materials, the windows should be stored on the job for several days before application so that they can take on the same moisture content as the materials on which they will be installed. Check the windows for size on arrival, however, to be sure that each window will fit the opening. It is also wise to check immediately for any damage in shipping. Do not remove any packing clips or bracing, however. These can be used to protect the window until it is in the opening and ready to be operated. Installation procedures are similar to prefabricated metal windows. Figure 7-2 shows typical installation details. Most units can be installed in either wood frame, masonry or concrete openings.

# Chapter 8

# DOOR BUCKS AND FRAMES

Wherever there is to be a doorway in a masonry or frame wall, a wooden frame should be provided. If the frame is for a wooden partition, it is generally made of finished lumber and to the finish dimensions of the door. This type is called a door jamb. If the door opening is in a masonry wall, a door buck or false jamb is provided to guide the mason in laying up the masonry. A separate finished jamb is often fitted to the door buck.

Door bucks are generally made of rough stock 1 5/8 inch thick and as wide as the masonry wall plus the thickness of the furring and the plaster coats on the inside of the wall. They are made in much the same way as the head and side jambs of a cellar frame but the sill is omitted. There is a temporary brace to hold the buck at this point. The buck is further braced to hold it square and it is then erected in the wall and braced in a plumb and level position.

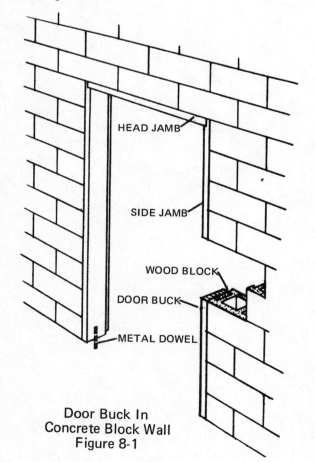

Door Buck In
Concrete Block Wall
Figure 8-1

Provision is made for anchoring the buck in a masonry wall by placing wooden blocks in the wall as it is being laid up. The buck is nailed to these blocks after the wall is set and before the braces are taken off the buck (figure 8-1). Metal anchors are also used for this purpose. If the buck is set on a masonry floor, the bottom ends of the buck are anchored to the floor as shown in figure 8-1. This figure shows a buck placed in a concrete block wall where casings are not required.

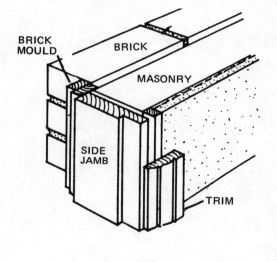

Door Jam
In Masonry Wall
Figure 8-2

Figure 8-2 shows a combination door buck and jamb in a masonry wall that is wider than the jamb. An outside casing provides a recess for a storm or screen door. The buck is kept flush with the inside plaster line and finished with a door casing as shown.

### How To Make A Door Buck

1. Measure the thickness of the masonry wall and select stock 1 5/8 inch thick and as wide as the wall is thick. Cut the stock for the header and sides of the jamb frame, allowing 3 inches extra on the length.

2. Plane the face and edges straight and smooth.

3. Determine the height of the header from the floor and lay out the dado joint in the side jamb. This is done in the same way as for the basement frame.

4. Lay out a right and left hand side jamb and cut the dado joints ¾ inch deep.

5. Lay out and square both ends of the head jamb to a length 1½ inch longer than the width of the door that is to be used in the opening.

6. Assemble the head and side jambs. Keep the edges flush and drive three 16d common nails in each dado joint.

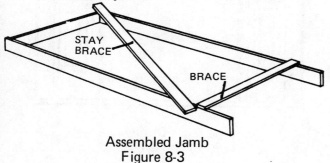

Assembled Jamb
Figure 8-3

7. Brace the assembled jamb as shown in figure 8-3. Put on the cross brace first keeping the two side jambs the same distance apart at the bottom and top of the frame. Hold the jamb square with a diagonal brace solidly nailed.

## How To Set A Door Buck

1. Determine the distance between the bottom face of the head jamb and the top of the finish floor. This distance may also be found by measuring the height of the door that is to be used.

2. Check the levelness of the floor across the door opening.

3. Mark the two side jambs to the length found in step 1. If the floor is level at the opening, cut the side jambs off at these marks. If the floor is not level, determine the low side and allow this difference on the length of one side jamb.

4. Place the door buck in the opening and center it according to the dimensions given on the floor plans and the thickness of the wall.

*NOTE:* If the bottoms of the buck are to be anchored to masonry floors, place a ½ inch metal dowel into the jamb and floor as shown in figure 8-1 or anchor it to the wooden blocks placed in the masonry wall.

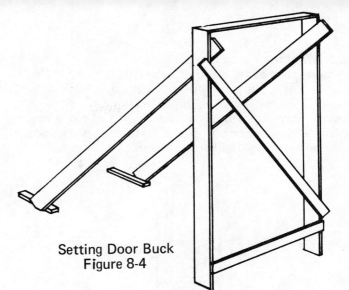

Setting Door Buck
Figure 8-4

5. Brace and plumb the door buck as shown in figure 8-4. Be sure the braces are nailed to solid wood members such as floor joists or blocks of wood spiked through the subflooring and into the joints.

6. Check the head to see if it is square with the side jambs at each corner. Test the side jambs with the straight edge. If they are bowed, bring them into alignment and place braces to hold them in position.

*NOTE:* Figure 8-2 shows a door buck that is set flush with the inside of the wall so that a casing may be nailed to the edge of the buck and also to the plaster ground on the wall. The outside edge of the jamb is finished by running a casing and brick mould from the edge of the jamb to the masonry wall. This type of buck should be erected and braced before the wall is laid up. Nailing blocks would also have to be set in the wall. The procedures are the same as previously described.

Door frames are usually made of material 1 5/16 inch thick. The dimensions of the members of a door frame vary widely but a typical exterior frame is shown in figures 8-5 and 8-6.

In exterior door frames the sill is usually made of oak though other materials are often used if metal wear strips are included. The frame is nailed to studs and headers of the rough opening through the outside casing. The sill must rest firmly on the header or stringer joist of the floor framing, which commonly must be trimmed with a saw and hand ax or other means. After finish flooring is in place, a hardwood or metal threshold with a plastic weatherstop covers the joints between the floor and sill. Exterior doors are 1¾ inches thick and not less than 6 feet 8 inches high. The main extrance door is usually at least 3 feet wide and the side or rear service door 2 feet 8 inches wide. The main extrance to a house is often the most prominent feature of the exterior trim. In some types of architecture, such as the Colonial, the finish of the building is quite simple while the design of the principal doorway may be quite elaborate. A door frame may be composed of a single door opening of, if a more elaborate frame is desired, a transom and side window lights may be built into the frame.

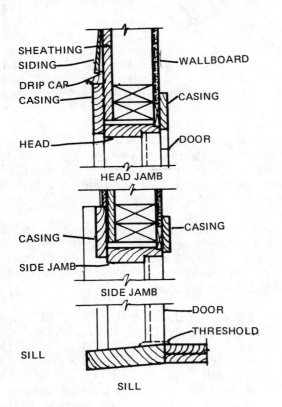

Door Frame
Figure 8-5

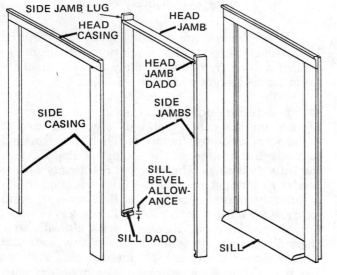

Parts Of An Exterior Frame
Figure 8-6

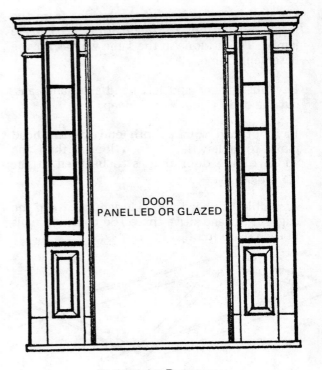

Side Light Doorway
Figure 8-7

Figure 8-7 shows a door frame with side lights. The general makeup of the frame is similar to that of the single frame with the addition of the side window units which extend from the head casing about two thirds of the way down the door. The remaining space is made up of a solid panel. In some cases the mullions and side casings are finished to represent a column or pilaster. The head casing is composed of a wide drip cap and built-up fascia to receive the caps of the pilasters. Sometimes, a curved or square transom is included over the door.

### How To Set An Outside Door Frame

In balloon frame construction a sill header must be framed between the trimmer studs, flush with the outer faces of the studs, to support the sill and the lower ends of the side jambs (figure 8-8). In platform frame construction, the sill and the bottom ends of the side jambs rest on the sub-flooring.

1. Plumb an outside door frame in the rough opening. Use thin shingle - type wedges, five to each side, inserted at intervals up the side jambs and the trimmer studs.

*NOTE:* Before the assembled frame is set in the rough opening, a strip of building paper 10 or 12 inches wide should be tacked to the sheathing around the rough opening.

66

2. Place the frame in the rough opening and set a brace against it to hold it in place during the process of plumbing and wedging.

3. Place a level on the sill, and if the sill is not level, wedge it up as necessary until it is.

4. Insert the side jamb wedges, and drive the corresponding wedges on each jamb part way alternately, until the space between the side jamb and trimmer stud is the same on both sides of the frame.

5. Drive a 16d casing nail through the side casing, and into the trimmer stud on both side casings near the bottom of the door to hold the sill level. Drive the nails part way. Do not drive the nails flush until all nails have been placed and a final check has been made for level and plumb.

6. Place the level against one of the side jambs and drive the upper wedges on that side to bring the jamb plumb and true on that side. Repeat the process on the other side.

7. Make a final all-around check for level and plumb. Then fasten the frame in place with 16d casing nails. The nails should be ¾ inch from the outer edges of the casings and spaced 16 inches apart. Drive the nails through the casings into the trimmer studs and the rough-frame door header. Set all nails with a nail set.

Interior trim, door frames, and doors are normally installed after the finish floor is in place. Some contractors may install the interior door frames before the finish door is in place, allowing for the flooring at the bottom of the jambs. This is usually done when the jambs act as plaster grounds. However, because excessive moisture is present and edges of the jambs are often marred, this practice is usually undesirable.

An interior door frame consists only of the jambs because the casings are considered part of the inside wall covering. Rough openings in the stud walls for interior doors are usually framed out to be 3 inches more than the door height and 2½ inches more than the door width. This provides for the frame and its plumbing and leveling in the opening. Interior door frames are made up of two side jambs and a head jamb and include stop mouldings upon which the door closes. The most common of these jambs is the one-piece type (figure 8-9,A). Jambs may be obtained in standard 5¼ inch widths for plaster walls and 4 5/8 inch widths for walls with ½ inch dry-wall finish. The two and three piece adjustable jambs are also standard types (figure 8-9, B and C). Their principal advantage is in being adaptable to a variety of wall thicknesses.

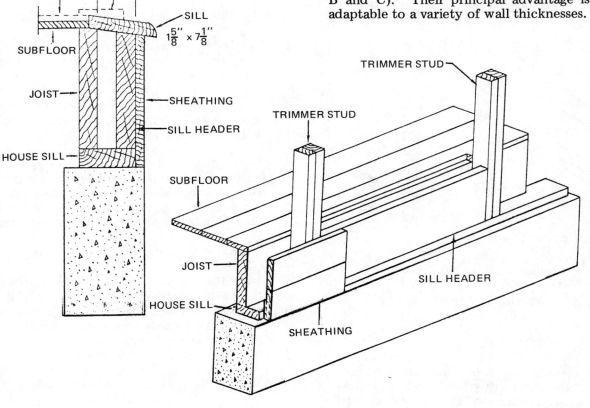

Outside-Door Sill Installation, Balloon Framing
Figure 8-8

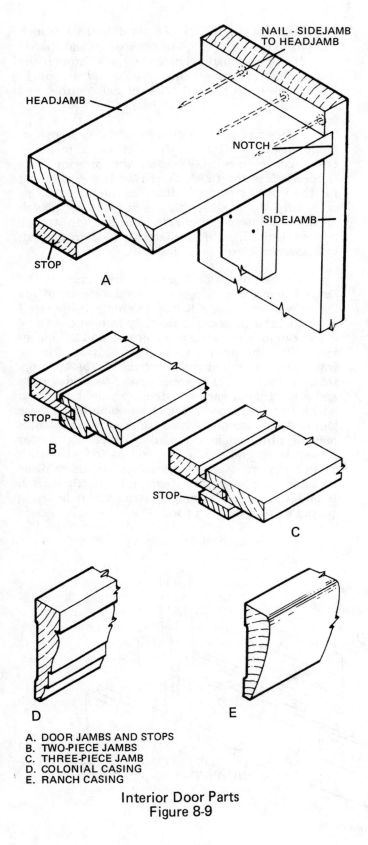

A. DOOR JAMBS AND STOPS
B. TWO-PIECE JAMBS
C. THREE-PIECE JAMB
D. COLONIAL CASING
E. RANCH CASING

Interior Door Parts
Figure 8-9

Some manufacturers produce interior door frames with the door fitted and prehung, ready for installing. Application of the casing completes the job. When used with two or three piece jambs, casings can even be installed at the factory.

Common minimum widths for single interior doors are: (a) Bedroom and other habitable rooms, 2 feet 6 inches; (b) bathrooms, 2 feet 4 inches; (c) small closet and linen closets, 2 feet. These sizes vary a great deal, and sliding doors, folding door units, and similar types are often used for wardrobes and may be 6 feet or more in width. However, in most cases, the jamb, stop, and casing parts are used in some manner to frame and finish the opening.

Standard interior and exterior door heights are 6 feet 8 inches for first floors, but 6 foot 6 inch doors are sometimes used on the upper floors.

Door frames, like window frames, may be made on the job or ordered from the mill in prefabricated or assembled condition. A door frame is built in about the same manner as a window frame. However, the blind stop and the parting strip are omitted in the door frame. The opening between the rabbeted edges of the side and head jambs must be of the proper size to accommodate the door that is to be used in the frame. The door frame is squared and braced in the same manner as the window frame. In framing the hardwood sill, it is well to use a rip saw rather than a chisel when cutting out the end of the sill where the jamb and the casing meet at the sill line. This rip cut should be parallel to the outside edge of the sill.

**How To Build And Set Interior Door Jambs**

1. Select the door jamb stock and lay out the head and side jambs in the same way as for door bucks.

2. Cut the dado joints 3/8 inch deep if the jamb stock is 25/32 inch thick and ½ inch deep if it is 1 1/16 inch thick.

3. Determine the distance that the bottom face of the head jamb is to be from the finished floor. This distance is often measured from the height of the window jambs and the door jambs made to line up with the window jambs.

4. Mark this distance on each side jamb.

5. Joint the side and head jambs to the width of the partition, beveling them about 1/16 inch so that the casings will fit tightly against the edges of the jamb. See figure 8-10. Sometimes the casings are beveled and it is not necessary to bevel the edges of the jambs.

6. Assemble the head jamb and side jambs.

7. Set the assembled jamb temporarily into the door opening and level it.

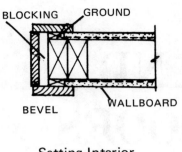

BLOCKING   GROUND

BEVEL   WALLBOARD

Setting Interior
Door Jambs
Figure 8-10

8. Mark the cut on the side jambs as described above for door bucks.

9. Remove the jamb and cut the side jambs to length.

10. Nail ¾" x 3" blocks about 14 inches apart up the hinge side of the door opening. The blocks should be as long as the jamb is wide. Arrange the blocks so that one will be placed behind the hinges of the door to form a solid base back of the hinges (figure 8-11).

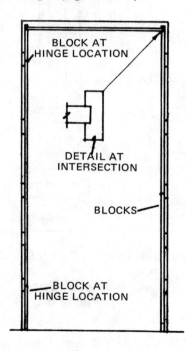

BLOCK AT
HINGE LOCATION

DETAIL AT
INTERSECTION

BLOCKS

BLOCK AT
HINGE LOCATION

Blocking At Door Jamb
Figure 8-11

11. Place the jamb against these blocks. Place a small block of finished flooring under the bottom end of this side jamb if the finished floor has not been laid.

12. Plumb this jamb, keeping it flush with the faces of the finished wall. Nail the jamb temporarily at the top and bottom.

13. Test the face of the jamb with the straight-edge. If it is straight over its entire length and flush with both walls, fasten it to the blocks by toenailing it with 8d finishing nails through the edges of the jamb. Set the nails and be careful not to mar the jamb with hammer marks.

14. Place blocks in a similar fashion at the opposite side of the door opening. Cut a small strip of wood as long as the inside width of the jamb at the head. Place this strip between the two side jambs at the floor line.

15. Place the loose side jamb on top of a block of finish floor the same as at the nailed jamb.

16. Square the head jamb with the jamb that is nailed to the blocks. If it is square, temporarily nail the loose jamb to the blocks at the top and bottom.

17. Wedge behind all the blocks with shingles at least 2½ inches wide.

*NOTE:* If the opening between the back of the jamb and the face of the blocks is about ½ inch, it may be filled by wedging shingles from both sides of the wall. Point the thin edges toward each other and wedge them until they fit tightly against the back of the jamb. Do not force the shingles but bring the jamb into alignment with the straight edge and the strip at the bottom of the jamb.

18. When the jamb is straight, toenail it into the blocks. Straighten the head jamb in a similar way.

*Caution:* Re-check both side jambs for straightness and plumbness as one side of the jamb is often disturbed or bowed when the nails are driven home and set.

# Chapter 9

# FITTING AND HANGING DOORS

Interior and exterior doors are made in many styles and types of construction. Perhaps the best description of a particular type of door is that supplied by the mill where the door is to be obtained.

Doors are identified by their size, system of paneling and construction. The stiles are either solid or built up of several pieces of lumber machined and glued together and covered with veneer on the exposed surfaces. These stiles and rails are moulded in any one of several forms to support the door. See figure 9-1.

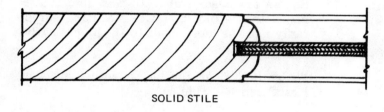

SOLID STILE

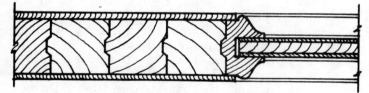

BUILT-UP STILE

Sections Of Door Stiles And Panels
Figure 9-1

Doors are made of any one of several kinds of wood but pine and fir are most frequently used. Exterior doors are generally made of solid pine in standard paneling and glass light sizes. Veneered outside doors are made in so many styles that it is best to refer to a mill catalog for a complete description.

Exterior doors and outside combination and storm doors can be obtained in a number of designs to fit the style of almost any house. Doors in the traditional pattern are usually the panel type (figure 9-2, A). They consist of stiles (solid vertical members), rails (solid cross members), and filler panels in a number of designs. Glazed upper panels are combined with raised wood or plywood lower panels.

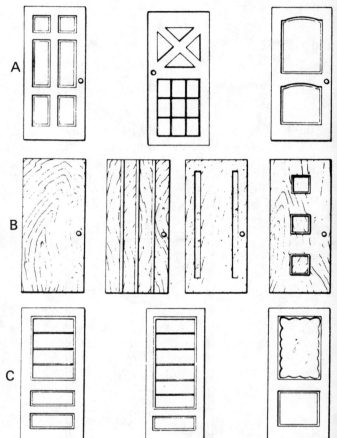

A. Traditional Panel  B. Flush  C. Combination

Exterior Doors
Figure 9-2

Exterior flush doors should be of the solid-core type rather than hollowcore to minimize warping during the heating season. (Warping is caused by a difference in moisture content on the exposed and unexposed faces.)

Flush doors consist of thin plywood faces over a framework of wood with a woodblock or particle board core. Many combinations of designs can be obtained, ranging from plain flush doors to others with a variety of panels and glazed openings (figure 9-2, B).

Wood combination doors (storm and screen) are available in several styles (figure 9-2, C). Panels which include screen and storm inserts are normally located in the upper portion of the door. Some types can be obtained with self-storing features, similar to window combination units. Heat loss through metal combination doors is greater than through similar type wood doors.

As in exterior door styles, the two general interior types are the flush and the panel door. Novelty doors, such as the folding door unit, might be flush or louvered. Most standard interior doors are 1 3/8 inches thick.

The flush interior door is usually made up with a hollow core of light framework of some type with thin plywood or hardboard (figure 9-3, A). Plywood faced flush doors may be obtained in gum, birch, oak, mahogany, and woods of other species, most of which are suitable for natural finish. Nonselected grades are usually painted as are hardboard-faced doors.

The panel door consists of solid stiles (vertical side members), rails (cross pieces), and panel filters of various types. The five-cross panel and the Colonial type panel doors are perhaps the most common of this style (figure 9-3, B and C). The louvered door (figure 9-3, D) is also popular and is commonly used for closets because it provides some ventilation. Large openings for wardrobes are finished with sliding or folding doors, or with flush or louvered doors (figure 9-3, E). Such doors are usually 1 1/8 inches thick.

Hinged doors should open or swing in the direction of natural entry, against a blank wall whenever possible, and should not be obstructed by other swinging doors. Doors should never be hinged to swing into a hallway.

Doors should not be delivered to the job until all the interior trim has been applied. The storage place should be dry and protected from moisture and the doors should be set upright on end. If they are left standing against a plastered wall, the door nearest the wall should be covered with building paper to protect it from moisture.

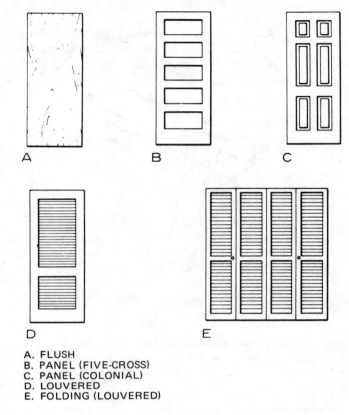

A. FLUSH
B. PANEL (FIVE-CROSS)
C. PANEL (COLONIAL)
D. LOUVERED
E. FOLDING (LOUVERED)

Interior Doors
Figure 9-3

**How To Build A Bench Vise And Fit The Door**

If a number of doors are to be fitted and hung, a bench vise or door jack should be made to hold the doors while edges are trimmed and finished and hardware is installed.

1. Nail two 2 inch by 4 inch blocks about 6 inches long on a piece of stock ½" x 2" x 18". Keep the blocks as far apart as the thickness of the doors. See figure 9-4.

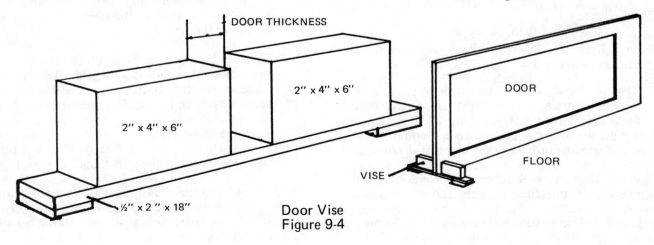

Door Vise
Figure 9-4

2. Nail the piece on the floor and place the door in an upright position in the slot between the blocks. This will hold the door so that the side rail may be planed.

*NOTE:* Another way to support the door is to nail two cleats to the top of a sawhorse as shown in figure 9-5.

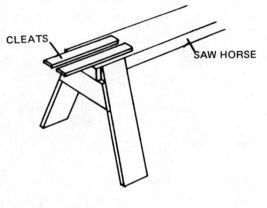

Door Vise
Figure 9-5

3. Toenail the sawhorses and the vise to the floor. See figure 9-6.

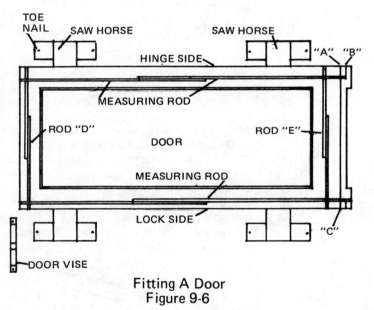

Fitting A Door
Figure 9-6

4. Test the head jamb of the door opening with a steel square to see if it is square with both side jambs. If it is, lay a door on the sawhorses and cut the horns off square with the stile and flush with the top of the top rail.

5. Plane the top end of the door smooth and round off the four corners about 1/8 inch.

6. Make two measuring rods long enough to measure the height of the door opening. Mark

the distance of the door clearance above the floor on the end of one rod. This distance is generally ¾ inch. See A and B, figure 9-6.

7. Hold the two rods together and measure the height of the head jamb above the floor at the hinge side of the door opening. Keep the rod having the clearance mark on top of the floor.

8. Transfer this distance to the hinge stile of the door on the horses. Keep the section of the rod which was against the head jamb flush with the top edge of the door and mark the clearance mark on the bottom rail of the door. See A, figure 9-6.

9. Use the rods in the same way to measure the distance from the head jamb to the floor on the lock side of the opening. Transfer this distance to the lock stile of the door and mark the clearance mark C on the bottom rail of the door.

10. Connect the marks A and C with a straight line. Use a fine combination blade saw to cut through the stiles of the door along this line and to cut along the line on the rail. Plane the edge smooth and round the corners.

11. Test the side jambs with a straightedge to see if their surfaces are straight. If so, place the door on its edge in the floor vise and plane the lock stile of the door straight and square.

*NOTE:* Some carpenters prefer to put a slight bevel toward the stop side of the door stile. Actually this is not necessary on 1 3/8 inch doors unless the door is less than 2 feet wide.

12. Replace the door flat on the sawhorses.

13. Use short measuring rods to measure the distance between the side jambs at the head of the opening. Transfer this distance to the top of the door, measuring from the planed edge. Mark this distance on the hinge stile. See Rod D, figure 9-6.

14. Measure the distance between the jambs at the bottom of the door opening and transfer this distance to the bottom of the door in the same way. See Rod at E, figure 9-6.

15. Connect the two points on the top and bottom of the door with a straight line and plane the edge of the stile to this line.

*NOTE:* If the door stops are not on the jambs, tack blocks to the jambs to prevent the door from going into the door opening beyond the thickness of the door.

16. Place the door in the opening and examine the fit at the head and side jambs. Plane the edges of the door to fit the contour of the face of the jambs. Allow a clearance of about 3/32 inch on the sides and head and about ¾ inch on the bottom of the door.

17. Slightly round the edges with sandpaper and remove any marks made on the surfaces.

*NOTE:* In fitting doors for double action hinges, the fitting of the door into the opening is similar to the procedure outlined above with the exception that much more clearance is required at the sides of the door. The side edges of the door would have to be rounded to allow the door to swing both ways.

The hardware needed for an average door consists of a pair of butt hinges, a lock and a door stop. Exterior doors are usually hung with three butt hinges and may have an ornamental lockset on the outside.

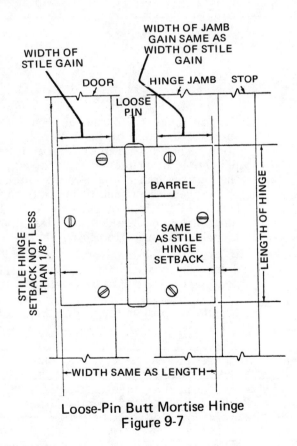

Loose-Pin Butt Mortise Hinge
Figure 9-7

The butt hinge shown in figure 9-7 consists of two leaves and a loose pin. Since these hinges are mortised into the door and jamb, they are slightly offset or swaged to permit the leaves to come close together. See the folded hinge in figure 9-8. One leaf of each hinge is attached to the jamb and the other leaf to the door. When the door is set in its

proper position, the loose pin may be placed in the hole and the two halves of the hinge will be held together. The hinge is called a mortise hinge because the leaves are mortised into gains cut in the hinge stile of the door and the hinge jamb of the frame. Butt hinges are made in different sizes, weights and types of bearing surfaces. However, only a few different sizes are used in ordinary frame buildings. The size is determined by the length of the leaf and the distance between the outer edges of the two leaves when the hinge is open. The length of the leaf is always stated first.

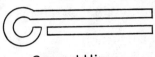

Swaged Hinge
Figure 9-8

The first step in fitting a door is to determine from the floor plan which stile is the hinge stile and which the lock stile, and to mark the stiles and the corresponding jambs accordingly. Next, carefully measure the height of the finished opening along both side jambs and the width at both top and bottom. The finished opening should be rectangular, but it might not be, and your job is to fit the door to the opening regardless of the shape of the opening.

A well fitted door, when hung, should conform to the shape of the finished opening with a clearance of 1/16 inch at sides and top. For an inside door without sill or threshold there should be a bottom clearance above the finish floor of from 3/8 to ½ inch. This is required to ensure that the door will swing clear of carpeting. For extra thick carpeting the clearance would have to be greater than ½ inch. For a door with a sill and no threshold, the bottom clearance should be 1/16 inch above the sill or threshold.

Lay off the measured dimensions of the opening, less clearance allowances, on the door. Check the jambs for trueness, and if you find any irregularities, transfer them to the corresponding stiles. Then place the door in the vise and plane to the lines, checking for fit repeatedly as you near the line dimension on the second stile you plane, by setting the door in the opening.

### How To Fit Hinges On The Door

There are many types of hardware and methods of applying them. This book will only describe the application in a general way. Much hardware comes in package form together with directions and templets. Directions should be carefully followed.

NOTE: Before hardware is applied, screwdriver bits should be selected and fitted so that they will fit the types of screws that are to be driven. Only the solid type of screwdriver should be used as the spiral automatic type often slips and injures the surfaces of the trim. If mortising machines or door butt machines are used, the wood surfaces should be thoroughly protected.

It is assumed that the door is fitted to the opening to allow for swing clearance. Doors 1 3/8 inches thick or less require no bevel at the lock side for swing clearance. Doors 1¾ inches thick require a bevel of only 1/8 inch on this edge.

1. Select hinges large enough to clear the casings of the door trim.

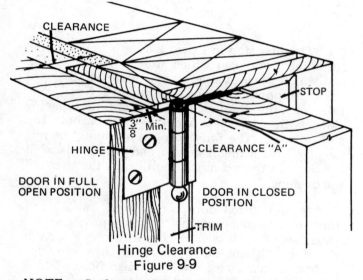

Hinge Clearance
Figure 9-9

NOTE: In locating full butt hinges on any type of a door that is flush with the edge of the jamb, there should be a clearance from the edge of the jamb to the center of the hinge pin. This clearance varies with the thickness of the door, the thickness of the trim and the size of the hinge. Clearance A, figure 9-9, shows the projection of the hinge beyond the face of the door. This clearance must be at least one half the overall thickness of the door trim.

2. Locate the position of the hinges on the jamb in reference to the height from the floor.

NOTE: Inside doors up to and including 6 feet 8 inches high take two butts. Those from 6 feet 8 inches to 90 inches high take three butts. If three butts are used, the middle butt should be half way between the top and bottom hinges. See figure 9-10. When two butts are used,

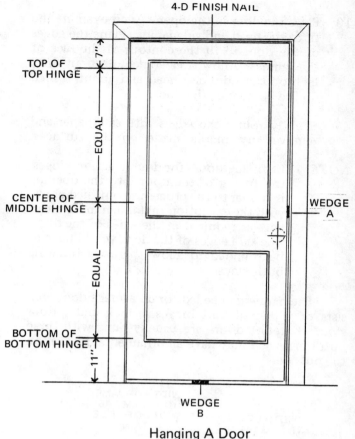

Hanging A Door
Figure 9-10

the top hinge pin should be in line with the bottom edge of the top rail of the door. The bottom of the bottom hinge pin should be in line with the top edge of the bottom rail. In no case should the top hinge be less than 6 inches from the top of a 1 3/8 inch or 1¾ inch door. The bottom hinge should not be less than 9 inches above the floor. On 1 1/8 inch thick doors the hinges may be from 2 to 4 inches from the top and bottom, depending on the height of the door.

Select the proper hinge size from table 9-11.

| FRAME THICKNESS OF DOOR | WIDTH OF DOOR | SIZE OF HINGE |
|---|---|---|
| 1-1/8" to 1-3/8" | Up to 32" | 3-1/2 |
| 1-1/8" to 1-3/8" | 32" to 37" | 4 |
| 1-3/8" to 1-7/8" | Up to 32" | 4-1/2 |
| 1-3/8" to 1-7/8" | 32" to 37" | 5 |
| 1-3/8" to 1-7/8" | 37" to 43" | 5 extra heavy |
| Over 1-7/8" | Up to 43" | 5 extra heavy |
| 1-7/8" | Over 43" | 6 extra heavy |

The size of a loose-pin butt mortise hinge is designated by the length (longer dimension) of the leaf in inches.

Hinge Selection
Table 9-11

74

3. Make a gauge line on the edge of the door and on the face of the jamb at the hinge locations so the center of the hinge pin will project the correct distance beyond the face of the door. See clearance A, figure 9-9.

4. Place the hinge on the door along the gauged line and mark the length of the hinge. Square these marks across and use a knife to cut the outline of the hinge about 1/16 inch deep. See figure 9-12. Follow the same procedure for the jamb.

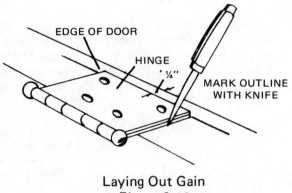

Laying Out Gain
Figure 9-12

5. Gauge the thickness of the hinge along the edge of the jamb and the face of the door. See figure 9-13.

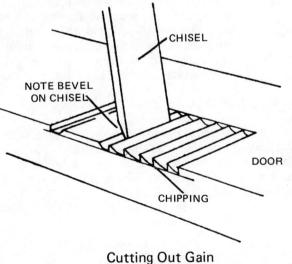

Cutting Out Gain
Figure 9-13

6. Use a 1½ inch butt chisel to chip out the outlined butt gain. Tap the chisel with a hammer so that the chisel will enter the wood as deep as the thickness of the butt. See figure 9-13.

7. Chip out the entire area of the gain, holding the bevel of the chisel toward the wood surface.

8. Pare the chips from the gain, holding the back of the chisel toward the bottom of the gain

and paring along the gauge line which shows the depth of the gain. See figure 9-14.

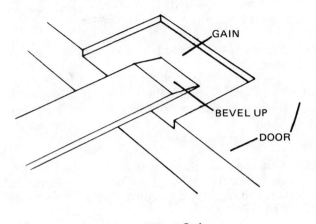

Paring Butt Gain
Figure 9-14

9. Finish paring the bottom of the gain to the depth shown by the gauge mark on the face of the door in figure 9-13.

10. Use the chisel to cut the shoulders of the gain deeper if the chips do not pare out neatly at these points.

11. Try the hinge in the gain to see that the top surface of the hinge is flush with the edge of the door.

NOTE: This is very important as it will affect the fit of the door after it is hung. If the hinge surface is below the door surface, shim it up with cardboard until it is flush. If the hinge is above the surface, pare the gain until the butt is flush.

12. Place the butt in the gain and if it fits perfectly, punch holes with a nail set at the screw locations. Be sure to hold the nail set in a vertical position so that the screws will go into the wood straight and will fit flat on the butt surface. Fasten the butt with the screws.

NOTE: It is best to fit the half butts to the door in their proper locations first. Then place the door in the opening in the proper relation to the jambs and lightly wedge it in place so that the clearances are the same on the top and sides of the door. Mark the location of the hinges on the jambs. A 4d finish nail placed between the top of the door and the head jamb will give the door the proper spacing at the head jamb.

13. Fit the opposite half of the butt to the door jamb in exactly the same manner the first half was fitted to the door.

14. Fit the other door butts in exactly the same manner.

15. Hang the door on the hinges of the jamb by placing the loose pin in the top butt first. Then tap the bottom half butts together and insert the lower pin.

16. Test the door to see if it swings into the opening properly. If it does not fit well, do not force it into the opening but find the difficulty.

*NOTE:* Some of the most common causes and remedies of a poor fit at this point are:

A  If the door strikes on the jamb at the lock side: Examine the door butts to see that the flat head screws are perfectly flat with the surface of the butt. If they are not, they may be preventing the hinge from closing properly.

Check the depth of the butt gains to see that the surfaces of the butts are not above the surface of the door or jamb. If they are, make them flush or even a little below the surface.

B  If the door binds: The door butts are generally too far below the surfaces of the door or jamb and should be shimmed up.

The conditions in A and B may also be corrected by beveling the bottom of the gain in the door so the butt pin center is shifted toward or away from the lock jamb. This pulls the edge of the door toward or away from this jamb (figure 9-15).

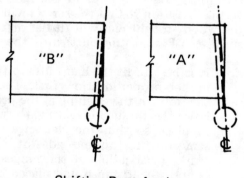

Shifting Butt Angle
Figure 9-15

C  If the top or bottom of the door strikes: The only remedy is to plane it off. Do not try to drive the hinge butts up or down to correct this condition.

## How To Fit Half Surface And Half Butt Hinges

*NOTE:* These hinges are located and marked in about the same manner as full butt hinges. The butt part of the hinge should be fitted to the jamb of the door in exactly the same way as the half of the full butt hinge.

1. Screw this part of the hinge into the gains at the top and bottom of the door jamb. Assemble the surface part of the hinge to the butt part.

2. Place the door into the door opening and lightly wedge it from the surface of the floor so that it is the same distance from the top and side jambs, and so that there is enough clearance at the bottom of the door to clear rugs or floor covering. This is usually ¾ inch.

3. Mark the locations of the hinges on the surface of the door by folding the surface part of the hinge over the surface of the door and lightly punch marking the door surface through the screw openings in the hinges.

4. Fasten the surface part of the hinge to the door and test for swing clearance.

NOTE: The full surface hinges are used where the casing is flush with the face of the door. In this case the hinges are located and fastened to the door and casings in about the same way as the surface part of the half surface and half butt hinge.

## How To Install Locks

After placing hinges in position, mark off the position of the lock on the lock stile. The lock is placed about 36 inches from the floor level. The parts of an ordinary cylinder-type lock for a door are shown in figure 9-16.

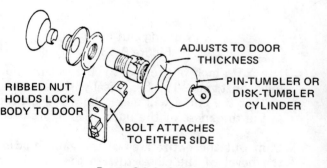

Parts Of A Cylinder Lock
Figure 9-16

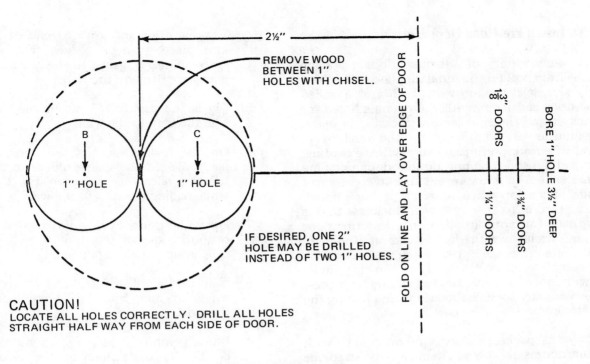

REMOVE WOOD BETWEEN 1" HOLES WITH CHISEL.

B
1" HOLE

C
1" HOLE

IF DESIRED, ONE 2" HOLE MAY BE DRILLED INSTEAD OF TWO 1" HOLES.

2½"

FOLD ON LINE AND LAY OVER EDGE OF DOOR

BORE 1" HOLE 3½" DEEP

1⅜" DOORS

1¾" DOORS

1½" DOORS

**CAUTION!**
LOCATE ALL HOLES CORRECTLY. DRILL ALL HOLES STRAIGHT HALF WAY FROM EACH SIDE OF DOOR.

One Type Of Template
Figure 9-17

1. Open the door to a convenient working position and check it in place with wedges under the bottom near the outer edge.

2. Measure up 36 inches from the floor (the usual knob height), and square a line across the face and edge of the lock stile.

3. Use the template that is usually supplied with a cylinder lock; place the template on the face of the door (at proper height and alignment with layout lines) and mark the center of holes to be drilled. See figure 9-17.

4. Drill the holes through the face of the door. Then drill the one through the edge to receive the latch bolt; it should be slightly deeper than the length of the bolt.

5. Rout a gain for the face plate and install the latch unit. (figure 9-18).

6. Install exterior and interior knobs.

7. Find the position of the strike plate and install it in the jamb. (figure 9-19).

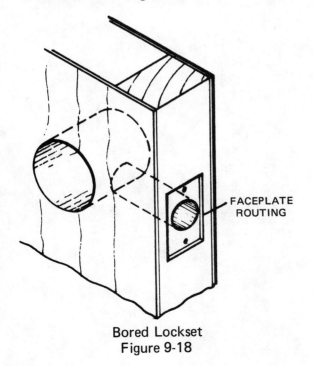

FACEPLATE ROUTING

Bored Lockset
Figure 9-18

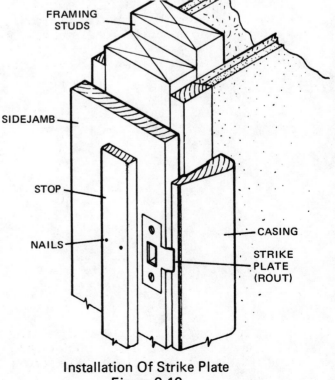

FRAMING STUDS

SIDEJAMB

STOP

NAILS

CASING

STRIKE PLATE (ROUT)

Installation Of Strike Plate
Figure 9-19

## How To Install Pre-Hung Door Units

A wide variety of pre-hung door units are available from building material suppliers. The door usually arrives at the job with the hinges installed on the door and jamb, with the opening bored for the lockset and the split jamb and casing in place. These units are placed directly into the rough opening and often are prefinished to eliminate sanding, prime and finish. Prehung double door units are also available. It is important to know the exact opening dimension when ordering prehung doors. Also, be careful to specify a wall thickness that is appropriate for your installation. Exterior door units are available with the sill and threshold installed. Most packaged pre-hung doors arrive with fairly complete instructions. The following guidelines will apply in most cases but should be supplemented with any specific directions supplied by the manufacturer.

1. Lay the packaged door unit on 2 x 4's with the door side down. Remove any straps or banding material.

2. Remove the top and bottom caps and the spacer blocks which keep the casing halves apart. The two halves will then come apart easily.

3. Remove any nails that have been driven through the jamb to make the unit rigid.

4. Lift the door and grooved half of the casing into place. Check to see that the upper spacer block is against the header and that the jambs are flush on the floor.

5. Check the trim for plumb on the hinged side. Nail the trim to the wall.

6. On the lockset side of the door, push the jambs against the spacer blocks to maintain a uniform clearance between the door jamb while nailing the trim to the wall.

7. Open the door. Use shims behind the jamb on both sides of the door to make the unit snug against the rough opening.

8. Nail through the jamb and shims into the rough opening frame. Do not nail through the stop.

9. Block behind the jambs and remove any spacer blocks that remain on the installed half.

10. Fit the opposite half against the installed jamb. Nail the trim of this opposite half to the wall.

11. Nail through the stop into the jambs. This secures the two halves firmly together.

12. Install the knobs for the lockset and check the operation of the door.

# Chapter 10

# DOOR TRIM

Defects in the appearance of door trim will be very apparent for the life of the structure. Sound craftsmanship requires that trim be selected and installed with great care. There should be no dent in the surface and all joints must be tight and permanent. Exposed nail holes should be as few as possible because each one must be filled up prior to the finishing coats. Door trim is generally applied before the flooring is laid.

A door casing is the wooden trim attached to both sides and to the head of the door jamb. Its primary uses are to protect the edges of the wall covering at the door openings and to form an ornamental finish for the door jamb. It also furnishes a surface to which the base may be fitted.

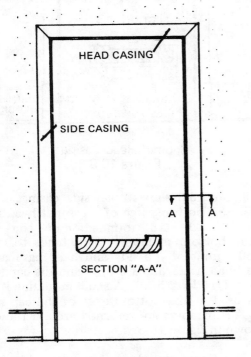

HEAD CASING

SIDE CASING

A    A

SECTION "A-A"

Mitered Casing
Figure 10-1

Figure 10-1 shows a plain casing using dimensioned and surfaced boards. The material is usually 15/32 inch by 3 inches to 4 inches. Pine or other wood suitable for interior trim is usually used. The outside edges are rounded and the back is cupped to permit a tight fit between it and the wall. See section A-A, figure 10-1. The side and head casings are connected with a mitered joint. This joint should be fastened with a spline and glued to

help overcome the tendency of this type of joint to open up and show a crack. The plain casing may be assembled with a butt joint instead of a miter joint. In this case, the head casing is made thicker than the side casing. The resulting slight overhang tends to conceal the joint.

### How To Fit Plain Door Casing

*NOTE:* Assume that the casings shown in figure 10-1 are to be fitted and installed and that the casing stock is dimensioned and sanded.

1. Select straight casing stock and lay off the lengths for the side and head casings. Allow enough material for the joints.

2. Cut the bottom ends of the two side casings square.

3. Place one in position on the side jamb. Allow a margin of 3/16 inch between the edge of the casing and the edge of the jamb.

4. Mark a point 3/16 inch above the bottom face of the head jamb on the inside edge of the casing. This point shows the short end of the 45 degree cut to be made at the casing. Mark the two side casings in this manner.

*NOTE:* A convenient way of scribing a true margin along the edge of the jamb is to set the combination square so that the blade projects 3/16 inch beyond the face of the square head. The square then may be used as a gauge to mark the margin.

5. Place the head casing in position on the head jamb. Allow a 3/16 inch margin and mark a point on the inside lower edge of the casing 3/16 inch beyond the inside edge of the side jamb. Mark both ends of the head casing in the same way. These points show the short end of the miter cuts. Mark the miter cuts.

6. Cut the miters on the casings in the miter box and finish the surfaces with a plane if necessary.

7. Form a kerf for the spline in the miter cuts by running a saw cut in the edge of the miter to a depth of 1 inch (figure 10-2).

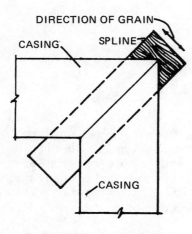

**Splined Mitered Joints**
**Figure 10-2**

*NOTE:* This may be conveniently done with an electric saw. The saw blade should be set so as to form a saw kerf of about 3/16 inch or a double cut may be made by running the saw through, first with the fence against one face and then with it against the other. A hand rip saw may also be used for this purpose.

8. Make a spline about ¼" x 6" x 2" and fit it into the kerfs of both parts of the mitered joint. Assemble the joint to see if the spline is fitted properly and holds the joint together. If it does not, refit the spline.

*NOTE:* Special splines of metal or wood may be purchased for this purpose. There are also several fasteners that may be used.

9. Nail the side casing to the edge of the side jamb with 8d finishing nails, starting at the bottom. Space the nails about every 14 inches and maintain the 3/16 inch margin as the nails are being driven.

*NOTE:* In trying to maintain the 3/16 inch margin, be sure the jamb is not pulled out of line. Sometimes even a nail driven in with too much slant will pull the jamb out of alignment.

10. Nail the opposite edge of the casing to the grounds and studs keeping the nails opposite those driven into the jamb. Set the nails.

*NOTE:* In spacing the nails, be sure not to locate a nail where the lock strike plate will come in the jamb.

11. Nail the opposite side casing in the same manner.

12. Cover the splines with glue and place them in the miter cuts of the head casing.

13. Slip the casing in place and nail it the same as the side casings. Slant the nails driven into the studs so the miter joint will be pulled up tight.

14. Trim the edges of the spline off flush with the casing edges with a sharp chisel and sand the edges smooth.

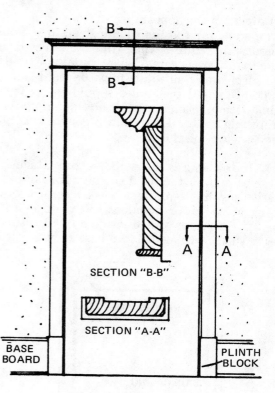

**Cabinet Head Casing**
**Figure 10-3**

Figure 10-3 shows plain side casings butting against the bottom edge of a cabinet head casing. A fillet ¼" x 1 1/16" rounded on one edge is used for the bottom member. This tends to conceal the butt joint of the side and head casings. The fascia board is 25/32" x 5 5/8" and the cap moulding is 1 1/16" x 2 5/8". A small moulding is sometimes used at the bottom edge of the cap moulding. All members are returned around the corner as shown in figure 10-3.

This figure also shows how plinth blocks may be used at the floor. These blocks are generally 1 1/16 inch thick, slightly wider than the door casing and about 1 inch higher than the baseboard. They are nailed to the door jamb the same as the casing and form a surface to which the casing and the baseboard may be fitted.

**How To Build And Fit A Cabinet Head Casing**

*NOTE:* Cabinet head casings are generally built as a unit on a bench, fastened in place on the head jamb and the side casings are then fitted to them.

1. Place a small piece of side casing in position on each of the side jambs and mark the outside edges on the wall. The distance between these two marks is the length of the fascia. See figure 10-4.

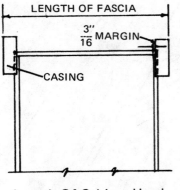

LENGTH OF FASCIA

$\frac{3''}{16}$ MARGIN

CASING

Length Of Cabinet Head
Figure 10-4

2. Mark and cut the fascia to length and plane the end grain smooth.

3. Cut the fillet to length, allowing it to project ½ inch over each end of the fascia. Round off the ends the same as the edge.

4. Cut the cap moulding long enough to project over each end of the fascia so that it may be returned.

5. Make a return on each end of the cap moulding.

*NOTE:* The return may be formed by mitering a short piece to each end or the cap may be returned on its own profile.

6. Nail the cap moulding on the top edge of the fascia with 8d finishing nails. Keep the square edge of the moulding flush with the back of the fascia. See section B-B, figure 10-3.

7. Cut, fit and nail the pressed moulding if one is needed. Nail the fillet with 1½d finishing nails to the bottom edge of the fascia, allowing it to project ½ inch over each end of the fascia. The square edge should be flush with the back of the fascia.

8. Set the nails and sand the whole cabinet head.

9. Nail the cabinet head with 8d finishing nails to the head jamb, keeping the fillet parallel to the head jamb and showing a 3/16 inch margin on this jamb. The ends of the cabinet head should be in line with the marks on the wall.

## How To Fit Casings To A Cabinet Head

*NOTE:* Figure 10-3 shows a cabinet head with plinth blocks and casings.

1. Select plinth block stock approximately 1 1/16 inch thick and a little wider than the side casing and longer than the height of the baseboard.

2. Lay out and cut two plinth blocks to size. Slightly round off the top outer edge and sand the surfaces that will show when the block is placed.

3. Nail the block to the door jamb and grounds with 8d nails, leaving a margin of 1/8 inch between the edge of the block and the face of the jamb. The bottom of the block should be even with the top of the finished floor. Fasten a block on the opposite jamb in the same way.

4. Select the two side casings. Square the bottom ends and place the squared end of one casing on top of a plinth block and the back of the top end against the fillet of the cabinet head as shown in figure 10-5.

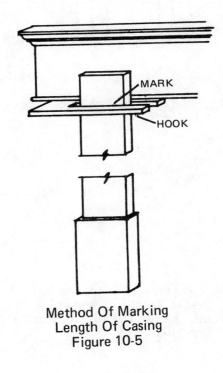

MARK

HOOK

Method Of Marking
Length Of Casing
Figure 10-5

5. Slip a base hook over the casing and along the bottom side of the fillet. Hold it tightly against the fillet and mark the face of the casing along the top side of the hook with a hard sharpened pencil.

6. Saw along the line with a fine crosscut saw.

7. Replace the casing on the jamb and line it up so that it shows a 3/16 inch margin. Inspect the top and bottom fits. If they are correct, nail the casing. Repeat these operations on the opposite jamb.

### How To Fit Moulded Casings

A moulded casing may have only one edge shaped to a moulding or the entire surface may be moulded (figure 10-6). The latter type is usually fitted together with a miter joint, preferably splined. The side casing moulded only on the inside edge may be fitted to a similar head casing by a coped joint or, if the bottom edge of the top casing is square, the side casing could be butted to it.

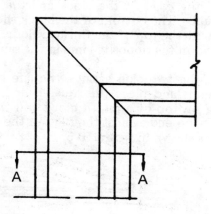

SECTION "A-A"

Moulded Trim
Figure 10-6

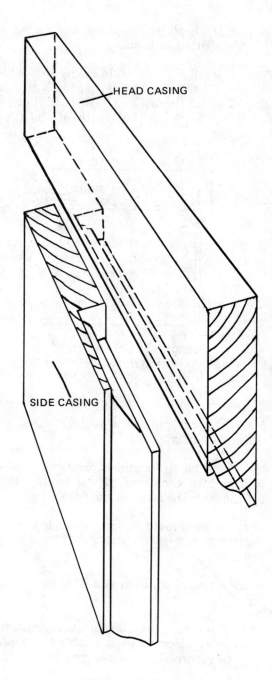

Cutout Bead And
Coped Side Casing
Figure 10-7

1. Select the head casing stock and cut it off to the proper length as shown in figure 10-4. Cut out the ends of the head casing as shown in figure 10-7.

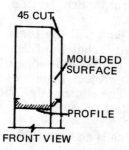

Coped Casing
Figure 10-8

2. Set the head casing in place on the head jamb with a 3/16 inch margin and nail it.

3.  Cut a miter on the moulded surface of the side casing (figure 10-8). The cut will show the profile of the moulded surface. Cut and carve along this line to the flat surface of the casing so that the coped surface will fit against the curved surface of the head casing. Cut the flat surface square so that it will fit against the cut out part of the bottom edge of the head casing (figure 10-7).

4.  Cut the bottom end of the casing to fit the plinth block or finished floor as the case may be.

5.  Select the stock for the head and side casings. Measure the length from the plinth block or floor to the top of the head casing. This gives the short cut of the miter for the back band. Cut the miter in a miter box and nail the back bank in place. Cut, fit and nail the opposite back band in the same way.

6.  Fit the top back band between the miter cuts of the side back bands and nail it in place.

*NOTE:* Sometimes in using moulded casings that are to be mitered at the head casing, it is difficult to provide a spline such as shown in figure 10-2 because the casing is too thin. If this is the case, a spline may be rabbeted into the back of each casing at the miter as shown in figure 10-9.

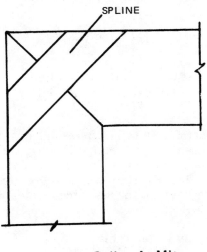

Rabbet Spline At Miter
Figure 10-9

**How To Fit And Install Door Stops**

Door stops are fitted to the head and side jambs in such a position that they will stop the door at its proper position on the door jamb. They are generally about ½ inch thick and 1½ inch wide. If the edge of the casing is rounded, the outside edge of the stop is usually rounded. If the edge of the casing is moulded, the edge of the stop is moulded. One edge of the stop is square to fit against the surface of the door.

1.  Select the door stop material and cut the head stop to fit between the two side jambs.

2.  Cut door stops for both side jambs long enough to reach from the head jamb to the bottom of the side jamb.

3.  Cope the top ends of the side stops so that they fit the contour of the head stop.

4.  Mark the thickness of the door on the face of the head and side jambs as shown by the line in figure 10-10.

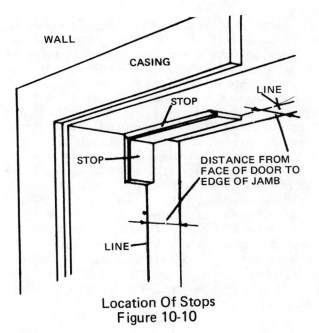

Location Of Stops
Figure 10-10

5.  Temporarily nail the head and side stops in place along these marks. When the door is closed, the square edge of the stop should be against the face of the door.

*NOTE:* After the door has been hung and the lock fitted, the stops may be adjusted so that the door will close properly and will not rattle.

# Chapter 11

# SIDING

Because siding and other types of covering used for exterior walls have an important influence on the appearance as well as on the maintenance of the house, a careful selection should be made. The builder now has a choice of many wood and wood base materials which may be used to cover exterior walls. Masonry, veneers, metal or plastic siding, and other nonwood materials are additional choices. Wood siding can be obtained in many different patterns and can be finished naturally, stained, or painted. Wood shingles, plywood, wood siding or paneling, fiberboard, and hardboard are some of the materials used as exterior coverings. Many prefinished sidings are available, and the coatings and films applied to several types of base materials may eliminate the need of refinishing for many years.

Before outside trim is applied, the sheathing should be fully face nailed and prepared at the corners so that the trim may be placed on a straight and true surface. Waterproof building paper or felt should cover the entire surface. The laps of the successive layers of paper should point down so if water finds its way behind the siding, it will not drain into the sheathing. The outside wall covering is usually applied after door and window frames have been set. Before siding is applied a water table is often installed. The water table of a frame building is that section of the exterior trim that is immediately below the bottom course of the siding material. Its purpose is to keep the water which drains off the side of the house from running down the foundation. It is also used to form a starting point for the siding material and to improve the exterior appearance of the building. A water table is usually used with wood siding laid in a horizontal pattern.

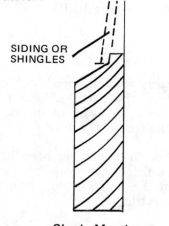

SIDING OR
SHINGLES

Single Member
Water Table
Figure 11-1

There are two general types of water tables. The single member water table is composed of a solid board, generally 1 1/16" x 5 5/8" surfaced four sides (S4S) and machined to the cross section shown in figure 11-1. The dotted line shows how the siding fits onto the top of the water table when both are nailed in place on the wall.

The built-up type of water table may be composed of several members. Generally a board ¾" x 5 5/8" (S4S), a drip cap, and a moulding are assembled as shown in figure 11-2. This type of water table is built up according to the style of the trim and may include additional members.

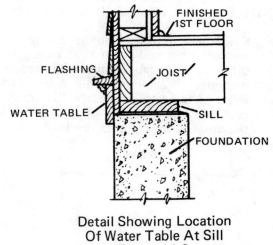

FINISHED
1ST FLOOR

FLASHING

JOIST

WATER TABLE

SILL

FOUNDATION

Detail Showing Location
Of Water Table At Sill
Figure 11-2

In general, any type of assembled water table should be flashed with metal at the drip cap. There should be a quirk (curve) provided in the underside of the drip cap to prevent water from working into the joints of the assembled water table and causing decay.

### How To Apply Water Table

1. Apply a strip of building paper horizontally over the sheathing where the water table and the first courses of siding material are to be placed. Tack it in place using scrap pieces of wood nailed temporarily with shingle nails.

*NOTE:* This keeps the paper from tearing loose from the nails.

2. Locate a point on the sheathing at one end of the building to represent the top of the water table.

NOTE: The distance between this point and the bottom edge of the sheathing should be ½ inch less than the width of the water table. See figure 11-3. This will permit the water table to extend below the lower edge of the sheathing.

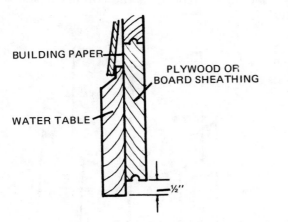

BUILDING PAPER

PLYWOOD OR BOARD SHEATHING

WATER TABLE

½"

Section Of Water Table
Figure 11-3

3. Locate a similar point on the opposite end of the building.

4. Snap a chalk line from one point to the other. Check the mark to see that it is level.

5. Temporarily nail the water table so the top is on the line.

6. Miter the water table at the outside corners and butt the joint at the internal corners.

7. Sight along the bottom edge of the water table to note any irregularities. If it is straight, nail the boards permanently in place using two 8d casing or common nails at each stud.

8. Set the nails with a nail set.

9. Apply the water table to the other walls in a like manner.

## Corner Treatments

The method of finishing wood siding or other materials at exterior corners is often influenced by the overall design of the house. A mitered corner effect on horizontal siding or the use of corner boards are perhaps the most common methods of treatment.

Mitering corners (figure 11-4A) of bevel and similar sidings, unless carefully done to prevent openings, is not always satisfactory. To maintain a good joint, it is necessary that the joint fit tightly the full depth of the miter. It is also good practice to treat the ends with a water-repellent preservative prior to nailing.

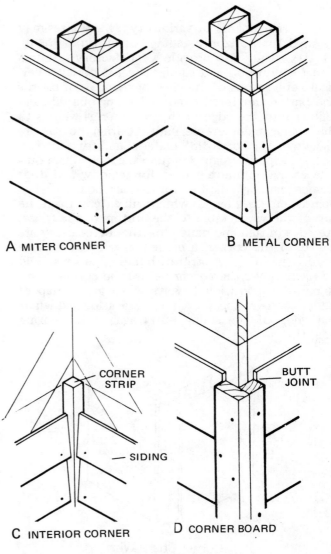

A MITER CORNER

B METAL CORNER

CORNER STRIP

SIDING

BUTT JOINT

C INTERIOR CORNER

D CORNER BOARD

Corner Treatments
Figure 11-4

Metal corners (figure 11-4B) are perhaps more commonly used than the mitered corner and give a mitered effect. They are easily placed over each corner as the siding is installed. The metal corners should fit tightly without openings and be nailed on each side to the sheathing or corner stud beneath. If made of galvanized iron, they should be cleaned with a mild acid wash and primed with a metal primer before the house is painted to prevent early peeling of the paint. Weathering of the metal will also prepare it for the prime paint coat.

Prefinished shingle or shake exteriors sometimes are used with color matched metal corners. They can also be lapped over the adjacent corner shingle, alternating each course. This is called "lacing." This type of corner treatment usually requires that some kind of flashing be used beneath.

Interior corners (figure 11-4C) are butted against a square corner board of nominal 1¼" or 1 3/8" size, depending on the thickness of the siding.

Corner boards of various types and sizes may be used for horizontal sidings of all types (figure 11-4D). They also provide a satisfactory termination for plywood and similar sheet materials. Vertical applications of matched paneling or of boards and battens are terminated by lapping one side and nailing into the edge of this member as well as to the nailing members beneath. Corner boards are usually 1 1/8" or 1 3/8" material and for a distinctive appearance might be quite narrow. Plain outside casing commonly used for window and door frames can be adapted for corner boards. The boards, cut to a length which will extend from the top of the water table to the bottom of the frieze, are edge-butted and nailed together before they are nailed to the corner, a procedure which ensures a good tight joint. A strip of building paper should be tacked over the corner before the corner board is nailed in position (always allow an overlap of paper to cover the subsequent crack formed where the ends of the siding butts against the corner board).

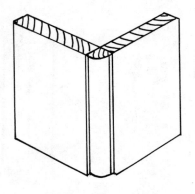

Corner Board With
Quarter Round
Figure 11-5

Figure 11-5 shows another method of forming a corner. This type is composed of two corner boards of the same thickness and width and a quarter round or cove moulding.

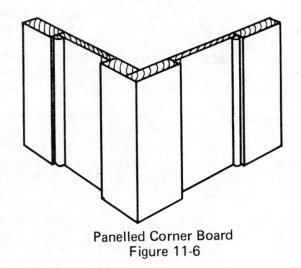

Panelled Corner Board
Figure 11-6

Figure 11-6 shows a more elaborate corner board built up of two plain corner boards spaced about 4 inches apart. A piece of siding is placed between the boards to form a panel which is trimmed with cove or quarter round moulding. When shingles are used on the walls without corner boards, they should be lapped at the corners as shown in figure 11-7.

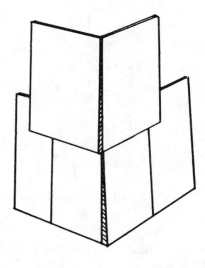

Shingled External Corner
Figure 11-7

**How To Apply Corner Boards**

1. Cut strips of building paper about 5 feet long and the full width of the roll.

2. Fold the paper lengthwise down the middle.

3. Apply the paper to all external and internal corners before the corner boards are placed. Place the fold in the paper vertically on the corner, thus covering the sheathing 18 inches on each side of the corner.

4. Tack the building paper in place using scrap pieces of wood nailed temporarily with shingle nails.

5. Select a straight piece of 1 1/8 inch lumber. Use a piece at least 8 feet long.

6. Lay out the bottom end as shown in figure 11-8.

7. Cut the board on these marks and fit it over the top of the water table.

8. Temporarily nail the corner board flush with the outside edge of the sheathing at the corner of the building (figure 11-9, Board A).

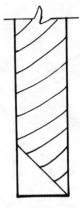

Side View Showing Cut
Figure 11-8

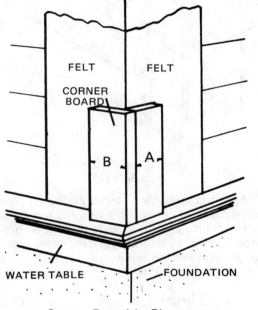

Corner Board In Place
Figure 11-9

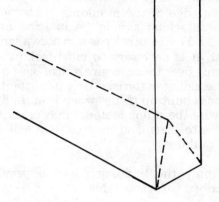

Bottom Cut Of Overlapping
Corner Board
Figure 11-10

## How To Apply Belt Courses

A belt course is made up the same as a water table. It is really a continuous water table around the building. Its function is to shed water from the walls and also to decorate the side of the building. Belt courses are generally used where the siding material of the lower story is not the same as on the upper section of the wall. Belt courses may be made up of one or of several members. They often consists of a few courses of siding material arranged in a different fashion from the ones above or below.

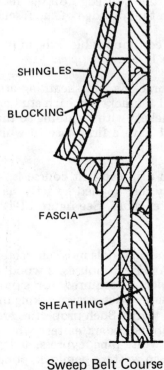

Sweep Belt Course
Figure 11-11

9. Nail enough additional pieces to extend it up to meet the bottom of the frieze or cornice.

10. Mark the bottom edge of another 1 1/8 inch board in a similar manner. However, the bottom cut that fits over the water table does not go through both edges (figure 11-10).

11. Nail this board flush with the outside edge of corner board A as shown in figure 11-9 and extend additional pieces up to the frieze.

12. Straighten both boards up and nail them permanently in place using 8d nails spaced about 14 inches.

13. Set the nails with a nail set.

Figure 11-11 shows a belt course with a sweep formed on the siding or shingles by nailing them over the edge of the moulding. In some cases continuous blocking should be inserted as shown in figure 11-11. In other cases, where a large sweep is desired, it is necessary to cut brackets and to nail sheathing over them to give a firm base on which to nail the siding material. It is important to have a solid base built up if the sweep is more than 1 inch. Otherwise the siding material may crack from being forced into place and may cause a leak in the side of the building.

1. Apply the building paper as previously described for water table.

2. Locate the height of the belt course. Snap a chalked line and check for levelness.

3. Tack small blocks of wood at the location of each stud and about 1½ inch above the bottom of the fascia of the belt course (figure 11-11).

*NOTE:* These blocks should be the same thickness as the top of the siding material that is to be used back of the belt course.

4. Tack similar blocks at the location of the top of the fascia.

5. Nail the fascia of the belt course in the same manner as the water table.

6. Nail the bed or crown moulding to the fascia, keeping the top edge of the moulding on a line with the top edge of the fascia.

7. Nail the continuous blocking in place as shown in figure 11-11.

*NOTE:* If brackets and sheathing are to be used, nail a bracket at each stud and cover the brackets with sheathing so that the siding will have a firm base to which it can be nailed.

If a drip cap belt course is to be used it may be applied exactly as a drip cap water table. See figure 11-12.

**Wood Siding**

One of the materials most characteristic of the exteriors of American houses is wood siding. The essential properties required for siding are good painting characteristics, easy working qualities, and freedom from warp. Such properties are present to a high degree in the cedars, eastern white pine, sugar pine, western white pine, cypress, and redwood; to a good degree in western hemlock, ponderosa pine, the spruces, and yellow-poplar; and to a fair degree in Douglas-fir, western larch, and southern pine.

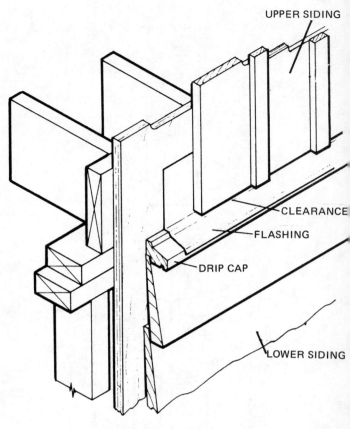

Drip Cap Belt Course
Figure 11-12

Material used for exterior siding which is to be painted, should preferably be of a high grade and free from knots, pitch pockets, and waney edges. Vertical grain and mixed grain (both vertical and flat) are available in some species such as redwood and western red cedar.

The moisture content at the time of application should be that which it would attain in service. This would be approximately 10 to 12 percent except in the dry Southwestern States where the moisture content should average about 8 to 9 percent. To minimize seasonal movement due to changes in moisture content, vertical grain (edge-grain) siding is preferred. While this is not as important for a stained finish, the use of edge-grain siding for a paint finish will result in longer paint life. A 3 minute dip in a water repellent preservative before siding is installed will not only result in longer paint life, but also will resist moisture entry and decay. Some manufacturers supply siding with this treatment. Freshly cut ends should be brush treated on the job.

One of the important factors in successful performance of various siding materials is the type of fasteners used. Nails are the most common of these, and it is poor economy indeed to use them sparingly. Corrosion resistant nails, galvanized or made of aluminum, stainless steel, or similar metals, may cost more, but their use will insure spot free siding under adverse conditions.

Two types of nails are commonly used with siding, the finishing nail having a small head and the siding nail having a moderate size flat head. The small head finishing nail is set (driven with a nail set) about 1/16 inch below the face of the siding, and the hole is filled with putty after the prime coat of paint is applied. The flathead siding nail, most commonly used, is driven flush with the face of the siding and the head later covered with paint.

Ordinary steel wire nails tend to rust in a short time and cause a disfiguring stain on the face of the siding. In some cases, the small head nails will show rust spots through the putty and paint. Non-corrosive nails that will not cause rust are readily available.

Siding to be "natural finished" with a water-repellent preservative or stain should be fastened with stainless steel or aluminum nails. In some types of prefinished sidings, nails with color matched heads are supplied.

In recent years, nails with modified shanks have become quite popular. These include the annularly threaded shank nail and the helically threaded shank nail. Both have greater withdrawal resistance than the smooth shank nail and, for this reason, a shorter nail is often used.

Exposed nails in siding should be driven just flush with the surface of the wood. Overdriving may not only show the hammer mark, but may also cause objectionable splitting and crushing of the wood. In sidings with prefinished surfaces or overlays, the nails should be driven so as not to damage the finished surface.

## Bevel Siding

Plain bevel siding can be obtained in sizes from ½" x 4" to ½" x 8", and also in sizes of ¾" x 8" to ¾" x 12" (figure 11-13). "Anzac" siding (figure 11-13) is ¾" x 12" in size. Usually the finished width of bevel siding is about ½ inch less than the size listed. One side of bevel siding has a smooth planed surface, while the other has a rough resawn surface. For a stained finish, the rough or sawn side is exposed because wood stain is most successful and longer lasting on rough wood surfaces.

Installed plain bevel siding is shown in figure 11-13. The top edge varies from 3/16 inch to ½ inch in thickness and the bottom edge from 3/8 inch to ¾ inch. Redwood "Anzac" siding is made as wide as 12 inches and as thick as ¾ inch at the lower edge. Most siding comes in bundles of from 4 feet to 16 feet in length.

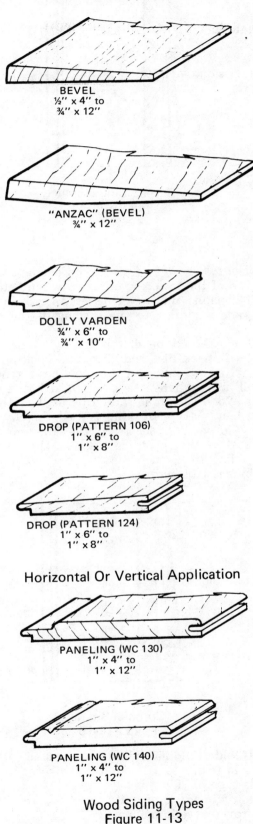

**Horizontal Application**

BEVEL
½" x 4" to
¾" x 12"

"ANZAC" (BEVEL)
¾" x 12"

DOLLY VARDEN
¾" x 6" to
¾" x 10"

DROP (PATTERN 106)
1" x 6" to
1" x 8"

DROP (PATTERN 124)
1" x 6" to
1" x 8"

**Horizontal Or Vertical Application**

PANELING (WC 130)
1" x 4" to
1" x 12"

PANELING (WC 140)
1" x 4" to
1" x 12"

Wood Siding Types
Figure 11-13

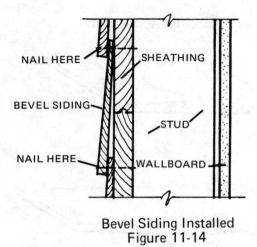

Bevel Siding Installed
Figure 11-14

The lower edge of one board overlaps the upper edge of the lower board as shown in figure 11-14. This lap should never be less than ¾ inch but may vary according to the spacing of the siding.

Nails should be driven through both thicknesses of the siding and into the sheathing and studs. Narrow siding of this type has a tendency to pull apart where it is overlapped between the studs. Wood sheathing should be used on the side walls when this type of siding is used, thereby forming a solid base. If necessary, the siding may then be nailed to the sheathing between the studs. If wide siding of ¾ inch butt is used, composition sheathing is satisfactory.

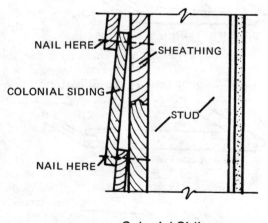

Colonial Siding
Figure 11-15

If wide Colonial siding is to be used, the type shown in figure 11-15 is quite satisfactory. Some of this type of siding is beveled at the back. This allows the board to lie quite close to the sheathing, thus providing solid nailing.

Dolly Varden siding is similar to true bevel siding except that shiplap edges are used, resulting in a constant exposure distance (figure 11-13). Be-

cause it lies flat against the studs, it is sometimes used for garages and similar buildings without sheathing. Diagonal bracing is then needed to provide racking resistance to the wall.

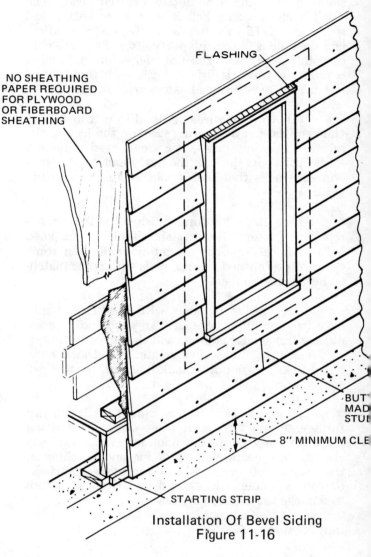

Installation Of Bevel Siding
Figure 11-16

The average exposure distance is usually determined by the distance from the underside of the window sill to the top of the drip cap (figure 11-16). From the standpoint of weather resistance and appearance, the butt edge of the first course of siding above the window should coincide with the top of the window drip cap. In many one-story houses with an overhang, this course of siding is often replaced with a frieze board. It is also desirable that the bottom of a siding course be flush with the underside of the window sill. However, this may not always be possible because of varying window heights and types that might be used in a house.

One of two systems used to determine the siding exposure width so that it is about equal both above and below the window sill is described below:

Divide the overall height of the window frame by the approximate recommended exposure distance for the siding used (4 for 6 inch wide siding, 6 for 8 inch siding, 8 for 10 inch siding, and 10 for 12 inch siding). This will result in the number of courses between the top and bottom of the window. For example, the overall height of our sample window from top of the drip cap to the bottom of the sill is 61 inches. If 12 inch siding is used, the number of courses would be 61/100=6.0 or six courses. To obtain the exact exposure distance, divide 61 by 6 and the result would be 10-1/6 inches. The next step is to determine the exposure distance from the bottom of the sill to just below the top of the foundation wall. If this is 31 inches, three courses at 10-1/3 inches each would be used. Thus, the exposure distance above and below the window would be almost the same (figure 11-16).

When this system is not satisfactory because of big differences in the two areas, it is preferable to use an equal exposure distance for the entire wall height and notch the siding at the window sill. The fit should be tight to prevent moisture entry.

It is good practice to avoid butt joints whenever possible. Use the longer sections of siding under windows and other long stretches and utilize the shorter lengths for areas between windows and doors. If unavoidable, butt joints should be made over a stud and staggered between courses as much as practical (figure 11-16).

Siding should be square-cut to provide a good joint at window and door casings and at butt joints. Open joints permit moisture to enter, often leading to paint deterioration. It is good practice to brush or dip the fresh cut ends of the siding in a water-repellent preservative before boards are nailed in place. Using a small finger actuated oil can to apply the water-repellent preservative at end and butt joints after siding is in place is also helpful.

## How To Install Bevel Siding With Corner Boards

1. Starting at the bottom, apply a full width strip of building paper.

*NOTE:* Each strip of paper should lap over the proceeding one about 4 inches. Tuck the paper up tightly into the grooves under all window frames. Do not cover a large area with paper at one time but apply the strips as the application of the siding progresses.

2. Secure a piece of stock about ¾" x 3" and long enough to reach from the bottom of the sheathing to the top of the first floor windows.

3. With one end of this rod ½ inch below the bottom edge of the sheathing, mark the location of the bottom of the window sill and of the top of the drip cap (figure 11-17).

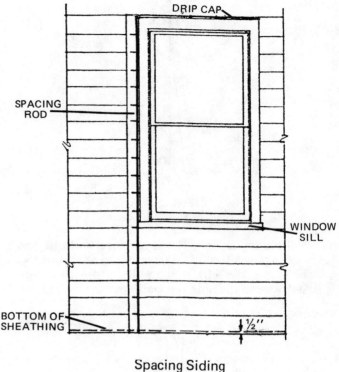

Spacing Siding
Figure 11-17

4. Mark the spacing of the courses of siding on the rod with dividers.

*NOTE:* The width of these spacings will be determined by the type of siding and the exposure of each course. The dividers should be adjusted so that the spaces are equal and so that the bottom edge of the siding comes to the sill and to the cap of the window. If the spacing below and at the sides of the windows do not come out equal, they should be changed slightly so they appear equal.

The position of the courses may be stepped off directly on the building without using a rod. However, this process would then have to be repeated at each side of the building.

5. To start the first courses, make a mark on each end of the building where the top edge of the first course will come.

6. Snap a chalk line between these two marks to show the top edge of the first course.

7. Nail furring strips along the bottom edge of the sheathing (figure 11-18).

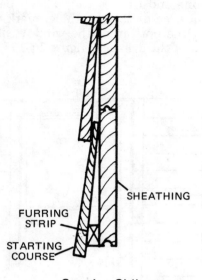

Starting Siding
Figure 11-18

8. Square the ends of the first board and put one end against the left corner board with the top edge on the chalk line. Tack the top edge with small nails driven part way in. See figure 11-19.

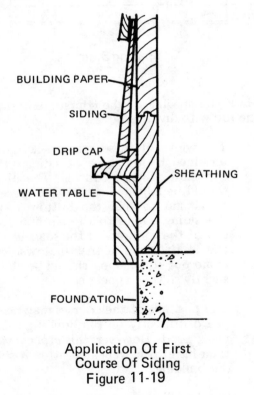

Application Of First
Course Of Siding
Figure 11-19

9. Continue the siding across in the same manner and fit it to the right corner board.

10. Sight across the bottom of the first course and, if satisfactory, nail it in place securely. Nail through the thick part of the board into the furring strip at the bottom.

*NOTE:* Siding should be nailed to each stud or on 16 inch centers. When plywood or wood sheathing or spaced wood nailing strips are used over nonwood sheathing, 7d or 8d nails (2¼ and 2½ inches long) may be used for ¾ inch thick siding. However, if gypsum or fiberboard sheathing is used, the 10d nail is recommended to penetrate into the stud. For ½ inch thick siding, nails may be ¼ inch shorter than those used for ¾ inch siding.

The nails should be located far enough up from the butt to miss the top of the lower siding course (figure 11-20). This clearance distance is usually 1/8 inch. This allows for slight movement of the siding due to moisture changes without causing splitting. Such an allowances is especially required for the wider sidings of 8 to 12 inches wide.

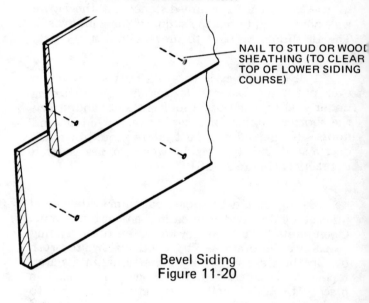

Bevel Siding
Figure 11-20

11. With the spacing rod, mark for the second course, strike a line and continue in the same way.

12. Use a siding hook as shown in figure 11-21 to mark the length of the pieces of siding between the corner boards or window casings. Be sure the siding is in a level position while the mark is being made.

**How To Apply Beveled Siding With Mitered Corners**

1. Allow a piece of siding of the first course to project beyond the corner of the building (figure 11-22). Make a mark on the outside face at the bottom of the siding at a distance from the corner of the building equal to the thickness of the bottom edge of the siding (A, figure 11-22).

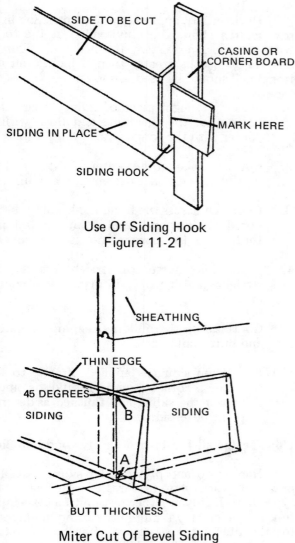

Use Of Siding Hook
Figure 11-21

Miter Cut Of Bevel Siding
For Starting Course
Figure 11-22

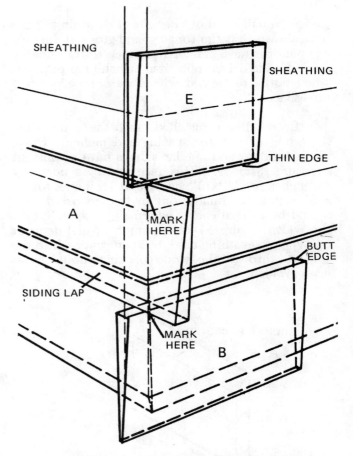

Cut Of Bevel For Succeeding Courses
Figure 11-23

2. Make a mark at the top of the siding at a distance from the corner of the building equal to the thickness of the top edge of the siding (B, figure 11-22).

3. Connect these points with a straight line on the face of the siding. This gives the long point of the miter cut. Mark a 45 degree angle from this line across the edge of the piece.

4. Cut the board along this line with a fine tooth saw.

5. Mark and cut the siding for the opposite side of the corner in a similar manner and nail both boards in place.

6. Place a board for the next course in position (A, figure 11-23).

7. Place a short piece of siding B underneath the piece A and against the face of the first course in the position shown in figure 11-23.

8. Mark the outside face of piece A opposite the outside edge of piece B.

9. Put the short piece B in the position shown at E with the thin edge down.

10. Mark the top of the outside face of piece A opposite the outside edge of E.

11. Draw the line connecting the two marks, lay out the angle and make the cut as before.

12. Mark and cut the piece for the other side of the corner and for succeeding courses in the same manner. Nail the boards in position as they are cut.

### How To Apply Drop, Lap Or Matched Siding

Regular drop sidings can be obtained in several patterns, two of which are shown in figure 11-13. This siding, with matched or shiplap edges, can be obtained in 1" x 6" and 1" x 8" sizes. This type is commonly used for lower cost dwellings and for garages, usually without benefit of sheathing. Tests have shown that the tongued-and-grooved (matched) patterns have greater resistance to the penetration of wind-driven rain than the shiplap patterns, when both are treated with a water-repellent preservative.

Drop siding is installed much the same as bevel siding except for spacing and nailing. Drop, Dolly Varden, and similar sidings have a constant exposure distance. This face width is normally 5¼ inches for 1" x 6" siding and 7¼ inches for 1" x 8" siding. Normally, one or two 8d or 9d nails should be used at each stud crossing, depending on the width (figure 11-24). Length of nail depends on type of sheathing used, but penetration into the stud or through the wood backing should be at least 1½ inches.

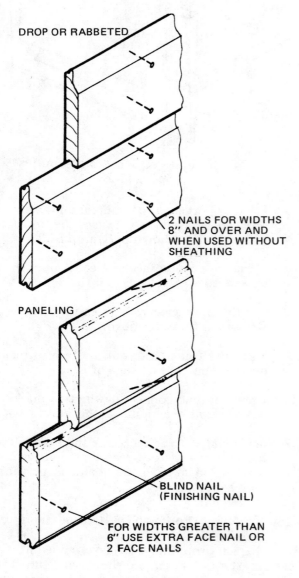

DROP OR RABBETED

2 NAILS FOR WIDTHS
8" AND OVER AND
WHEN USED WITHOUT
SHEATHING

PANELING

BLIND NAIL
(FINISHING NAIL)

FOR WIDTHS GREATER THAN
6" USE EXTRA FACE NAIL OR
2 FACE NAILS

**Nailing Of Siding
Figure 11-24**

Horizontally applied matched paneling in narrow widths should be blind-nailed at the tongue with a corrosion-resistant finished nail (figure 11-24). For widths greater than 6 inches, an additional nail should be used as shown.

1. Select a straight piece of siding. Start at the bottom of the sheathing and flush with the corner with the tongue up.

2. Cut the piece on the center of a stud and tack it in place with nails driven part way in.

3. Continue across the building, keeping the first board straight and level. Cut the last piece flush with the corner and tack it in place.

4. Sight this course for straightness. If it is straight, nail it firmly in place with two nails at each stud.

5. Continue up the building keeping all matched and butt joints tight.

*NOTE:* When siding is applied directly to studding, corner boards should be applied over the siding and finished as described for bevel siding.

### How To Install Hardboard Or Plywood Lap Siding

Hardboard and plywood lap siding is available in a wide variety of textures and finishes. Many types have highly weather resistant factory-applied finishes which may require little or no maintenance for the life of the structure. Hardboard and plywood lap siding also offer superior resistance to shrinking and warping and often can be applied over unsheathed studs 16 inches on center. Adequate diagonal bracing must be provided, however. Building paper or a felt wind barrier must be used on all sides and a vapor barrier of polyethylene film or foil backed gypsum board should be used on the interior side of the insulation in the wall when hardboard or plywood siding is used. This vapor barrier will prevent condensation from forming within the wall.

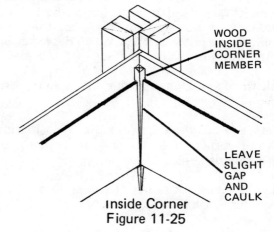

WOOD
INSIDE
CORNER
MEMBER

LEAVE
SLIGHT
GAP
AND
CAULK

Inside Corner
Figure 11-25

1. Install the required inside corners. See figure 11-25. The corner material should be at least 1¼" thick and long enough to reach between the top edge of the siding and ¼ inch below the bottom of the sheathing or sill plate.

2. Install a starter strip of 3/8" x 1½" wood lath or a 2 inch strip of siding material around the bottom edge of the sheathing or sill plate. This strip should be level all around the building. See figure 11-26.

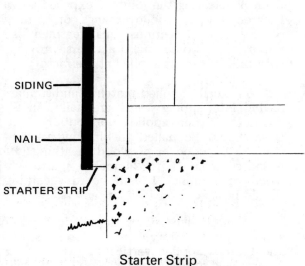

Starter Strip
Figure 11-26

3. Nail the first course of siding. The bottom edge should be level and 1/8 inch below the starter strip. Use 8d galvanized nails with a head at least 3/16 inch in diameter. If the siding is being applied over ¾ inch sheathing a 10d nail should be used. Checkered head nails should be used where a smooth head would contrast with a textured siding finish. Nails should be at least ½ inch from the bottom edge and ends. Nails should not be more than 16 inches apart.

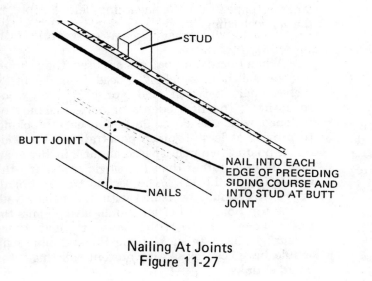

Nailing At Joints
Figure 11-27

4. Butt joints should occur only when both ends can be nailed over a stud. Use two nails in each board end. Adjacent boards should just fit snugly. Don't force to wedge them into place. See figure 11-27.

*NOTE:* Hardboard or plywood siding should be cut with a fine toothed band saw or a power saw with a combination blade. Cut from the back side.

5. The second and following courses must have at least a 1 inch lap. Figure the correct lap using either of the two methods described previously for bevel siding. Nails should go through both siding courses at the lap. See figure 11-28. Joints of adjacent courses should always be staggered between studs. Where the siding butts against trim leave a 1/8 inch space and fill this space with butyl caulk. See figure 11-29.

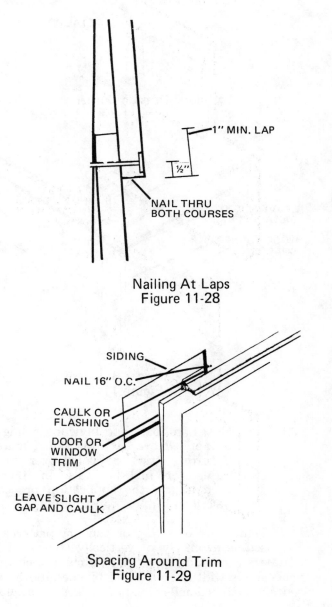

Nailing At Laps
Figure 11-28

Spacing Around Trim
Figure 11-29

6. Most prefinished hardboard and plywood siding is available with metal corner tabs prefinished to match the siding in color and texture. They should be installed by inserting the tab behind the lower edge of siding and nailing each corner at the top. See figure 11-30. If corner boards are used they should be at least 1 1/8 inch thick and should be caulked at the edges with butyl caulk. (See figure 11-31).

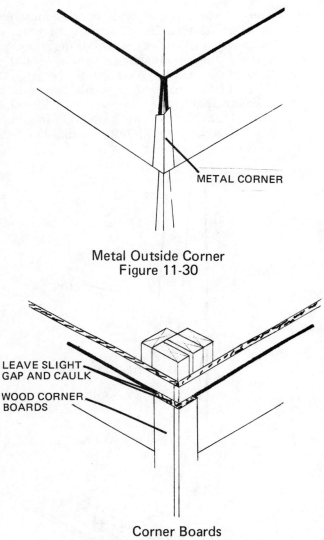

Metal Outside Corner
Figure 11-30

Corner Boards
Figure 11-31

*NOTE:* Most hardboard and plywood siding can be applied over existing siding material if furring strips are nailed over the old siding at 16 inch intervals. In other respects follow the application procedure described for new construction.

A number of siding or paneling patterns can be used horizontally or vertically (figure 11-13). These are manufactured in nominal 1 inch thickness and in widths from 4 to 12 inches. Both dressed and matched and shiplapped edges are available.

The narrow and medium width patterns will likely be more satisfactory when there are moderate moisture content changes. Wide patterns are more successful if they are vertical grain to keep shrinkage to a minimum. The correct moisture content is also important when tongued and grooved siding is wide, to prevent shrinkage to a point where the tongue is exposed.

Treating the edges of both drop and the matched and shiplapped sidings with water-repellent preservative usually prevents wind-driven rain from penetrating the joints if exposed to weather. In areas under wide overhangs, or in porches or other protected sections, this treatment is not as important. Some manufacturers provide siding with this treatment applied at the factory.

Vertically applied matched and similar sidings having interlapping joints are nailed in the same manner as when applied horizontally. However, they should be nailed to blocking used between studs or to wood or plywood sheathing. Blocking is spaced from 16 to 24 inches apart. With plywood or nominal 1 inch board sheathing, nails should be spaced on 16 inch centers.

A method of siding application, popular for some architectural styles, utilizes rough-sawn boards and battens applied vertically. These boards can be arranged in several ways: (a) Board and batten, (b) batten and boards, and (c) board and board (figure 11-32). As in the vertical application of most siding materials, nominal 1 inch sheathing boards or plywood sheathing 5/8 or ¾ inch thick should be used for nailing surfaces. When other types of sheathing materials or thinner plywoods are used, nailing blocks between studs commonly provide the nailing areas. Nailers of 1 by 4 inches, laid horizontally and spaced from 16 to 24 inches apart vertically can be used over nonwood sheathing. However, special or thicker casing is sometimes required around doors and window frames when this system is used. It is good practice to use a building paper over the sheathing before applying the vertical siding.

When boards and battens are used, they should also be nailed to blocking spaced from 16 to 24 inches apart between studs, or closer for wood sheathing. The first boards or battens should be fastened with one 8d or 9d nail at each blocking, to provide at least 1½ inch penetration. For wide under boards, two nails spaced about 2 inches apart may be used rather than the single row along the center (figure 11-32). The second or top boards or battens should be nailed with 12d nails. Nails of the top board or batten should always miss the under boards and not be nailed through them. (Figure 11-32). In such applications, double nails should be spaced closely to prevent splitting if the board shrinks.

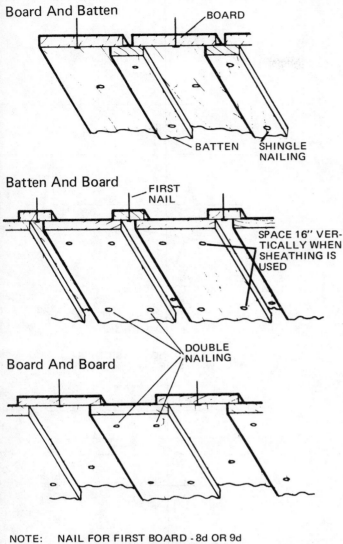

**Board And Batten**

BOARD

BATTEN    SHINGLE
NAILING

**Batten And Board**

FIRST
NAIL

SPACE 16" VER-
TICALLY WHEN
SHEATHING IS
USED

**Board And Board**

DOUBLE
NAILING

NOTE:    NAIL FOR FIRST BOARD - 8d OR 9d
        NAIL FOR SECOND BOARD - 12d

Vertical Board Siding
Figure 11-32

## Sheet Siding

A number of sheet materials are now available for use as siding. These include plywood in a variety of face treatments and species, overlaid plywood, and hardboard. Plywood or overlaid plywood is sometimes used without sheathing and is known as panel siding with 3/8 inch often considered the minimum thickness for such use for 16 inch stud spacing. However, from the standpoint of stiffness and strength, better performance is usually obtained by using 3/4 or 5/8 inch thickness. Hardboard panel siding 3/8 inch thick can be used with studs spaced at 16 inches. For studs spaced at 24 inches at least 5/8 inch hardboard should be used. Be sure to check local building code requirements.

For sheet siding, girts must be nailed between the studs along the lines where joints between panels will occur. Both the horizontal and the vertical joints between panels must be made weather-tight. Horizontal joints may be protected by flashing laid on the girts and shaped so as to protrude through the joint and overhang the upper edge of the lower panel. The horizontal edges of the panels may be rabbeted so they will join together in an overlapping joint like that between strips of ship-lap. Vertical joints may be closed by nailing vertical battens over them; by leaving a slight space between the edges of panels, rabbeting the edges, and gluing in a spline; by a vertical joint sealed by caulking compound.

Exterior grade plywood, overlaid plywood, hardboard and similar sheet materials used for siding are usually applied vertically. When used over sheathing, plywood should be at least 1/4 inch thick, although 5/16 and 3/8 inch will normally provide a more even surface. Hardboard should be 1/4 inch thick and materials such as medium-density fiberboard should be 1/2 inch.

All nailing should be over studs and total effective penetration into wood should be at least 1 1/2 inches. For example, 3/8 inch plywood siding over 3/4 inch wood sheathing would require about a 7d nail, which is 2 1/4 inches long. This would result in a 1 1/8 inch penetration into the stud, but a total effective penetration of 1 7/8 inches into wood.

Plywood should be nailed at 6 inch intervals around the perimeter and 12 inches at intermediate members. Hardboard siding should be nailed at 4 and 8 inch intervals. All types of sheet material should have a joint caulked with mastic unless the joints are of the interlapping or matched type or battens are installed. A strip of 15 pound asphalt felt under uncaulked joints is good practice. As with hardboard or plywood lap siding, a vapor barrier must be used on the interior side of the insulation.

### How To Install Sheet Siding

A few simple precautions will prevent warping and splitting of the siding after it is applied. If siding is to be applied over sheathing, the sheathing should be dry. Don't try to apply siding over sheathing soaked by rain. The siding should be stored unwrapped at the job site about 5 days before it is applied so that its moisture content is as nearly as possible the same as the studs and the sheathing.

All joints between siding sheets and between siding and trim should leave a 1/8 to 1/16 inch gap to allow for expansion. Be careful not to trap any moisture in the wall when applying siding.

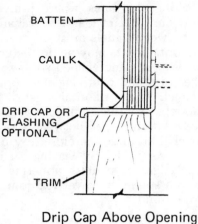

Drip Cap Above Opening
Figure 11-33

1. Cut the siding to length so that the bottom edge laps the foundation by 1½ inch and extends at least 3 inches above the top of the studs. Sheet paneling is usually installed vertically with the face grain running up and down the wall. Cut off excess material with a fine toothed hand saw or a power saw with a combination blade. Always cut and mark siding on the back side. A drip cap or flashing is usually installed above openings (figure 11-33) and drip cap may be installed at the base of the siding (figure 11-34).

Drip Cap At Foundation
Figure 11-34

2. If a joint does not fall on a framing member, nail a girt behind the joint and nail the siding edges to the girt. Battens are usually placed over vertical joints (figure 11-35) unless ship-lap edges are formed into the siding. (Figure 11-36). Do not spring or force the panels into place. Remember to leave a 1/16 inch to 1/8 inch space between panels and caulk the joints.

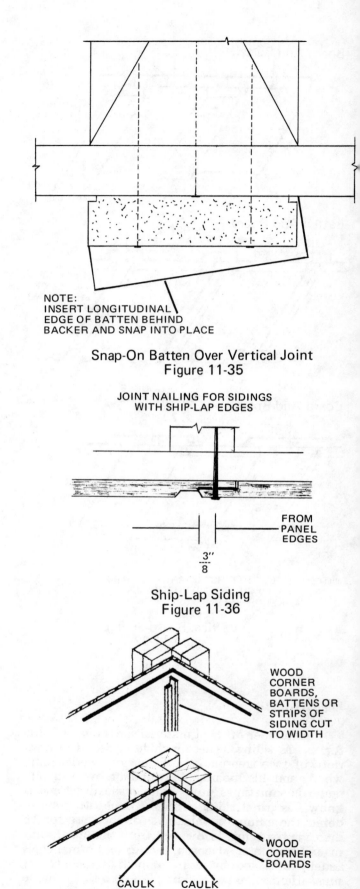

NOTE:
INSERT LONGITUDINAL EDGE OF BATTEN BEHIND BACKER AND SNAP INTO PLACE

Snap-On Batten Over Vertical Joint
Figure 11-35

JOINT NAILING FOR SIDINGS WITH SHIP-LAP EDGES

FROM PANEL EDGES

$\frac{3''}{8}$

Ship-Lap Siding
Figure 11-36

WOOD CORNER BOARDS, BATTENS OR STRIPS OF SIDING CUT TO WIDTH

WOOD CORNER BOARDS

CAULK     CAULK

Two Inside Corner Details
Figure 11-37

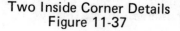

*NOTE:* Plywood paneling may not require caulking on joints covered by battens or joints made by beveling the edges. Follow the manufacturer's instructions.

3.  Form inside and outside corners by installing battens, wood corner boards or strips of siding. See figures 11-37 and 11-38.

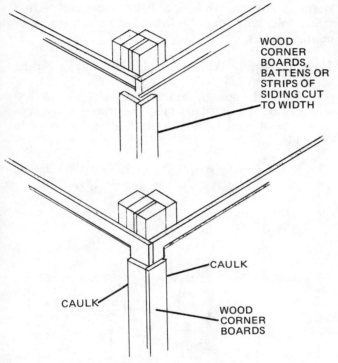

Outside Corner Details
Figure 11-38

## Wood Shingles And Shakes

Wood shingles and shakes are applied in a single or double course pattern. They may be used over wood or plywood sheathing after the wall has been covered with building paper. If sheathing is 3/8 inch plywood, use threaded nails. For non-wood sheathing, 1" x 3" or 1" x 4" wood nailing strips are used as a base. In the single course method, one course is simply laid over the other as lap siding is applied. The shingles can be second grade because only one half or less of the butt portion is exposed (figure 11-39). Shingles should not be soaked before application but should usually be laid up with about 1/8 to ¼ inch space between adjacent shingles to allow for expansion during rainy weather. When a "siding effect" is desired, shingles should be laid up so that they are only lightly in contact. Prestained or treated shingles provide the best results for this system.

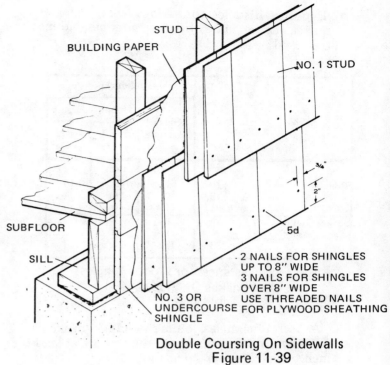

Double Coursing On Sidewalls
Figure 11-39

In a double course system, the undercourse is applied over the wall and the top course nailed directly over a ¼ to ½ inch projection of the butt (figure 11-40). The first course should be nailed only enough to hold it in place while the outer course is being applied. The first shingles can be a lower quality, such as third grade or the undercourse grade. The top course, because much of the shingle length is exposed, should be first grade shingles.

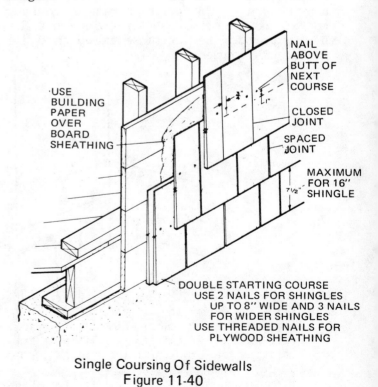

Single Coursing Of Sidewalls
Figure 11-40

Exposure distance for various length shingles and shakes can be guided by the recommendations in table 11-41.

| Material | Length | Maximum exposure | | |
|---|---|---|---|---|
| | | Single coursing | Double coursing | |
| | | | No. 1 grade | No. 2 grade |
| | Inch | Inch | Inch | Inch |
| Shingles | 16 | 7½ | 12 | 10 |
| | 18 | 8½ | 14 | 11 |
| | 24 | 11½ | 16 | 14 |
| Shakes (hand split and resawn) | 18 | 8½ | 14 | -------- |
| | 24 | 11½ | 20 | -------- |
| | 32 | 15 | -------- | -------- |

Exposure Distance For Wood Shingles
And Shakes On Sidewalls
Table 11-41

As in roof shingles, joints should be "broken" so that butt joints of the upper shingles are at least 1½ inch from the under shingle joints.

Closed or open joints may be used in the application of shingles to sidewalls at the discretion of the builder (figure 11-39). Spacing of ¼ to 3/8 inch produces an individual effect, while close spacing produces a shadow line similar to bevel siding.

Shingles and shakes should be applied with rust-resistant nails long enough to penetrate into the wood backing strips or sheathing. In single coursing, a 3d or 4d zinc-coated "shingle" nail is commonly used. In double coursing, where nails are exposed, a 5d zinc-coated nail with a small flat head is used for the top course and 3d or 4d size for the undercourse.

Nails should be placed in from the edge of the shingle a distance of ¾ inch (figure 11-39). Use two nails for each shingle up to 8 inches wide and three nails for shingles over 8 inches. In single course applications, nails should be placed 1 inch above the butt line of the next higher course. In double coursing, the use of a piece of shiplap sheathing as a guide allows the outer course to extend ½ inch below the undercourse, producing a shadow line (figure 11-40). Nails should be placed 2 inches above the bottom of the shingle or shake. Rived or fluted processed shakes, usually factory stained, are available and have a distinct effect when laid with closely fitted edges in a double course pattern.

### How To Apply Wood Shingle And Shake Siding

1. Space the shingle courses the same way as described for bevel siding. The maximum exposure should not exceed the figures in table 11-41.

2. Nail a furring strip around the bottom edge of the building as shown in figure 11-42.

3. Locate the bottom edge of the first course of shingles with the layout rod.

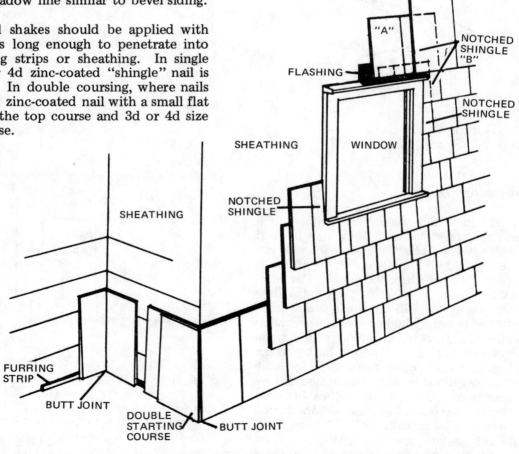

Application Of Wood Siding Shingles
Figure 11-42

4. Tack a shingle on both corners and in the middle of the building. Keep the bottom of the shingles level and at the proper height.

5. Drive a small nail into the bottom end of the first shingle and hook a line on this nail. Stretch the line across the building and hook it on the bottom edge of the middle and the opposite corner shingle.

6. Lay the first course of shingles with the butts against this line. Do not force the line downward.

*NOTE:* Keep the edges of the shingles which butt against one another plumb. Use a spirit level to level the bottom of the shingles of the internal corner with those of the external corner shown in figure 11-42.

7. Lap the shingles at the external and internal corners butting them as shown in figure 11-42. Corners may also be mitered, woven or jointed as with roofing shingles.

8. Double the first course of shingles the same as the starting course on a roof. Alternate the lap of the corner shingles.

9. Determine the location of the second course with the layout rod. Snap a chalk line to show the butt line of the second course.

10. Lay the second course of shingles to the chalk line.

11. Lap the corners opposite to the lower course. No joint should occur in any course directly over one in the preceding course. Make the break at least 1¼ inch from the joint below.

12. Apply the third course in the same manner but again reverse the lap at the corners.

*NOTE:* When fitting shingles around the bottom of windows, do not allow the joints to come directly under the casing edge. If the tips of the shingles run above the window sill, notch them as shown in figure 11-42 so they will slide up into the groove of the sill.

## How To Shingle Above Windows

1. Flash the drip cap (figure 11-42). Notice how the shingle B is cut to fit around the drip cap and how those over the window (A) are cut off at the butts so the tips will line up.

*NOTE:* If the shingles are cut off at the tips to make them line up, a bulge will be formed in the shingles at this point.

2. Continue the shingles across the tops of all windows in a like manner.

3. Place the course that comes above the window in the same manner as the regular courses.

## How To Shingle Over Existing Siding

Shingles can be applied directly over wood siding. Building paper should be applied first. Then follow the steps outlined above for new construction. Moulding strips should be nailed around windows and doors before beginning to apply the shingles. Nail the moulding strips over the old casings so that the outer edge of the moulding meets flush against the shingles. When applying shingles over composition siding or stucco, apply horizontal nailing strips to the wall to provide a firm base for the shingle nails. The strips should be spaced as far apart as the exposure distance of each course and should be placed 2 inches above the butt line of each course.

## Asbestos Shingle Siding

Asbestos shingle siding, made principally of asbestos fiber and portland cement, is usually supplied in rectangular units with straight or wavy butt edges. Asbestos shingles are usually 12 to 24 inches, but other units may range from 9 to 16 inches in width and from 24 to 48 inches in length. Thickness ranges from 5/32 to 3/16 inch. The material is rigid, strong, fire-resistant, pestproof, and resists weathering. Colors are obtained by pigmentation or by embedding of colored mineral granules. The siding may be painted but does not require painting for preservation.

The only accessories furnished with asbestos-cement siding are face nails and backer or joint flashing strips. Nails and fasteners must be permanently and effectively corrosion resistant and nonstaining. Siding units are made with properly sized and located holes to receive exposed face nails, which serve as guides for the correct amount of headlap and exposure and unit alignment. Backer or joint flashing strips, asphalt saturated and coated, must always be applied back of each vertical joint between siding units. Underlayment material or sheathing paper should be asphalt saturated felt. Coal-tar-saturated felts should not be used because they may stain the siding.

Portable shingle cutting machines may be used to cut, punch, and notch asbestos siding. They save time and labor and do a superior job. The siding may be sawed with a hacksaw, or a power saw equipped with a fabric reinforced flexible abrasive wheel or a carbide tipped blade. Edges of the material may be dressed with a file. Holes may be drilled or punched with a special punching device mounted on the shingle cutter.

Much time and expense can be saved by planning the job properly. Make sure proper material storage facilities are on the job to protect the asbestos cement siding from all hazards and damage.

Siding from different lots or factory runs may have slight and unavoidable differences in colors. All surfaces to which siding is applied should be supported adequately, be smooth, clean and dry, and provide an adequate nailing base and support. Provide a suitable sheathing or surface for the siding that will serve as an adequate nailing base, capable of developing the full holding power of nails or fasteners that must be used, and that is substantially level, plumb, and smooth. When men are working on a structure that has been or is being sided with asbestos cement siding, they must be required to take adequate precautions not to damage, stain, or harm the exterior wall siding. This is especially important when painting or built-up roofing work is being done.

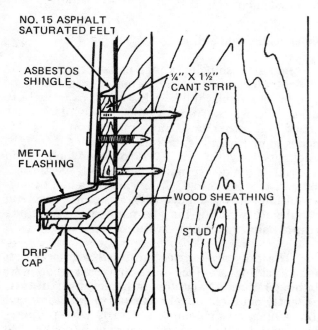

Flashing For Asbestos Siding
Figure 11-43

Where wall surfaces join at inside corners, the courses of siding are generally butted, although metal moulding or wood corner strip may be used. Outside corners can be handled by any one of several methods. For lapped adjoining courses at outside corners, temporarily place a whole shingle against each adjoining wall so that they meet and join at the corner. Scribe and cut the adjoining vertical edges of the siding units at the proper angle to form a lapped or woven corner joint. See figure 11-44. Corner joints should be lapped to the left and right in alternate courses. Courses on adjoining walls should meet and match at corners.

Flash over openings as illustrated in figure 11-43. Flash all outside corners and inside corners with a 12 inch wide strip of underlay material centered in or around the corner when corner boards are used. In other corner treatments, carry the underlayment felt around the corner of each sidewall so that a double thickness of felt results over the corner and use folded backer strips at each course of shingles at the corner.

Asbestos cement siding should be bedded in nonshrinking caulking compound at all corners and wherever it butts against wooden trim, masonry, or other projections. Care must be taken in applying the compound to avoid smearing the face of the shingles. Avoid applying visible or exposed caulking compound.

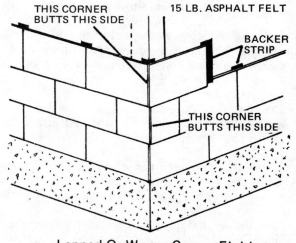

Lapped Or Woven Corner Finish
Figure 11-44

Wood corner boards are made of two pieces of nominal one inch lumber. A 1" x 3" member is nailed to the backside of the 1" x 4" member. This will form a face surface of equal dimension on each side of the corner. Corner boards, as well as all other exterior trim, should be face and back primed before assembly to the structure.

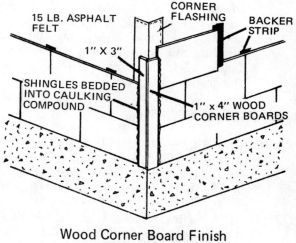

Wood Corner Board Finish
Figure 11-45

Several styles of nonstaining metal corner finish mouldings are available. Apply as recommended by the manufacturer.

**How To Apply Asbestos Siding**

*NOTE:* Assume that 12" x 24" siding panels are to be applied over plywood sheathing.

1. Determine where the bottom edge of the first course will be. This will be the lowest point of siding exposure on the building. All courses around the building must be level when the siding is completed.

2. Determine the total number of courses to complete one wall and lay out the job so that top courses under eves will not be too narrow or wedge shaped. Very few buildings are true and parallel. It is important to watch the relationship of the courses to the eve lines and make small adjustments to the exposure distances when necessary.

3. Remove all unnecessary projections for the wall.

4. Snap a level chalk line all around the building to fix the location of the top edge of the first course of siding as shown in figure 11-46.

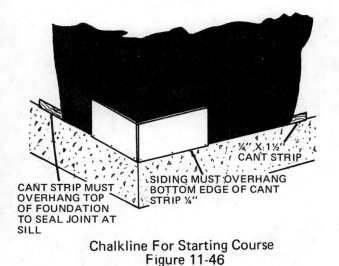

Chalkline For Starting Course
Figure 11-46

5. Nail a ¼" x 1½" cant strip along the bottom edge of the sheathing so that it is level and overhangs the top of the foundation enough to seal the joint between the top of the foundation, the wood sill, and the bottom of the sheathing. Locating the cant strip will be easier if a chalk line is snapped at the desired height below the line indicating the top of the first course of shingles. The bottom edge of the siding should extend ¼ inch below the lower edge of the cant strip.

6. Snap additional chalk lines to mark the top of each succeeding course. See figure 11-47. Remember to space the lines so that the exposure does not exceed the manufacturer's recommendation.

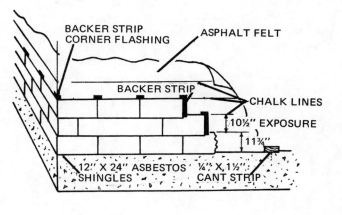

Chalklines For Filler Courses
Figure 11-47

7. Start the first course of shingles and each odd number course at the outside corner of the wall with a full size siding unit. Make sure this unit is placed plumb and level, and aligned with the chalk line, because it guides the lay of all other units. Use the proper face nails supplied with the siding for the type of sheathing and application method being used. Drive nails snug but not too tight. Before driving the last nail at the right hand end of the unit, insert a backer strip in place and secure it with the last nail. Backer strips must always be used and placed centered at the joint between siding units, and with the lower end overlapping the head of the cant strip or lower course. Continue to apply full size siding units in the first course, with their top edges aligned with the chalk line. The last unit in a course or at an opening should not be less than 6 inches wide. If a smaller space will remain to be filled, a few inches should be cut from the units applied earlier in the course. Punch any necessary face nail holes in short pieces of siding. Do not leave spaces between ends of units. Wedge shaped spaces between the ends of siding units are indications of incorrect application. Butt units tightly together end to end.

8. The second and every even course of shingles should start with other than a full size shingle. When using 12 by 24 inch siding, succeeding courses should have their vertical joints break on "halves." Start the second course with a half unit. When using 32 inch long units, break on "thirds." Start the second course of 48 inch long units with a 2/3 unit. Some bundles of siding contain units shorter than full length to provide the necessary shorter pieces for starting courses. Start at the left hand corner with a partial unit, having its head edge aligned with the chalk line and its lower edge overlapping the head of the next lower course the correct distance to provide the necessary head lap between courses. Insert a nail in a face nail hole, making sure the shank of the nail is resting on the top edge of the next lower course, thus establishing the proper amount of head lap. Then nail in place, and continue to work with full size units.

# Chapter 12

# PORCH TRIM

A porch may be defined, in general, as a covered projection at the entrance to the main building. Its chief functions are to provide protection from the weather, a means of exterior decoration and additional living space. A porch may be considered an individual building because it is composed of a foundation, frame, roof and trim similar to that of the main building.

There are many types and designs of porches, some with roof slopes continuous with the roof of the house itself. Other porch roofs may have just enough pitch to provide drainage. The fundamental construction principles, however, are somewhat alike no matter what type is built. Thus, a general description, together with several construction details, can apply to several types.

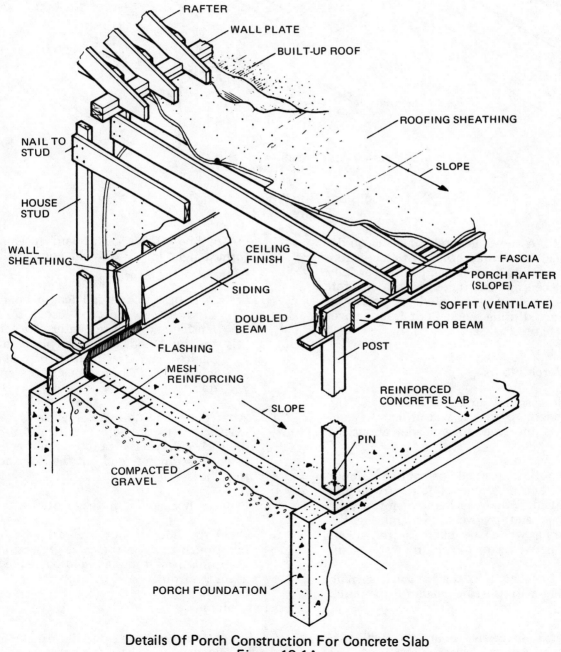

RAFTER
WALL PLATE
BUILT-UP ROOF
ROOFING SHEATHING
SLOPE
NAIL TO STUD
HOUSE STUD
WALL SHEATHING
CEILING FINISH
FASCIA
PORCH RAFTER (SLOPE)
SIDING
SOFFIT (VENTILATE)
DOUBLED BEAM
TRIM FOR BEAM
FLASHING
POST
MESH REINFORCING
SLOPE
REINFORCED CONCRETE SLAB
PIN
COMPACTED GRAVEL
PORCH FOUNDATION

Details Of Porch Construction For Concrete Slab
Figure 12-1A

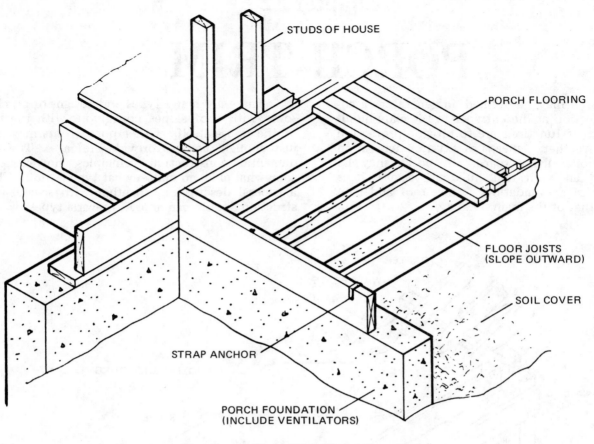

STUDS OF HOUSE

PORCH FLOORING

FLOOR JOISTS
(SLOPE OUTWARD)

SOIL COVER

STRAP ANCHOR

PORCH FOUNDATION
(INCLUDE VENTILATORS)

Porch Floor With Wood Framing
Figure 12-1B

Figure 12-1,A shows general construction details of a typical flat roofed porch with a concrete slab floor. An attached porch can be open or fully enclosed; or it can be constructed with a concrete slab floor, insulated or uninsulated. A porch can also be constructed using wood floor framing over a crawl space (figure 12-1, B).

## How To Lay Porch Floors

1. Select clear sound stock and cut it to the correct length so that it will project beyond the face of the front joist header about 3½ inches.

*NOTE:* Porch flooring should be painted on both faces and edges and left to dry before it is laid. Some mechanics paint just the tongue and groove edges and lay the flooring while the paint is wet. This tends to make the joint waterproof.

2. Start the first length by temporarily face nailing it in line with the side header of the porch joists.

3. Toenail each successive board to each joist, being careful not to drive the starting board out of line. Drive each board up enough to form a tight joint. Use 8d common coated nails.

*NOTE:* It is best to use full length boards. If short pieces must be used, the joints must come on the center of a joist and the butt ends of each piece must be painted and drawn up tight. Make no joints in the floor opposite the entrance door.

4. After the entire floor has been laid, mark the length it is to project over the front header on each side of the porch. Snap a line between these points and cut the flooring along this line.

5. Plane a nosing on the edge of the flooring.

6. Build the flooring out over the side headers far enough to form the same projection as on the front. Nail it in place and plane the nosing as on the front.

## Porch Columns

Supports for enclosed porches usually consist of full framed stud walls. The studs are doubled

106

at openings and at corners. Because both interior and exterior finish coverings are used, the walls are constructed much like the walls of the house. In open or partially open porches, however, solid or built-up posts or columns are used. A more finished or cased column is often made up of doubled 2 by 4's which are covered with 1" x 4" casing on two opposite sides and 1" x 6" finish casing on the other sides (figure 12-2, A). Solid posts, normally 4" x 4", are used mainly for open porches. An open railing may be used between posts.

A formal design of a large house entrance often includes the use of round built-up columns topped by Doric or Ionic capitals. These columns are factory made and ready for installation at the building site. (Figure 12-2, D).

The base of posts or columns in open porches should be designed so that no pockets are formed to retain moisture and encourage decay. In single posts, a steel pin may be used to locate the post and a large galvanized washer or similar spacer used to keep the bottom of the post above the concrete or wood floor. (Figure 12-2, B). The bottom of the post should be treated to minimize moisture penetration. Often single posts of this type are made from a decay resistant wood species. A cased post can be flashed under the base moulding. (Figure 12-2, C). Post anchors which provide connections to the floor and to the post are available commercially, as are post caps.

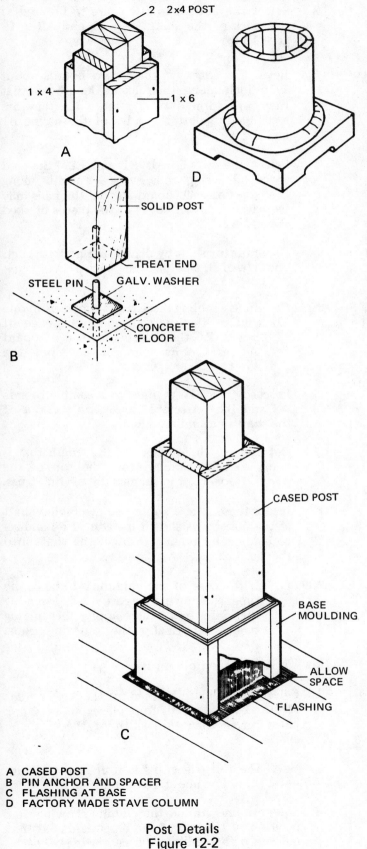

A  CASED POST
B  PIN ANCHOR AND SPACER
C  FLASHING AT BASE
D  FACTORY MADE STAVE COLUMN

Post Details
Figure 12-2

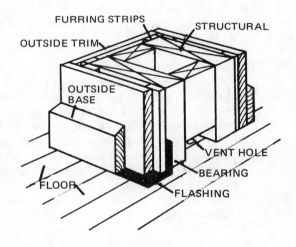

Base Of Built-Up Column
Figure 12-3

Figure 12-3 shows a method of protecting the base of a built-up column and providing ventilation. The surface of all members of the column at the base that are inaccessible to the painter should be thoroughly painted or treated with some wood preservative before they are permanently placed. Metal flashing should be installed at the base of the column where the water has a tendency to lodge. Note the flashing in figure 12-3. The outside trim that is nailed to the core of the column should be furred out at least ¼ inch to allow for ventilation between the back of the trim and the face of the core (figure 12-3).

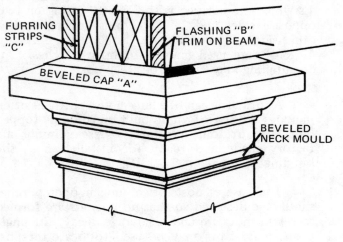

FURRING STRIPS "C"

FLASHING "B" TRIM ON BEAM

BEVELED CAP "A"

BEVELED NECK MOULD

Cap Of Built-Up Column
Figure 12-4

All neck mouldings and column caps should be beveled on the top surface to drain the water and prevent it from lodging and rotting the wood. See A, figure 12-4. Metal flashings are sometimes necessary at the top of the column to prevent the water being driven by wind into the bearing seat of the column and truss (B, figure 12-4). Furring strips should also be used at the back of the trim which is nailed on the sides and bottom of the porch truss (C, figure 12-4).

## How To Build The Column Shaft

*NOTE:* Many columns are still job built though a wide variety of wood and aluminum prefabricated columns are available. Often in repair or remodeling work a column can be built on the job at a cost below that of a custom fitted manufactured column. Occasionally a column must be made to match existing columns on the structure.

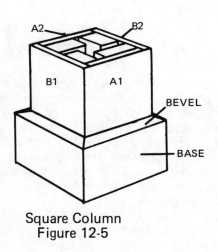

A2  B2

B1  A1

BEVEL

BASE

Square Column
Figure 12-5

1. Determine the horizontal and vertical dimensions of the column shaft and select clear, dressed stock. It should be long enough to reach from the floor up to the truss.

2. Select the two boards that are to be used as the sides of the shaft. See A1 and A2 in figure 12-5.

3. Bevel the edges of these two boards about 1/16 inch along their entire length so that they will form a tight joint when they are assembled against the sides of the casing B1 and B2.

4. Select the two boards B1 and B2. Set and space 8d casing nails every 14 inches along the edges of each board so that the nails may be driven into the edges of the pieces marked A1 and A2.

5. Assemble the shaft by driving the nails through one side of B1 and into one edge of A1.

*NOTE:* In assembling these edges, work from one end of the shaft, keeping the edge of board B1 flush with the face of board A1 as the nails are driven along the shaft.

6. Proceed in a like manner to assemble boards A2 and B2. Assemble these two sections of the shaft in a similar manner.

7. Cut four pieces of 2 x 4 to a length that is equal to the distance from the top of the porch floor to the underside of the truss.

8. Insert these 2 x 4's into the assembled shaft at the corners as shown in figure 12-4 and secure them by nailing through the shaft into the 2 x 4's.

*NOTE:* If the core of the column is to be of the type as shown in figure 12-3, assemble the core first, then apply the furring strips and finally the outside casing.

## How To Apply The Column Base

1. Select the stock to be used for the baseboards (figure 12-5) and cut four pieces about 4 inches longer than the width of the column shaft.

2. Bevel the top edges of the four pieces. This bevel should be about 10 degrees.

3. Square a line around the column showing the position of the top of the baseboards. If the column is tapered, mark a centerline on each

face of the column over its entire length. Square from this line instead of from the edge of the shaft.

NOTE: To simplify the marking of the miters of the baseboard, a base hook may be made from the same stock that is to be used for the base. The hook is slipped over the edge of one piece of base when it is placed at the corner of the column as shown in figure 12-6.

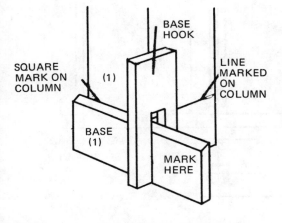

SQUARE MARK ON COLUMN (1) BASE HOOK LINE MARKED ON COLUMN BASE (1) MARK HERE

Use Of Base Hook
Figure 12-6

4. Place a piece of base in position at the bottom of the column. Keep the top edge of the base along the square mark on the column. Temporarily nail it in position.

5. Place the base hook over the base stock, holding it tightly against the column. Mark the base along the outside edge of the base hook. See figure 12-6. This mark shows the long edge of the miter cut.

6. Mark the top edge of the base at the corner of the column. This point shows the short point of the miter column.

7. Use a fine saw to cut the miter. Cut on the outside of the line, thus leaving a little stock in case the miter cut needs a little planing for fitting.

8. Mark the opposite end of the base in the same manner. Before taking the base stock off the column, mark the base and the side of the column so that the baseboard will be put on the same side of the column when it is permanently placed. See figure 12-6.

9. Place, mark and cut a piece of base in a similar way for each of the remaining sides of the column.

10. Replace each piece in its respective position

and check the joints for fit. Plane the joints if necessary to produce a tight fit.

NOTE: Leave the base nailed temporarily as it will have to be removed when the column is set in position on the porch.

This method of mitering the base is simpler than using the sliding T bevel or the miter box, especially if the column is tapered.

## How To Apply The Cap

NOTE: Figure 12-4 shows a typical cap composed of mouldings nailed around the column. The top of the upper member of this cap is flush with the top of the column (the bottom of the truss).

1. Cut four pieces of cap stock long enough to allow for the miter of each end of the stock. Bevel the top of the cap.

2. Place a piece of cap stock at the side of the column at the top and mark it at the corners of the column. These points mark the short point of the miter cut.

3. Cut the miters in a miter box and tack the piece temporarily in place.

4. Continue in the same manner on the other sides of the column. Check the joints for fit and plane them if necessary. When they fit, nail them in position permanently and set the nails.

NOTE: The same processes may be used in fitting the moulding around the column.

## How To Set Porch Columns

NOTE: The framework of the porch cornice and roof is generally supported by temporary columns during the framing of the building. These columns should not be placed in a position that will interfere with the setting of the permanent column unless the frame or core of the column is permanent as shown in figure 12-3.

All columns and deck posts should be set so that their centers line up with the center lines of the porch cornice box or lintel. This is illustrated in the porch floor plan shown in figure 12-7.

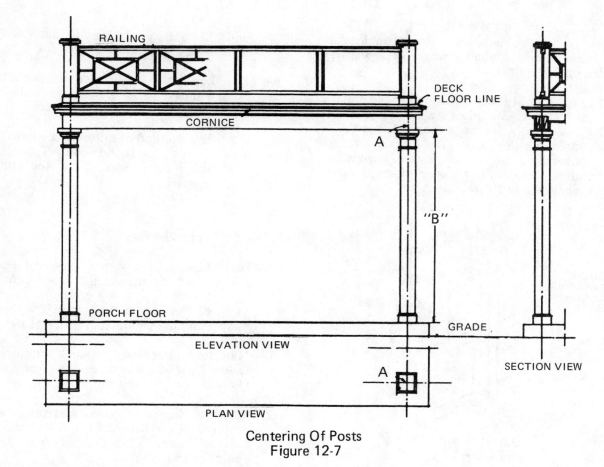

RAILING

DECK FLOOR LINE

CORNICE

A

"B"

PORCH FLOOR

GRADE

ELEVATION VIEW

SECTION VIEW

A

PLAN VIEW

Centering Of Posts
Figure 12-7

1. Locate the center lines of the side and front cornice boxes at the corner. The intersection of these lines gives the center of the top of the porch column. See A in the floor plan of figure 12-7 and A in the elevation.

2. Plumb down from this point to the porch floor with a plumb bob and line. This point on the floor locates the center of the column.

3. Lay out the base size of the column on the floor around the center mark. See the floor plan (figure 12-7). Repeat these operations for the opposite corner of the porch.

4. Remove the temporarily nailed base from the column.

5. Check the cornice box or truss framework to see that it is level. If so, measure the distance from the bottom of the box to the top of the floor. See B in the elevation, figure 12-7.

6. Mark this distance on the column, measuring from the top of the cap to the base of the column. Square a line around the column at this point, remembering to allow for the slope of the porch floor. Cut the column off along this line.

7. Thoroughly paint the floor surface which is to be covered by the column.

8. Place the column in position by temporarily raising the cornice box or truss about 1 inch. Nail the column to the box so that it lines up with the center lines. B1 or B2 of figure 12-5 shows the front of the column.

9. Lower the cornice box and check the column on both front and side for plumb. Nail the bottom of the column to the porch floor.

10. Insert the flashing at the base and top of the column and replace the base on the column.

*NOTE:* In replacing the base it will be necessary to taper the bottom of the base to fit the slope of the porch floor. It is best to replace the front piece of base first and then scribe the other pieces to the floor so that the tops of these pieces will be even with the square marks on the sides of the column.

Sometimes when metal flashing is used at the base of columns it is necessary to gouge out the back of the base to allow for the thickness of the metal and allow the miter joints to come up tight.

11. Have the base of the column and the back of the base painted and securely nail the base in place.

110

## Porch Steps

Many porch floors and porch steps are made of concrete or masonry. Often, however, the porch and steps in a conventional foundation structure are framed and surfaced in wood. Careful consideration in the layout of porch steps must be given to the porportioning of risers and treads. Because the surfaces of the treads on outside steps may become slippery during the winter months, they should be so made that the water will be drained from their surface and so that the underside of the steps will be ventilated. In no case should the width of the treads be less than 12 inches. This measurement includes the overhang of the nosing.

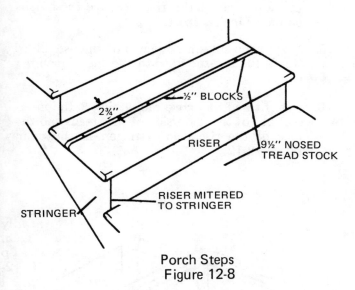

Porch Steps
Figure 12-8

Figure 12-8 shows a common method of draining the surfaces of treads. In some cases small holes are bored through the tops of the treads to provide drainage.

All wood used in porch steps should be painted on all surfaces or treated with some wood preservative before it is placed. The supporting members should rest on concrete piers and their bearing surfaces should be at least three inches off the ground

### How To Build Porch Steps

1. Lay out and cut the required number of stair carriages. The carriages should be made of sound stock at least 1 5/8" x 11½" and spaced in the stair frame no more than 2 feet apart.

2. Lay out and cut the side finish stringers the same as the carriages except that the riser cuts are mitered as shown in figure 12-9. This is to allow the riser to be mitered to the stringer at this point. See B, figure 12-9. The tread cuts on the finish stringer are cut square

the same as on the carriages. Cut a right and a left hand mitered stringer. This type of stringer may be ¾ inch thick and about 11½ inches wide.

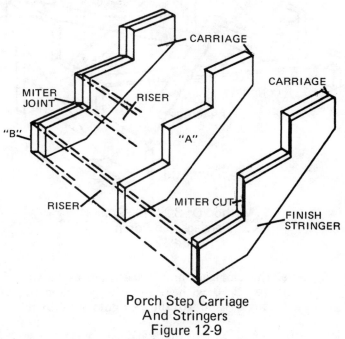

Porch Step Carriage
And Stringers
Figure 12-9

3. Assemble the mitered stringers to the carriages as shown in figure 12-9, keeping the tread cut of the stringer flush with the tread cut of the carriage and the short point of the riser miter cut flush with the riser cut of the carriage.

4. Cut the required number of finish riser boards. They should be as long as the width of the steps. Miter the ends of these boards.

5. Nail the riser boards to the mitered cuts of the finished stringers and to the stair carriages. See figure 12-9.

6. Place and secure the intermediate stair carriages (A, figure 12-9) to the riser boards, keeping the tread cuts of the carriages flush with the tops of the riser boards. Nail through the face of the riser boards into the carriages. Brace and square this framework.

7. Spike 2 x 4 uprights to the porch header at the position where the stair carriages are to be located on the header. See A, figure 12-10.

8. Spike the carriages to the sides of these uprights, making sure that the distance from the top of the stair carriage to the underside of the porch floor is the same as the height of a riser cut of the carriage.

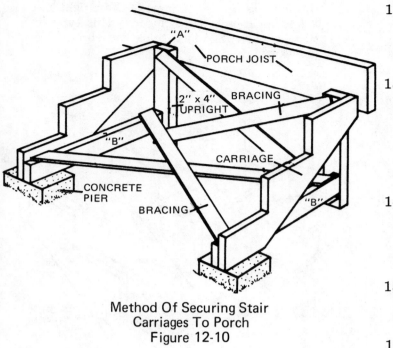

Method Of Securing Stair
Carriages To Porch
Figure 12-10

12. Nail the member B to the carriages as shown and also nail through the back of the riser boards into the edge of member B. Use 8d casing nails.

13. Cut parting strip blocks about 4 inches long and nail them to the edge of member C so that they will cover up the carriage and stringer edges and separate the members C and B. Nail these blocks at all points where the carriage edge will show from the top of the tread. See figure 12-11.

14. Nail the member C to the top of the carriage and tightly against the blocks. Also nail through the tread along the nosing line into the top edge of the riser. Space these nails about 12 inches apart.

15. Plane a nosing on the ends of the assembled treads to correspond to the nosing of member C.

16. Cut, fit and nail cove mouldings at the intersections of the underside of the treads and the face of the risers and stringers as shown in figure 12-12.

9. Level the carriages and brace them as shown in figure 12-10 with ¾" x 4" ties spiked to the stringers and to the uprights as shown.

10. Square and brace the carriages with cross braces as shown.

11. Cut the required number of treads long enough to project over the outside face of the finish stringer on each side the same distance they will project over the risers at the nosing. See A, figure 12-11.

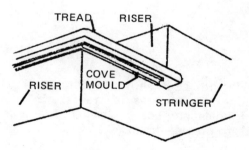

Location Of Cove Mould
Under Tread
Figure 12-12

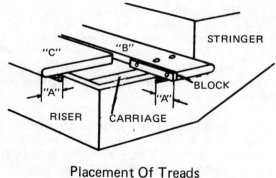

Placement Of Treads
Figure 12-11

*NOTE:* If the treads are to be made up of these members as shown in figure 12-11, stock 1 1/16" x 2 5/8" is generally used for the member B. Parting strip stock is used for the blocks that are nailed to this member. The member C is regular nosed tread stock 1 1/16 inch thick and 9½ inches or more wide, depending on the run of the step.

**Porch Balustrade**

A porch balustrade usually consists of one or two railings with balusters between them. They are designed for an open porch to provide protection and to improve the appearance. There are innumerable combinations and arrangements of them. A closed balustrade may be used with screens or combination windows above (figure 12-13, A). A balustrade with decorative railings may be used for an open porch (figure 12-13, B). This type can also be used with full-height removable screens.

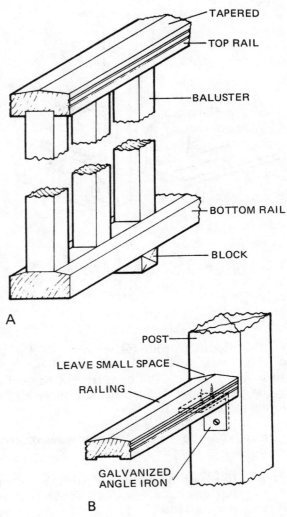

A

A Balustrade Assembly
B Rail-To-Post Connection

Railing Details
Figure 12-14

Connection of the railing with a post should be made in a way that prevents moisture from being trapped. One method provides a small space between the post and the end of the railing (figure 12-14, B). When the railing is treated with paint or water repellent preservative, this type connection should provide good service. Exposed members, such as posts, balusters, and railings, should be all heart wood stock of decay resistant or treated wood to minimize decay.

**How To Build Porch Balustrade**

*NOTE:* Figure 12-15 shows how the core of the balustrade post is supported by allowing it to run down through the porch deck to be attached to the joist or ceiling rafter. The core of the post runs through the flooring and is spiked to the side of a porch joist or rafter. This provides a rigid core upon which the post casing may be nailed.

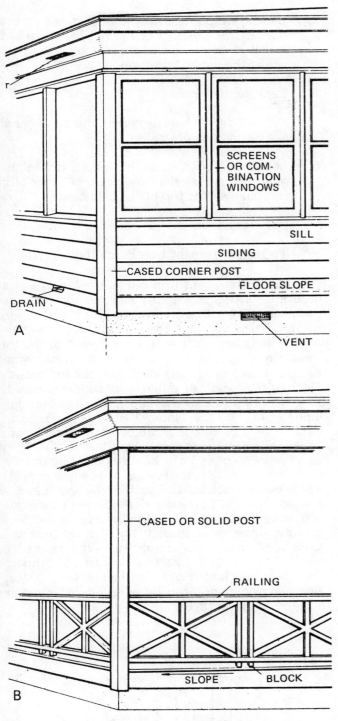

Types Of Balustrades: A, Closed; B, Open
Figure 12-13

All balustrade members that are exposed to water and snow should be designed to shed water. The top of the railing should be tapered and connections with balusters protected as much as possible (figure 12-14, A). Railings should not contact a concrete floor but should be blocked to provide a small space beneath. When wood must be in contact with the concrete, it should be treated to resist decay.

113

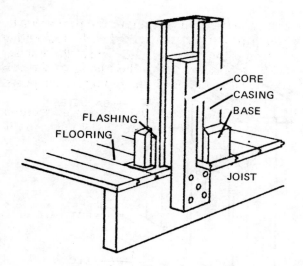

Desk Post Core Spiked To Joist
Figure 12-15

The flooring around the edges of the post should be well supported and should be flashed with metal flashing. The base trim of the column may be kept about ¼ inch off the surface of the flooring material.

1. Build up the core of the post according to the size of the finished post.

*NOTE:* It is not necessary to run the core the full height of the post, as the post supports no load.

2. Cut the core long enough so that it may be firmly spiked to the joists and so it will extend above the deck about 12 inches. See figure 12-15.

3. Locate the position of the post on the deck. Cut the flooring if it is already placed, and temporarily spike the core to the joists or to the blocking that is spiked between the joists.

4. Plumb the core and permanently spike it to the joist or blocking.

5. Place the headers around the core so as to support the deck flooring around the post core.

6. Replace the flooring and build the post casing around the core, following the same general processes as outlined for building porch columns. The procedures of placing the flashing, paint, baseboard, mouldings and cap are also similar. Set and build all posts in a similar manner.

## How To Fit The Rails (Figure 12-14)

1. Check to see that the deck posts are plumb.

2. Locate the position of the bottom rail on the sides of the posts. Cut the rail to length and nail it in the center of the width of the post and at the marked positions.

3. Remove the blocks.

4. Cut and fit the baluster stock into the top rail and against the posts.

5. Locate the position of the upper rail in the same manner as the lower rail. Cut and fit this rail over the top of the balusters.

6. Cut, fit and nail the rail cap.

## How To Install Wrought Iron Porch Rail

Modern wrought iron rail and columns add a decorative accent to porches and steps and can be installed easily with a minimum of tools and equipment. To determine the quantity of materials needed it is best to draw a scale layout of the installation. First locate all the end posts, intermediate posts and columns, if they are to be used. Measure the length of railing that will be required. In general, the distance between all posts and columns should be the same. Rail usually comes in either 4 foot or 6 foot sections. If the total length of rail does not divide evenly by 4 feet or 6 feet, an equal amount of rail will have to be cut before the rail is installed. Remember that the support posts add about 1½ inch to the length of rail and columns add about 9 to 11 inches depending on the style selected. Stair railing is usually made of 4 foot sections. Measure at an angle the distance from the front edge of the platform down to the front edge of the bottom step. Add one additional support post for any length greater than 4 feet. Most wrought iron railing can be adjusted to any stair angle. See figure 12-16.

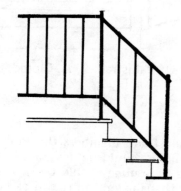

Step Installation
Figure 12-16

1. Rail post and column can be installed on the surface of masonry, concrete or wood or can be imbedded in concrete. Secure the post on column bases to the porch and temporarily mount each post. Be sure all posts are plumb.

2. Cut columns to the proper length and secure the columns to the bases and top plates.

3. Position the railing sections between the posts or columns and mark the sections the appropriate length. Cut the railing to fit.

4. Most porch posts must be shortened an inch or two depending on the desired railing height. Intermediate posts and bottom posts on stairs should be a full 35 inches high. Cut the excess material, if any, from the bottom of the post.

5. Slide connectors into grooves in the top and bottom of each rail. See figure 12-17. Attach all porch railing sections to posts and columns.

6. Slant the stair rail sections to the proper angle. The top and bottom rail of each stair railing section should be parallel when the correct angle is obtained. Cut the railing to the correct length and install the railing on the posts.

*NOTE:* Top and bottom rails of slanted sections must be cut parallel to the posts to eliminate gaps at the connection. (Figure 12-18).

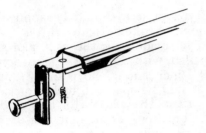

Attached Railing To Post
Figure 12-17

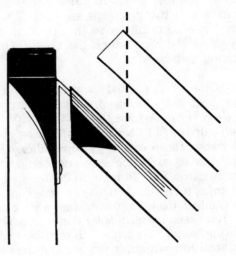

Slant Railing At Post
Figure 12-18

# Chapter 13
# INTERIOR WALL COVERING

## Plaster Bases

A plaster finish requires some type of base upon which the plaster is applied. The base must have bonding qualities so that plaster adheres, or is keyed to the base which has been fastened to the framing members.

One of the most common types of plaster base that may be used on sidewalls or ceiling is gypsum lath, which is 16" x 48" and is applied horizontally across the framing members. It has paper faces with a gypsum filler. For stud or joist spacing of 16 inches on center, 3/8 inch thickness is used. For 24 inch on-center spacing, ½ inch thickness is required. This material can be obtained with a foil back that serves as a vapor barrier. If the foil faces an air space, it also has reflective insulating value. Gypsum lath may be obtained with perforations, which, by improving the bond, would lengthen the time the plaster would remain intact when exposed to fire. The building codes in some cities require such perforation.

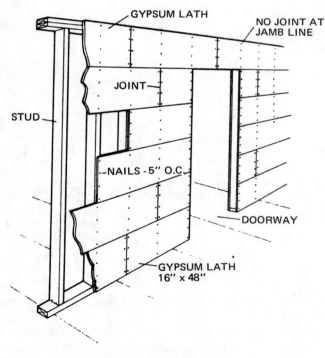

Application Of Gypsum Lath
Figure 13-1

Insulating fiberboard lath in ½ inch thickness and 16" x 48" in size is also used as a plaster base. It has greater insulating value than the gypsum lath, but horizontal joints must usually be reinforced with metal clips.

Metal lath in various forms such as diamond mesh, flat rib, and wire lath is another type of plaster base. It is usually 27" x 96" in size and is galvanized or painted to resist rusting.

Gypsum lath should be applied horizontally with joints broken (figure 13-1). Vertical joints should be made over the center of studs or joists and nailed with 12 or 13 gauge gypsum lathing nails 1½ inches long and with a 3/8 inch flat head. Nails should be spaced 5 inches on center, or four nails for the 16 inch height, and used at each stud or joist crossing. Some manufacturers specify the ring-shank nails with a slightly greater spacing. Lath joints over heads of openings should not occur at the jamb lines (figure 13-1).

### How To Apply Gypsum Lath

*NOTE:* Be sure all the corners and sections of the wall are solidly furred out to give good nailing surfaces for the ends of the plaster base.

1. Nail the lath with gypsum lathing nails and follow any special directions given by the manufacturer of the lath base being used. Break the joints on alternate studs, spacing the sheets ¼ inch apart at the ends and fastening them securely to the studs.

2. Lay out and cut panels that are to be fitted around corners and fixtures by using a knife or portable electric saw fitted with an abrasive cutting wheel.

3. Test the outer surfaces of the plaster base with a straight edge for straightness.

4. Apply a 4 inch strip of metal lath or wire fabric (cornerites) in all corners to reinforce the plaster and to reduce cracking. Special strips are sometimes provided for joints between the panels.

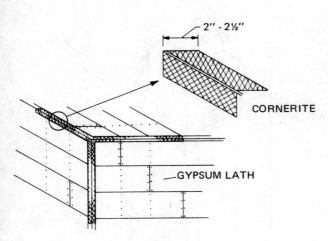

Reinforcing Of Plaster At Inside Corners
Figure 13-2

5. Apply the metal reinforcing strips, if specified, over the long joints in the panels by nailing them securely on top of the plaster base and overlapping the joint evenly. If tape or other material is to be used, apply it as specified by the manufacturer.

*NOTE:* If grounds are to be applied over the plaster base, a straight edge or chalked line should be used to set them in alignment for the interior trim.

6. Because some drying usually takes place in wood framing members after a house is completed, some shrinkage can be expected; in turn, this may cause plaster cracks to develop around openings and in corners. To minimize, if not eliminate, this cracking, expanded metal lath is used in certain key positions over the plaster-base material as reinforcement. Strips of expanded metal lath may be used over window and door openings (figure 13-3, A). A strip about 10" x 20" is placed diagonally across each upper corner of the opening and tacked in place.

7. Metal lath should also be used under flush ceiling beams to prevent plaster cracks (figure 13-3, B). On wood drop beams extending below the ceiling line, the metal lath is applied with self-furring nails to provide space for keying of the plaster.

8. Corner beads of expanded metal lath or of perforated metal should be installed on all exterior corners (figure 13-4). They should be applied plumb and level. The bead acts as a leveling edge when walls are plastered and reinforces the corner against mechanical damage.

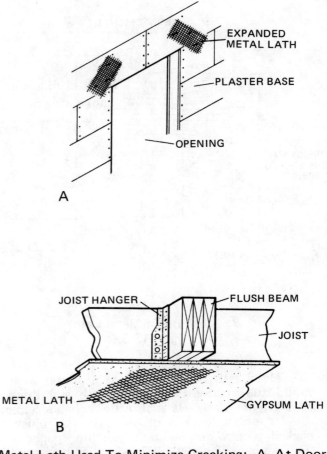

A

B

Metal Lath Used To Minimize Cracking: A, At Door And Window Openings; B, Under Flush Beams
Figure 13-3

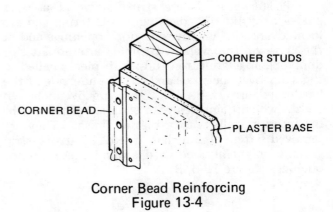

Corner Bead Reinforcing
Figure 13-4

Insulating lath should be installed much the same as gypsum lath, except that slightly longer blued nails should be used. A special waterproof facing is provided on one type of gypsum board for use as a ceramic tile base when the tile is applied with an adhesive.

117

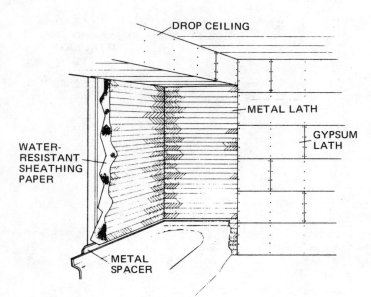

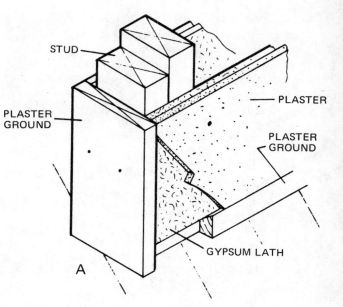

Application Of Metal Lath
Figure 13-5

Metal lath is often used as a plaster base a-round tub recesses and other bath and kitchen areas (figure 13-5). It is also used when a ceramic tile is applied over a plastic base. It must be backed with water resistant sheathing paper over the framing. The metal lath is applied horizontally over the waterproof backing with side and end joints lapped. It is nailed with No. 11 and No. 12 roofing nails long enough to provide about 1½ inch penetration into the framing member or blocking.

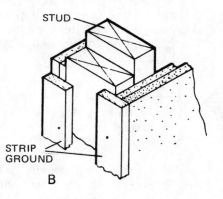

Plaster grounds are strips of wood used as guides or strike-off edges when plastering and are located around window and door openings and at the base of the walls. Grounds around interior door openings are often full-width pieces nailed to the sides over the studs and to the underside of the header (figure 13-6, A). They are 5¼ inches in width, which coincides with standard jamb widths for interior walls with a plaster finish. They are removed after plaster has dried. Narrow strip grounds might also be used around these interior openings (figure 13-6, B).

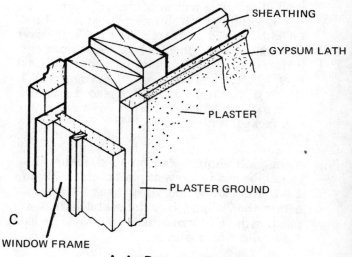

In window and exterior door openings, the frames are normally in place before plaster is applied. Thus, the inside edges of the side and head jamb can, and often do, serve as grounds. The edge of the window sill might also be used as a ground, or a narrow 7/8 inch thick ground strip is nailed to the edge of the 2" x 4" sill. Narrow 7/8" x 1" grounds might also be used around window and door openings (figure 13-6, C). These are normally left in place and are covered by the casing.

A At Doorway And Floor
B Strip Ground At Doorway
C Ground At Window

Plaster Grounds
Figure 13-6

A similar narrow ground or screed is used at the bottom of the wall in controlling thickness of the gypsum plaster and providing an even surface for the baseboard and moulding (figure 13-6, A). These strips are also left in place after plaster has been applied.

## Plaster

Plaster for interior finishing is made from combinations of sand, lime, or prepared plaster and water. Waterproof finish wall materials (Keene's cement) are available and should be used in bathrooms, especially in showers or tub recesses when tile is not used, and sometimes in the kitchen wainscot.

Plaster should be applied in three coat or two coat double up work. The minimum thickness over 3/8 inch gypsum lath should be about ½ inch. The first plaster coat over metal lath is called the scratch coat and is scratched, after a slight set has occurred, to insure a good bond for the second coat. The second coat is called the brown or leveling coat, and leveling is done during the application of this coat.

The double up work, combining the scratch and brown coat, is used on gypsum or insulating lath, and leveling and plumbing of walls and ceilings are done during application.

The final or finish coat consists of two general types - the sand-float and the putty finish. In the sand-float finish, lime is mixed with sand and results in a textured finish, the texture depending on the coarseness of the sand used. Putty finish is used without sand and has a smooth finish. This is common in kitchens and bathrooms where a gloss paint or enamel finish is used, and in other rooms where a smooth finish is desired. Keene's cement is often used as a finish plaster in bathrooms because of its durability.

The plastering operation should not be done in freezing weather without constant heat for protection from freezing. In normal construction, the heating unit is in place before plastering is started.

Insulating plaster, consisting of a vermiculite, perlite, or other aggregate with the plaster mix, may also be used for wall and ceiling finishes.

## Gypsum Wallboard (Drywall)

Gypsum board is a sheet material composed of a gypsum filler faced with paper. Sheets are normally 4 feet wide and 8 feet in length, but can be obtained in lengths up to 16 feet. The edges along the length are usually tapered, although some types are tapered on all edges. This allows for a filled and taped joint. This material may also be obtained with a foil back which serves as a vapor barrier on exterior walls. It is also available with vinyl or other prefinished surfaces. In new construction ½ inch thickness is recommended for single layer application. In laminated two ply applications two 3/8 inch thick sheets are used. The 3/8 inch thickness, while considered minimum for 16 inch stud spacing in single layer applications, is normally specified for repair and remodeling work.

| Installed long direction of sheet | Minimum thickness | Maximum spacing of supports (on center) | |
|---|---|---|---|
| | | Walls | Ceilings |
| | Inches | Inches | Inches |
| Parallel to framing members | ⅜ | 16 | |
| | ½ | 24 | 16 |
| | ⅝ | 24 | 16 |
| Right angles to framing members | ⅜ | 16 | 16 |
| | ½ | 24 | 24 |
| | ⅝ | 24 | 24 |

Single Layer Gypsum Wallboard Thicknesses
Table 13-7

Table 13-7 lists maximum member spacing for the various thicknesses of gypsum board.

When the single layer system is used, the 4 foot wide gypsum sheets are applied vertically or horizontally on the walls after the ceiling has been covered. Vertical application covers three stud spaces when studs are spaced 16 inches on center, and two when spacing is 24 inches. Edges should be centered on studs, and only moderate contract should be made between edges of the sheet.

Fivepenny cooler type nails (1 5/8 inch long) should be used with ½ inch gypsum, and fourpenny (1 3/8 inch long) with the 3/8 inch thick material. Ring shank nails, about 1/8 inch shorter, can also be used. Some manufacturers often recommend the use of special screws to reduce "bulging" of the surface ("nail-pops" caused by drying out of the frame members). If moisture content of the framing members is less than 15 percent when gypsum board is applied, "nail-pops" will be greatly reduced. It is good practice, when framing members have a high moisture content, to allow them to approach moisture equilibrium before application of the gypsum board. Nails should be spaced 6 to 8 inches for sidewalls and 5 to 7 inches for ceiling application (figure 13-8, A). Minimum edge distance is 3/8 inch.

The horizontal method of application is best adapted to rooms in which full length sheets can be used, as it minimizes the number of vertical joints. Where joints are necessary, they should be made at windows or doors. Nail spacing is the same

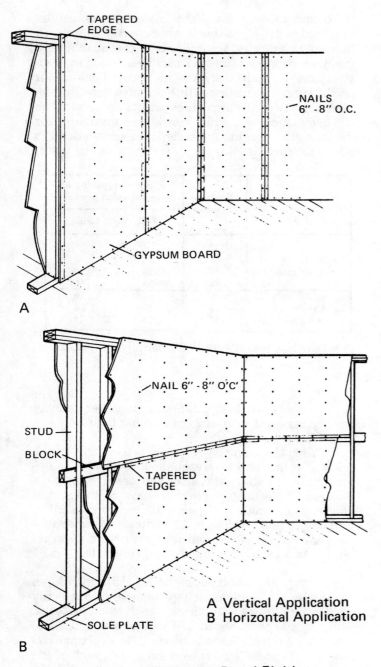

A

B

Application Of Gypsum Board Finish
Figure 13-8

as that used in vertical application. When studs are spaced 16 inches on center, horizontal nailing blocks between studs are normally not required when gypsum board is 3/8 inch or thicker. However, when spacing is greater, or an impact resistant joint is required, nailing blocks may be used (figure 13-8, B).

Another method of gypsum board application (laminated two ply) includes an undercourse of 3/8 inch material applied vertically and nailed in place. The finish 3/8 inch sheet is applied horizontally, usually in room size lengths, with an adhesive. This adhesive is either applied in ribbons, or is spread with a notched trowel. The manufacturer's recommendations should be followed in all respects.

Nails in the finish gypsum wallboard should be driven with the heads slightly below the surface. The crowned head of the hammer will form a small dimple in the wallboard (figure 13-9). A nail set should not be used, and care should be taken to avoid breaking the paper face.

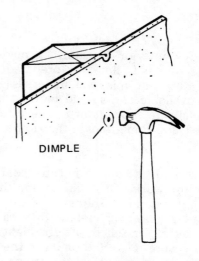

Nail Set With Crown Hammer
Figure 13-9

### How To Install Gypsum Wallboard

*NOTE:*  The use of thin sheet materials such as gypsum board requires that studs and ceiling joists have good alignment to provide a smooth, even surface. Wood sheathing will often correct misaligned studs on exterior walls. A "strong-back" provides for aligning of ceiling joists of unfinished attics (figure 13-10) and can be used at the center of the span when ceiling joists are uneven.

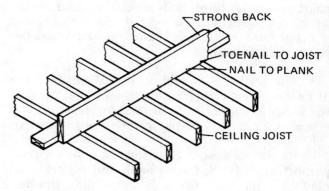

Strong Back Used To Align Joists
Figure 13-10

1.  Measure the length and width of the ceiling of the room to decide how the panels or units of wall board are to run.

2.  Apply nailing blocks to the joists where required so that the outside edges of each panel

will have a solid nailing surface. The blocks form a straight and true surface.

3. Back up or install blocks around all edges of fixtures and openings so that the panels or units may be nailed solidly around these edges.

4. Start the first row of panels by snapping a chalked line to keep them square and straight. Cut the board with a hand saw or with a knife by laying it across two saw horses. Cut the first paper layer and then break through the remaining thickness.

5. Fasten the panels following the instructions given by the maker of the type of board being used.

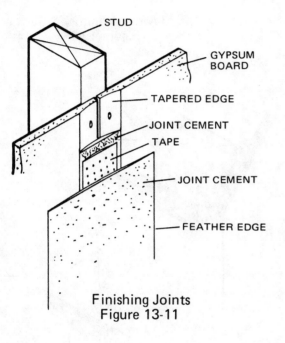

STUD

GYPSUM BOARD

TAPERED EDGE

JOINT CEMENT

TAPE

JOINT CEMENT

FEATHER EDGE

Finishing Joints
Figure 13-11

## How To Finish Joints

Joint cement is used to apply the tape over the tapered edge joints and to smooth and level the surface. It comes in powder form and is mixed with water to a soft putty consistency so that it can be easily spread with a trowel or putty knife. It can also be obtained in premixed form. The general procedure for taping (figure 13-11) is as follows:

1. Use a wide joint knife (5 inches) and spread the cement in the tapered edges, starting at the top of the wall.

2. Press the tape into the recess with the putty knife until the joint cement is forced through the perforations.

3. Cover the tape with additional cement, feathering the outer edges.

4. Allow to dry, sand the joint lightly, and then apply the second coat, feathering the edges. A steel trowel is sometimes used in applying the second coat. For best results, a third coat may be applied, feathering beyond the second coat.

5. After the joint cement is dry, sand smooth (an electric hand vibrating sander works well).

6. For hiding hammer indentations, fill with joint cement and sand smooth when dry. Repeat with the second coat when necessary.

*NOTE:* Interior corners may also be treated with tape. Fold the tape down the center to a right angle (figure 13-12) and (1) apply cement at the corner, (2) press the tape in place, and (3) finish the corner with joint cement. Sand smooth when dry and apply a second coat.

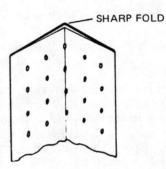

SHARP FOLD

Tape At Inside Corner
Figure 13-12

*NOTE:* The interior corners between walls and ceilings may be concealed with some type of moulding (figure 13-13). When mouldings are used, taping this joint is not necessary. Wallboard corner beads at exterior corners will prevent damage to the gypsum board. They are fastened in place and covered with the joint cement.

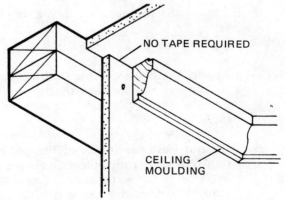

NO TAPE REQUIRED

CEILING MOULDING

Moulding Over Drywall Joint
Figure 13-13

121

## Wood Paneling

Many types of wood interior wall coverings are available. Paneling selection should include consideration of insulation value, decorative effect, texture, color, cost, durability, and ease of maintenance. Plywood, fiberboard, hardboard, hardwood paneling and many types of plastic veneers are available. Table 13-14 lists thicknesses required for various stud spacings.

| Framing spaced (inches) | Thickness | | |
|---|---|---|---|
| | Plywood | Fiberboard | Paneling |
| | Inch | Inch | Inch |
| 16 | 1/4 | 1/2 | 3/8 |
| 20 | 3/8 | 3/4 | 1/2 |
| 24 | 3/8 | 3/4 | 5/6 |

Minimum Panel Thicknesses For Stud Spacing
Figure 13-14

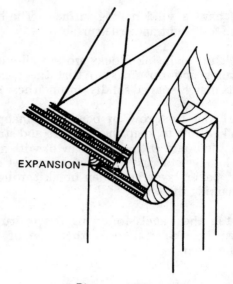

Plywood Window Trim
Figure 13-15

## How To Install Plywood Paneling

Prefinished plywood is available in a number of species, and its use should not be overlooked for accent walls or to cover entire room wall areas. Plywood for interior covering may be used in 4' x 8' and longer sheets. They may be applied vertically or horizontally, but with solid backing at all edges. Casing or finishing nails 1¼ to 1½ inches are used. Space them 8 inches apart on the walls and 6 inches apart on ceilings. Edge nailing distance should be not less than 3/8 inch. Allow 1/32 inch end and edge distance between sheets when installing. Most wood or wood base panel materials should be exposed to the conditions of the room before installation. Place them around the heated room for at least 24 hours.

1. Plan the layout of the panels according to the size of the room.

2. Install nailing blocks under joints and around panel ends.

3. Nail the panels to the studs, joists or nailing blocks.

*NOTE:* Figure 13-15 shows how to use plywood for furring on the face of the stud and also the use of plywood for window casings.

Do not butt the joints of the plywood tightly together but allow from 1/8 inch to ¼ inch for expansion. This is particularly true near window trim.

4. Use mouldings at corners formed by the walls as shown in figure 13-16.

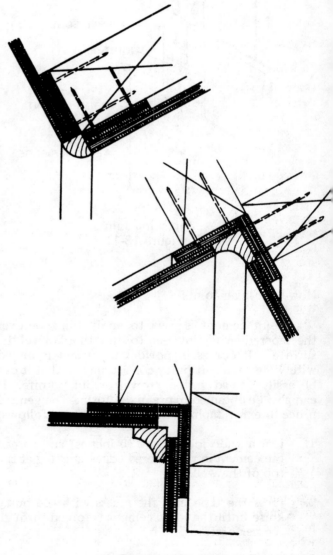

Finishing Corners
Figure 13-16

5. When prefinished paneling is used, nails should be covered with prefinished moulding or coated finishing nails should be used. Matching putty is often used to cover nail holes.

*NOTE:* Adhesives may also be used to fasten prefinished plywood and other sheet materials to wall studs. These panel adhesives usually eliminate the need for more than two guide nails for each sheet. Application usually conforms to the following procedure: (a) Position the sheet and fasten it with two nails for guides at the top or side, (b) remove plywood and spread contact or similar adhesive on the framing members, (c) press the plywood in place for full contact using the nails for positioning, (d) pull the plywood away from the studs and allow adhesive to set, and (e) press plywood against the framing members and tap lightly with a rubber mallet for full contact. Manufacturers of adhesives supply full instructions for application of sheet materials.

## How To Install Fiberboard And Hardboard

Fiberboards are made of wood or vegetable fibers compressed to form sheets or boards. They come in thicknesses of ½ inch to 1 inch, in widths of 4 feet and in lengths up to 12 feet. The boards are comparatively soft to provide good heat insulating and sound absorbing qualities. The surface is usually rough but some boards are available with finished surfaces. Some boards are scored to divide the surface into squares or other designs. Pieces 6 inches to 16 inches wide and up to 12 feet long are available. These are called planks. Small individual pieces are also available to give a tiled effect. All of these boards are usually fastened to the studs in such a way that no nail heads show.

Although hardboards are known by several trade names, they are all made by separating and treating wood fibers which are then subjected to heat and heavy pressure. This board is available in thicknesses of 1/16 inch to 5/16 inch. The most common size of sheet is 4 feet by 8 feet but smaller ones are available. This board may be obtained in a plain smooth surface or in any one of a number of glossy finishes.

Fiberboard and hardboard are installed using the same procedures as outlined for plywood. Fiberboard in tongued-and-grooved plank or sheet form must be ½ inch thick when frame members are spaced 16 inches on center and ¾ inch when 24 inch spacing is used. The casing or finished nails must be slightly longer than those used for plywood or hardboard; spacing is about the same. Fiberboard is also used in the ceiling as acoustic tile and may be nailed to strips fastened to ceiling joists. It is also installed in 12" x 12" or larger tile forms on wood or metal hangers which are hung from the ceiling joists. This system is called a "suspended ceiling".

## How To Apply Plastic Laminated Hardboard

Many plastic laminated hardboards are available. Most manufacturers recommend application with specific adhesives and provide metal moulding to complete the installation. Plastic laminated hardboard is usually installed as a finish material over wallboard or plaster.

1. Measure and cut all panels and mouldings to fit. Make all cut-outs necessary and smooth all edges. Cutting is done most easily with a small reciprocating hand saw.

2. Put the panels and mouldings in place to make sure they fit.

*NOTE:* Several manufacturers manufacture base mouldings which are applied by nailing before the panels are put in place.

3. Apply adhesive to the back of the hardboard. Some manufacturers recommend a standard paint roller for applying the adhesive.

4. Fit the panel to the wall. When the panel is in place, apply a firm pressure to the entire panel with a rubber roller or a wood block and hammer.

5. Replace the metal mouldings. Apply the horizontal face mouldings first and then the vertical mouldings. Some mouldings must be nailed in place while others snap firmly into place when tapped with a hammer and a wood block.

6. Where water is likely to be present, apply sealant around lower edges.

## How To Apply Wood Paneling

Various types and patterns of woods are available for application on walls to obtain desired decorative effects. For informal treatment, knotty pine, white-pocket Douglas-fir, sound wormy chestnut, and pecky cypress, finished natural or stained and varnished, may be used to cover one or more sides of a room. Wood paneling should be thoroughly seasoned to a moisture content near the average it reaches in service (In most areas about 8 percent). Allow the material to reach this condition by placing it around the wall of the heated room. Boards may be applied horizontally or vertically, but the same general methods of application should pertain to each.

1. Apply over a vapor barrier and insulation when application is on the exterior wall framing or blocking (figure 13-17).

2. Boards should not be wider than 8 inches except when a long tongue or matched edges are used.

3. Thickness should be at least 3/8 inch for 16 inch spacing of frame members, ½ inch for 20 inch spacing, and 5/8 inch for 24 inch spacing.

4. Maximum spacing of supports for nailing should be 24 inches on center (blocking for vertical applications).

5. Nails should be fivepenny or sixpenny casing or finishing nails.

Use two nails for boards 6 inches or less wide and three nails for 8 inch and wider boards. One nail can be blind-nailed in matched paneling.

Wood paneling in the form of small plywood squares can also be used for an interior wall covering. When used over framing and a vapor barrier, blocking should be so located that each edge has full bearing. Each edge should be fastened with casing or finish nails. When two sides are tongued and grooved, one edge (tongued side) may be blind-nailed. When paneling (16" x 48" or larger) crosses studs, it should also be nailed at each intermediate bearing. Matched (tongued-and-grooved) sides should be used when no horizontal blocking is provided or paneling is not used over a solid backing.

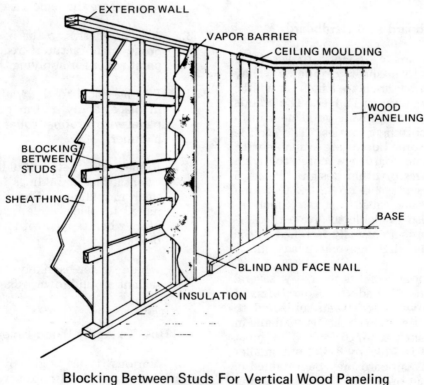

Blocking Between Studs For Vertical Wood Paneling
Figure 13-17

# Chapter 14

# STAIR LAYOUT AND CONSTRUCTION

The construction of stairs is most often left to the most experienced carpenter on the job. Yet, most journeymen carpenters would agree that more material and time have been wasted tearing down poorly designed or poorly built stairways than in any other framing job. No matter how experienced the craftsman, each stairway presents its own design and construction problems. Even in highly repetitive jobs where many similar stairways are constructed on one site, each stairway to be built may be somewhat unique. The floor to floor rise of each stairway built must be measured with accuracy and the craftsman must select the right tread and riser combination so that every rise and run is within ¼ inch of every other rise and run. Many times the plans are inadequate or the actual floor to floor dimension does not correspond with the floor to floor dimension on the plans. Consequently, the craftsman who actually builds the stairway is required to design the stairway before he builds it. More and more stairways are being designed since the increasing value of land recommends multiple story structures.

Stair design and construction is not complex and can be mastered by anyone with patience and and understanding of elementary carpentry. Let's assume that the first and second floors have been framed out and an opening has been left for the stairway. The long dimension of the stairway opening may be either parallel or at right angles to the joists. However, it is much easier to frame a stair-opening when its length is parallel to the joists.

For basement stairways the rough opening may be about 9 feet 6 inches long by 32 inches wide (two joist spaces). Openings in the second floor for main stairways are usually a minimum of 10 feet long. Widths may be 3 feet or more. Depending on the short header required for one or both ends, the opening is usually framed as shown in figure 14-1 when joists parallel the length of the opening. Nailing should conform to that shown in figure 14-2.

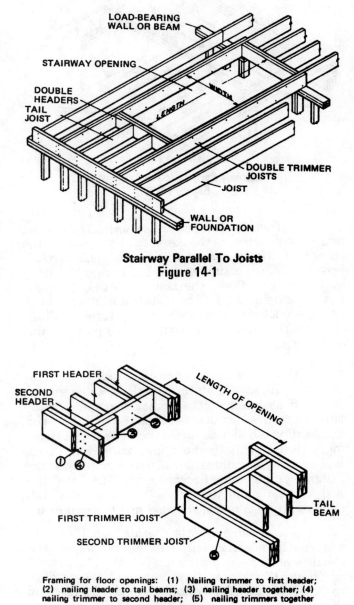

**Stairway Parallel To Joists**
**Figure 14-1**

Framing for floor openings: (1) Nailing trimmer to first header; (2) nailing header to tail beams; (3) nailing header together; (4) nailing trimmer to second header; (5) nailing trimmers together

**Figure 14-2**

When the length of the stair opening is perpendicular to the length of the joists, a long doubled header is required as in figure 14-3. A header under these conditions without a supporting wall beneath is usually limited to a 10 foot length. A load bearing wall under all or part of this opening simplifies the framing immensely, as the joists will then bear on the top plate of the wall rather than be supported at the header by joist hangers or other means.

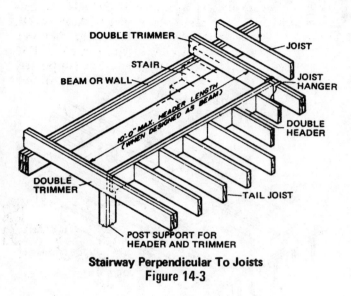

**Stairway Perpendicular To Joists**
**Figure 14-3**

The framing for an "L"-shaped stairway is usually supported in the basement by a post at the corner of the opening or by a load-bearing wall beneath. When a similar stair leads from the first to the second floor, the landing can be framed-out. See figure 14-4. The platform frame is nailed into the enclosing stud walls and provides a nailing area for the subfloor as well as a support for the stair carriages.

Once the rough opening is framed, measure the exact distance from the first floor to the second floor. If an intermediate landing is planned, measure the vertical distance between the first floor and the landing. Estimate how much the finish flooring material on both the upper and lower floors will increase or reduce this distance and adjust the distance you measured accordingly. Select the riser and tread combination that best suits the well opening, total run available and materials on hand.

The carriage supports the load on the stairs and can be made in either of several ways. No matter whether you are building a "cleat", "sawed" or "housed" stairway, you must cut the carriage to fit and locate the position of treads and risers on the carriage. Let's assume you are building a cut-out or sawed stair carriage. These stair carriages are made from 2 x 12 planks. The effective depth below the tread and riser notches must be at least 3½ inches (See figure 14-5). Such carriages are

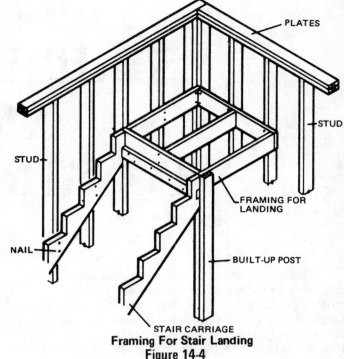

**Framing For Stair Landing**
**Figure 14-4**

usually placed only at each side of the stairs. However, an intermediate carriage is required at the center of the stairs when the treads are 1 1/16 inch thick and the stairs are wider than 2 feet 6 inches. Three carriages are also required when treads are 1 5/8 inch thick and stairs are wider than 3 feet. The carriages are fastened to the joist header at the top of the stairway or rest on a supporting ledger nailed to the header.

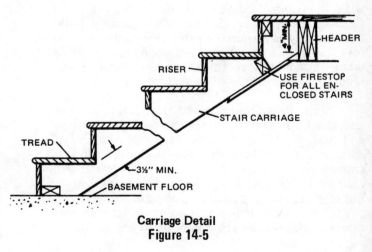

**Carriage Detail**
**Figure 14-5**

Select a sound 2 x 12, 18 to 20 inches longer than the carriage length. First you must cut the floor line which will rest squarely on the lower floor. Lay the body or long end of the framing square across one corner of the plank. Move the square so that the tread distance intersects the top of the plank on the body and the rise distance intersects the tongue on the top of the plank. See figure 14-6A.

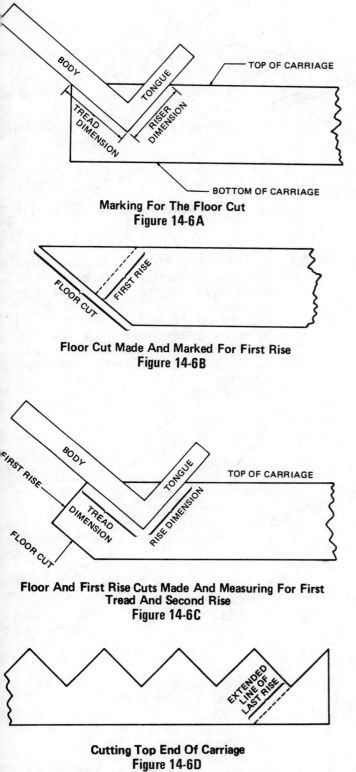

**Marking For The Floor Cut**
**Figure 14-6A**

**Floor Cut Made And Marked For First Rise**
**Figure 14-6B**

**Floor And First Rise Cuts Made And Measuring For First Tread And Second Rise**
**Figure 14-6C**

**Cutting Top End Of Carriage**
**Figure 14-6D**

Sound craftsmanship requires that these dimensions be marked and cut accurately. A set of stair gauges or some device to hold the correct dimensions will be useful here. Mark the outline of both the rise and tread dimensions on the plank. Extend the tread dimension in a straight line to the bottom edge of the material and cut along this line. This is the floor cut. If this is to be a cutout carriage, cut along the line marked for the first rise (see figure 14-6B).

Next, place the tread dimension on the square body so that it meets the top edge of the first rise and the rise dimension on the tongue so that it meets the top edge of the carriage. See figure 14-6C.

Repeat this process marking and cutting tread and rise dimensions for as many steps as there are in the stairway. When the last rise is reached, extend the line of the last rise to the bottom edge of the carriage. See figure 14-6D. Cut along this extended line if the carriage is to meet the end of the wellhole as illustrated in figure 14-7C. If the carriage is to meet the wellhole as in 14-7A or 14-7B, allow the appropriate additional material beyond the last rise and cut parallel to the last rise. For additional strength, the carriage may be supported below the header or extend beyond the end of the well opening below the upper floor.

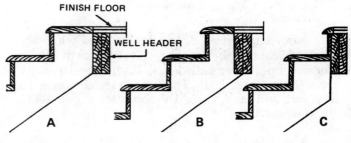

**Three Methods For Anchoring The Upper End Of A Stairway**
**Figure 14-7A   Full Tread Width Extension**
**Figure 14-7B   Partial Tread Width Extension**
**Figure 14-7C   Top Riser Flush Against Header**

After the carriages have been cut, they should be "dropped" or lowered to allow for the thickness of the tread and the finish flooring. You will recall that every rise dimension must be the same within a ¼ inch tolerance. The carriage has been designed to reach between the finished first floor and the finished second floor or landing. If the carriage is installed on the subfloor, it will be lower than the height you planned for by the thickness of the finished flooring material. However, the tread material will raise the level of the tread surface above the top of each cutout on the carriage. Usually the tread thickness will be greater than the depth of the finish flooring material. When this is the case, this difference must be cut from the bottom end of each carriage parallel to the floor cut. In figure 14-8A, 5/16'' has been marked to be cut off the lower end of the carriage. The height of the finish flooring material, ¾'' has been subtracted from the thickness of the tread material, 1 1/16 inch. When the stairway is completed, the rise of each step, including the first step and last step, will be 7½ inches. When the carriage rests on the finished floor level, the carriage should be "dropped" the full thickness of the treads. Once the carriage is cut and "dropped" it should be checked for fit. Each tread cutout should be level when the carriage is in place.

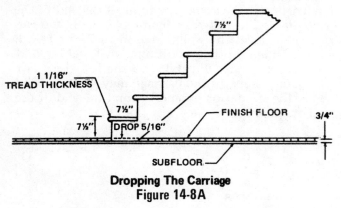

**Dropping The Carriage**
**Figure 14-8A**

Stair supports are usually installed when the carriage cannot be anchored to adjacent walls. These supports are called stair bridges and usually are of 2 x 4 material. They are framed similar to any partition except that the top plate is parallel to the stair carriage.

Cleat stairways (consisting only of a carriage and tread) should use 2" x 10" stock for the carriage. This design is not as desirable as the cutout carriage style where a wall is adjacent to one side of the stairway or where appearance of the finished stairway is important. The stringers should be at least 1 5/8 inch thick and wide enough to give a full width bearing for the tread. If cleats are used, they should be at least 25/32 inch thick, 3 inches wide and as long as the width of the tread. The treads can be only 1 1/16 inch thick unless the stairs are more than 3 feet wide.

A similar open stairway uses dado joints instead of cleats to support the treads. See figure 14-8B. This type of construction is quite common in steep stairs or ladders for attic or scuttle openings. If dado joints are used, they should be only one third as deep as the stringer is thick.

### How To Build Cleated Or Dadoed Stairs

1. Select the required stock. Use clear dressed stock free from defects.

2. Lay out the stringers in the same way as in laying out carriages.

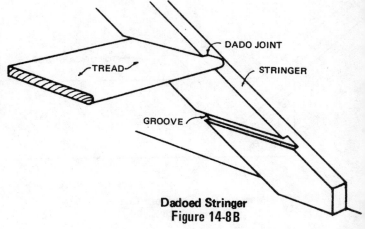

**Dadoed Stringer**
**Figure 14-8B**

*NOTE:* If the treads are to butt against the stringers and are to be supported by cleats, the tread marks on the stringers represent the tops of the finish treads and the top of the cleat should be the thickness of the tread below this line. See figure 14-9. If the treads are to be dadoed into the stringers, assume that the tread marks on the stringer represent the tops of the dado cuts.

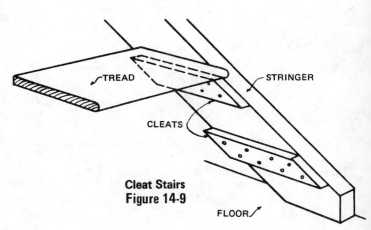

**Cleat Stairs**
**Figure 14-9**

3. Determine the length of the treads and cut the required number to this length.

4. Cut the required number of cleats and chamfer the edges that will show.

5. Nail the cleats to the proper marks below the tread marks on the stringers. Use nails long enough to reach within ½ inch of the combined thickness of the stringers and cleats.

6. Assemble the treads in place on the cleats or in the dadoes and nail through the stringers into the ends of the treads. Use 16d common nails if the stringers are 1 5/8 inch thick and cleats are used, or 10d casing nails if dado joints are used.

7. Square the assembled stairs and fasten them in place in about the same way as stair carriages are fastened.

*NOTE:* If the lower floor and side wall is of masonry, some means should be used to fasten the stringers firmly to these surfaces. Expansive shields and lag screws or wood blocks inserted into the masonry may be used for this purpose.

A somewhat more finished staircase for a fully enclosed stairway combines the rough notched carriage with a finish stringer along each side (figure 14-10). The finish stringer is fastened to the wall before carriages are fastened. Treads and risers are cut to fit snugly between the stringers and fastened to the rough carriage with finishing nails (figure 14-10). This may be varied somewhat by nailing the rough carriage directly to the wall and notching the finished stringer to fit (figure 14-11). The stringers are laid out with the same rise and run as the stair carriages, but they are cut out in reverse as shown in figure 14-11.

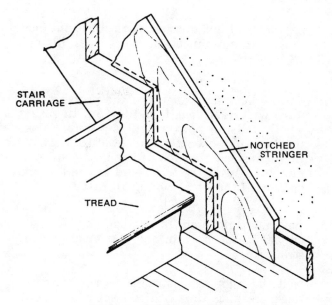

**Cut Out Or Notched Stringer**
**Figure 14-11**

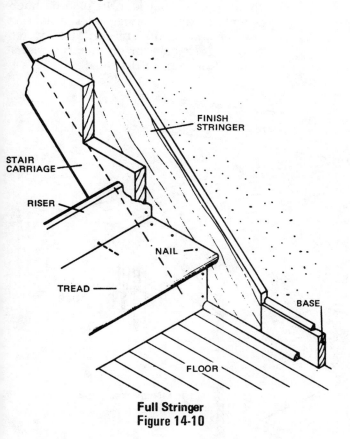

**Full Stringer**
**Figure 14-10**

The risers are butted and nailed to the riser cuts of the wall stringers and the assembled stringers and risers are laid over the carriage. The assembly is then adjusted and nailed so that the tread cuts of the stringers fit against the tread cuts of the carriages. The treads are then nailed on the tread cuts of the carriage and butted to the stringers the same as in figure 14-10. The finish stringer may be

25/32 inch or 1 1/16 inch thick and wide enough to cover the intersection of the tread and riser cut in the carriage and to reach about 2 inches beyond the tread nosing. This width is usually 12 inches to 14 inches. If the stringer is not cut out at the riser and tread marks, it is laid out in about the same way as a rough carriage. Only the level cut for the floor, the plumb cut for the header, and the plumb cuts at the top and bottom of the stringer for the baseboards are made. This is perhaps the best type of construction to use when the treads and risers are to be nailed to the carriages. This method saves time and labor in installing stairs but it is difficult to prevent squeaks when the stairs are stepped on. Another disadvantage is that any shrinkage of the frame of the building causes the joints to open up and to present an unsightly appearance. The notched stringer method has the advantage of having the two stringers tied together by the nailing of the risers to them. This prevents the two side stringers from spreading and showing open joints at the ends of the treads. Since the risers are nailed to the stringers, the face nailing of the risers to the carriage as in figure 14-10 is eliminated. This type of stringer is used where the carriages were fitted permanently to the bridgework at the time when the building was framed.

Sometimes the treads are allowed to run underneath the tread cut of the stringer. This makes it necessary to notch the tread at the nosing to fit around the stringer.

### How To Build Stairs With A Full Stringer

*NOTE:* It is assumed that the temporary carriages have been removed and that the finish lumber to be used in the stairs is clear stock and sanded.

1. Lay out and cut the stair carriages as outlined above for cut out stringer carriages. Use 1 5/8 inch stock.

2. Select the stair stringers of the proper thickness, width and length and lay out the exact length and the bottom and top cuts. Make the line of the bottom cut level to meet the floor line and the line of the baseboard cuts plumb to meet the baseboard at the top and bottom of the stair. See figure 14-12.

3. Lay out a right and a left hand stringer and cut along the bottom and top marks on the stringer.

4. Nail the right hand stringer to the stair carriage, keeping the bottom level cut of both pieces even and the top edge of the stringers at least 4 inches above the cutouts of the carriage. See figure 14-12.

*NOTE:* Be sure the bottom edge of the carriage is parallel with that of the stringer.

5. Nail the left hand stringer to a carriage in the same manner.

6. Place the built-up stringers in their proper places against the header and side walls of the stair opening. Nail them to the headers and side walls.

7. Select the required number of riser boards. These are generally 25/32 inch thick, 7½ inches wide and as long as the distance between the inside faces of the two stringers.

8. Rip a riser board for the first riser to a width equal to the height of the first tread cut of the carriage above the floor. See the bottom riser of figure 14-12. Square the ends of this riser to length so that it fits tightly against the finish stringer on each side of the stairs.

9. Face nail the riser board to the riser cuts of the three carriages with two 8d finishing nails in each carriage. Keep the nails about 1 inch from the top and bottom edges of the board. See figure 14-12.

*NOTE:* The nails at the top will be covered by the moulding that is to be placed underneath the tread nosing and the nails at the bottom of the riser will be covered by the floor shoe, or on the other risers, by the thickness of the tread.

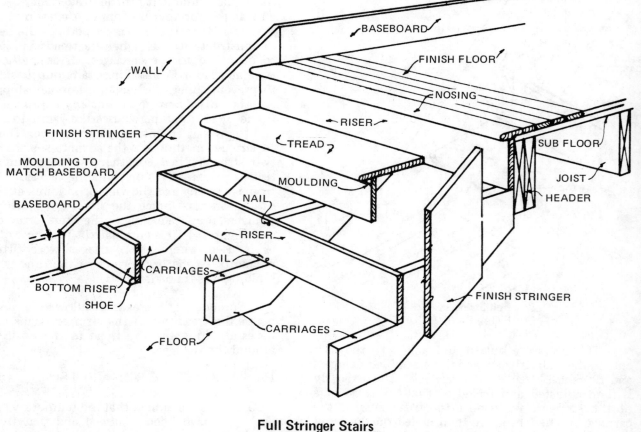

**Full Stringer Stairs**
**Figure 14-12**

10. Cut, fit and nail the remaining riser boards in a similar manner.

11. Cut the treads to the same length as the riser boards and fit them in place. Face nail them with three 8d finishing nails at each tread cut of each carriage.

*NOTE:* After each tread is face nailed, drive 8d common nails through the back of each riser board into the back edge of each tread. Space the nails every 8 inches between the carriages.

12. Cut a piece of rabbeted nosing stock to the same length as a tread and face nail it to the top edge of the top riser and to the subfloor. Set all nails that will show and sand the surfaces where necessary.

13. Fit and nail cove moulding under the nose of each tread.

## How To Build Stairs With Cut Out Stringers (Figure 14-11)

*NOTE:* When cut-out stringers are used, the same general procedure is followed except that the finish stringers are cut to fit against the tread cuts of the carriage and the face of the riser boards. The risers extend the full width of the stair opening. It is assumed that the carriages are permanently placed so the finish stringers, risers and treads will fit them.

1. Lay out the finish right and left hand stringers using the same figures as on the carriages. Mark the cuts at the top and bottom of the stringers for the floor and baseboard cuts. These cuts should be the same as shown in figure 14-12.

2. Lay out the riser and tread cuts.

3. Cut along these marks with a crosscut saw. Be careful not to break the wood where the riser and tread cuts meet.

4. Temporarily nail a stringer to the wall on the left hand side of the stair opening. Keep the riser cuts of the stringer approximately 1¼ inch from the riser cuts of the carriages and the tread cuts of the stringer on top of the tread cuts of the carriage.

5. Measure the distance between the finished walls at the top and bottom of the stairs to find the lengths of the riser boards.

6. Cut riser boards ½ inch shorter than these lengths.

7. Place the top riser board between the riser cut of the left hand stringer and the riser cut of the carriage.

8. Place the right hand stringer in the proper position on the right hand wall of the opening.

9. Mark the face of the riser board along the inside surface of both stringers. Be sure that there is a space of ¼ inch on each side between the outside of the stringers and the wall.

10. Follow the same procedure for the bottom and intermediate riser boards.

11. Remove the stringers and risers. Face nail the risers to the riser cuts of the stringer, keeping the tops of the risers tight against the tread cuts of the stringers and the face of the stringer in line with the marks on the faces of the risers. Nail the riser boards to both stringers in the same way.

12. Replace the assembled stringers on the carriages and adjust them so that the riser boards are tight against the riser cuts of the carriage and the tread cuts of the stringers are tight against the tread cuts of the carriages.

13. Nail the stringers to the walls in this location.

14. Cut, fit and nail the treads in the same way as for the built-up stringer.

*NOTE:* Some carpenters prefer to allow the treads to run under the stringers the same as the risers. See figure 14-13. The stairs in this case are built in practically the same way except that in laying out the cut-out stringer no deduction is made at the bottom riser mark for the thickness of the tread. The treads are notched to fit underneath the stringers at the nosings.

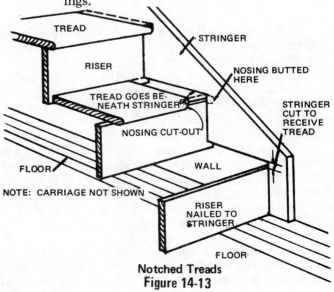

**Notched Treads**
**Figure 14-13**

## The Housed Stringer Stairway

Housed stair stringers are frequently considered a mill job but these stringers may be housed by the carpenter even if modern power woodworking tools are not available. The methods used in laying out the stringers, cutting the risers and treads and assembling the stairs are quite similar to these processes in other stairwork.

A closed type of housed stringer staircase is enclosed by walls on both sides of the staircase. The stringers are housed out to receive the ends of the treads and risers. This type is similar to the cut-out stringer stairway in which the treads and risers extend through the thickness of the stringer. In this case they only extend approximately 3/8 inch into the stringers. The treads and riser boards are then wedged into the dado joints of the stringers.

order to form the proper dado outlines for the risers, treads and wedges, riser and tread templets are made and placed at the riser and tread marks on the stringer as shown in B, figure 14-14.

The tread templet is laid out by drawing a straight line on the face of a board about ¼ inch by 2 inches by 14 inches. On this line is drawn the exact end section of the tread stock to be used

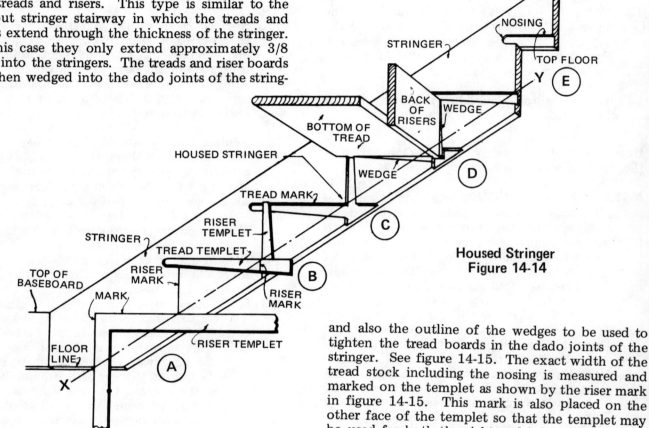

**Housed Stringer
Figure 14-14**

Figure 14-14 shows a housed stringer in various stages of construction. The lay out of the treads and risers is similar to that of the cut-out type of stair stringer except that before the stringer is laid out, a mark is gauged about 1½ inches from the bottom edge on the face of each stringer. See line X-Y, figure 14-14. This line acts as a measuring line the same as in laying out roof rafters. The purpose of using this line instead of the edge of the stringer is to provide room for the riser and tread boards to be supported by the wedges. The steel square at A, figure 14-14, shows the position in which the square is used on the gauge line in laying out the stringer.

The marks of the individual risers and treads represent the outside faces of the tread and riser boards when they are placed in the stringers. In

and also the outline of the wedges to be used to tighten the tread boards in the dado joints of the stringer. See figure 14-15. The exact width of the tread stock including the nosing is measured and marked on the templet as shown by the riser mark in figure 14-15. This mark is also placed on the other face of the templet so that the templet may be used for both the right and left hand stringers. The center of the nosing profile is also located as shown in figure 14-15. This mark is transferred to the other side by drilling a small hole through the templet.

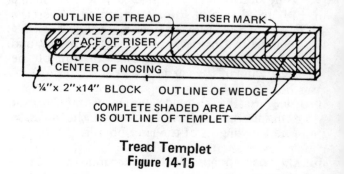

**Tread Templet
Figure 14-15**

The riser templet is laid out in the same way by using the end section of a riser board and the wedge outline on a thin piece of board for the tread templet. See figure 14-16. This templet is placed with its straight edge along the riser marks on the stringer. The outline of the templet is then marked along the tapered side of the templet on the stringer face. See B, figure 14-14.

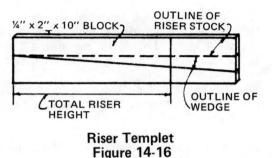

**Riser Templet**
**Figure 14-16**

The tread templet is placed in a similar manner with its straight edge on the tread mark of the stringer and the riser mark (figure 14-15) in line with the riser mark on the stringer. See B figure 14-14. The location of the hole in the templet is marked on the stringer with a scratch awl. This point shows the center of the hole that is to be bored in the stringer to form the round end of the dado to fit the nosing of the tread.

The layout at the top end of the stringer where the baseboard and the stringer meet is shown in E, figure 14-14. The nosing at the floor line is laid out with the tread templet to show the same nosing projection from the face of the riser as on the other treads. The nosing should be housed out in the same manner as the other treads. The riser cut directly below the nosing is cut completely through the stringer and the top riser is nailed to this surface. The depth of the tread and riser dado cuts is shown at C, figure 14-14.

The length of the treads is determined and they are inserted into the tread dadoes. They are then wedged, glued, and nailed from the outside of the stringers and into the ends of the treads. All risers, except the top one, are cut to the same length as the treads. The top riser is about 1¼ inch longer as it does not fit into the dado cuts but extends to the outside of the stringers. The other riser boards are inserted, wedged, glued and nailed into the riser dadoes the same as the treads. Moulding is sometimes fitted between the stringers under the nosing of the treads. Figure 14-14 at D shows one riser and tread in place in the housed dadoes and the wedges glued to the undersides of the treads and risers.

Some stairs are built with a rabbeted joint at the back of the tread and also at the top of the riser. However, if the treads and risers are properly jointed, driven up tight, wedged and nailed in this position, the butt joint is satisfactory and saves much labor.

Stock for the various parts of stairs is generally obtained from a mill in partially finished form. Treads and risers may be obtained completely machined and sanded but somewhat oversize. Rabbeted nosing stock for the edge of a landing or for the top step is usually obtainable in rough lengths. Standard wedges are also available. If the mill is furnished with the exact dimensions of the stair well, the parts can be completely machined and then assembled on the job.

### How To Build Housed Stringers

The first step in building a housed stringer stairway is the making of the tread and riser templet. It will be assumed that the tread stock is 1 1/16 inch thick and is nosed.

1. Select a straight piece of stock approximately ¼ inch thick, 2 inches wide and 14 inches long.

2. Lay out and plane one edge of the templet straight and square and taper the opposite edge as shown in figure 14-15.

*NOTE:* Be sure the width of the templet at the nosing is exactly 1 inch.

3. Select a similar piece of wood and lay out and cut the templet for the risers. See figure 14-16.

### How To Lay Out And House The Stringers

1. Select the stringer stock. This should be at least 1 1/16 inch thick and from 10½ to 14 inches wide. The length depends on the length of the stairs. Allow about one foot at each end for the top and bottom cuts of the stringer.

2. Sometimes regular tread stock is used for stringers. If so, plane the nosed surface flat so that moulding may be fitted to this surface after the stairs are in place.

3. Plane the bottom edge of the stringer straight.

4. Set a marking gauge to about 1½ inches and gauge a line from this edge. See line X-Y, figure 14-14.

5. Lay out the tread and riser marks with a steel square. Use a scratch awl or a fine hard lead pencil in marking the stringers.

133

NOTE: It is well to make a pitch board or to use a "fence" on the steel square. Both side stringers must be cut to exactly the same dimensions so that the stairs are square and sound.

6. Lay out the right and left hand stringers and check them for accuracy and length before doing any templet or housing work. Figure 14-17 shows how to check the stringers for length and accuracy of layout.

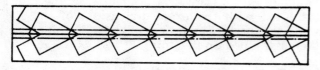

**Checking Stair Layout**
**Figure 14-17**

7. Place the tread templet with its straight edge exactly over a tread mark on the stringer. Adjust it so that the riser mark on the templet is also exactly in line with the riser mark on the stringer. Make a point on the stringer by putting the scratch awl through the hole in the templet to locate the center of the nosing. Also mark along both sides of the templet on the stringer. See B, figure 14-14.

8. Bore a hole with a Forstner or center bit using the point marked through the tread templet as a center. Bore the hole approximately 3/8 inch deep. Locate the center of a second hole so it will overlap the first and be within the top and bottom lines of the tread. See figure 14-18.

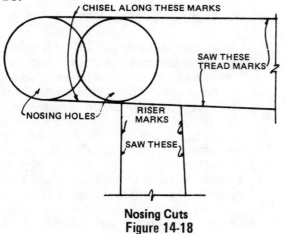

**Nosing Cuts**
**Figure 14-18**

9. Use the back of a 1½ inch butt chisel to chisel along the tread marks between the holes (figure 14-18).

10. Cut 3/8 inch deep along the tread marks with a saw. Start with the tip of the saw at the holes and continue back the length of the tread mark.

NOTE: If using the back saw to cut the housed joints, tip the saw a trifle so that the edges of the joint will be undercut. This will allow a tighter joint between the top of the tread and the stringer cut and will help hold the wedge in between the bottom of the tread and the edge of the housing.

11. Chisel out the stock between the cuts. Take this stock out carefully and to a depth of about ¼ inch. Leave the remaining 1/8 inch to be taken out smoothly by the router plane.

12. Set the router plane blade to take a cut 3/8 inch deep and use it to bottom out the joint to an even depth.

13. Cut the other tread housings in the same manner. Naturally, a power router will speed and simplify steps 8 to 13 above and steps 15 and 16 below.

14. Mark the riser cuts by placing the riser templet with its straight edge exactly over the riser mark on the stringer. Mark along the opposite edge of the templet on the stringer.

15. Cut along these lines with the back saw. Chisel and rout out the stock the same as for the treads.

16. Finish cutting and routing for all the treads and risers including the nosings at the top of both stringers.

17. Make the top and bottom cuts of both stringers with a crosscut saw.

## How To Assemble The Stairs

1. Select the tread stock. Use only clear stock free from imperfections and sanded to a finish on all surfaces that will show in the assembled stairs.

2. Square the pieces and cut them to length.

NOTE: Assume that the distance between the two walls of the stair well is 3 feet 6 inches.

3. Check the width of the stair well at the top and bottom and several intermediate points to see that no distance is less than 3 feet 6 inches so that the assembled stairs will easily fit between the walls.

4. Deduct from this assumed distance of 3 feet 6 inches twice the thickness of a stringer from the bottom of the housed joint to the outside face of the stringer (figure 14-19). From this figure subtract 1 inch.

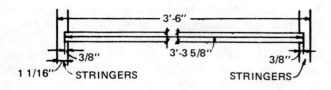

**Length Of Treads**
**Figure 14-19**

*NOTE:* Assuming that the stringers are 1 1/16 inch thick, the distance from the bottom of the housed joint to the outside face of the stringer would be 11/16 inch. Adding 11/16 inch for the other stringer would give 22/16 or 1 3/8 inch. 3 feet 6 inches minus 1 3/8 inches = 3 feet 4 5/8 inches. Subtracting 1 inch more would give 3 feet 3 5/8 inches, the length of the treads. The 1 inch is an allowance for fitting the assembled stairs in the well hole. This allowance is also made because the stairs have a tendency to spread when being assembled and the ends of all of the joints may not come up tight. The space between the stringer and wall will later be covered up with moulding.

5. Square and cut the treads and the nosed piece for the top step to length.

6. Rip the required number of wedges for both risers and treads or obtain them already cut.

7. Place the stringers on saw horses which are toenailed to the subfloor and spaced far enough apart to properly support the length of the stringers. See figure 14-20.

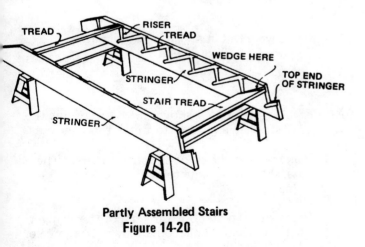

**Partly Assembled Stairs**
**Figure 14-20**

8. Apply glue to the housed joint in which the tread is to be inserted.

9. Insert a tread in the top housing of one stringer and tap it so the nosed section fits into the curved part of the housed joint.

10. Glue the wedge and drive it between the bottom side of the tread and the edge of the housing. Drive the tread and the wedge alternately until the tread nosing and the top surface of the tread fit perfectly against the edges of the housed joint that will show in the assembled stairs. The back edge of the tread must also be in line with the riser cut of the riser housing.

11. Drive an 8d common nail through the stringer into the nosing to pull the stringer up tightly against the tread end. Drive at least two more nails into the tread but use more if it is necessary to bring the tread up tightly against the bottom of the housed joint.

12. Insert the bottom tread in the bottom housing of the same stringer and fasten it to the stringer in the same manner.

13. Insert the opposite ends of these treads in the top and bottom housings of the opposite stringer and fasten them in the same manner.

14. Toenail the top edge of one stringer with 8d finishing nails to the tops of both saw horses. Be sure the stringer is straight. Place the steel square between the back edge of the top tread and the surface of the stringer. Bring the stairs into a square position at this point and toenail the loose stringer to the saw horses. Check the diagonally opposite corners of the stairs for squareness.

15. Insert the remaining treads and fasten them into the housings in the same manner.

*NOTE:* Be sure the back edge of each tread is perfectly flush with the front cut of each riser housing. If it does not reach this point, chisel off the riser cut until it is even with the back edge of the tread. If the tread projects beyond this point, plane or chisel off the back edge of the tread very carefully to a straight line.

16. Cut the risers to the same length as the treads. The top riser will be about 1 3/8 inch longer than the rest as it must be face nailed to the stringers at the top cut.

17. Nail the top riser to the stringers and to the back edge of the top tread. Be sure the top of this riser is even with the bottom of the housed joint of the nosing.

18. Rip the bottom riser to width and insert it into the bottom riser housings in the same general manner as the treads.

19. Install the remaining risers and fasten them the same as the treads.

20. Nail the back of the risers to the back edges of the treads with 8d common nails. Space the nails about 8 inches apart.

21. Cut angle blocks from a 2 x 4 and glue and nail them in place with shingle nails. Put one block in the middle of the stair width at the intersection of the back surface of each riser and tread. See figure 14-21.

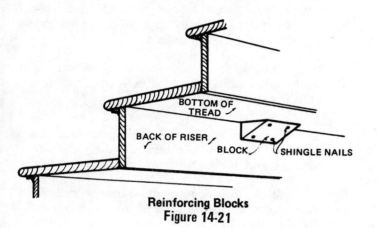

**Reinforcing Blocks**
**Figure 14-21**

22. Loosen the stringers from the horses, turn the stairs over and fit mouldings underneath the nosing. Nail them to both the riser and tread surfaces with 1¼ inch brads.

23. Nail through the top surfaces of the treads into the risers with 8d finishing nails. Space the nails about 8 inches apart and set these nails.

Finally, place the stairs in the well hole.

1. Place the stairs in the well hole with the top riser against the header. Adjust the top edge of the housed joint for the nosing so it is level with the top of the finished floor. To do this, it may be necessary to shim the back of the top riser out from the face of the header on one side of the well.

2. Center the stairs between the two sides of the well and nail the riser securely to the header.

*NOTE:* If the finish floor has not been laid, be sure to use blocks of finish floor stock under the bottom ends of the stringers.

3. Locate the studs in the side walls and nail through the stringers into them with 10d or 12d finishing nails.

4. Insert the rabbeted nosed piece into the top nosing housed joints and fur it solidly to the

top of the sub-floor or header over its entire length. Nail it to the header so that it will be forced tightly into the housed joints.

5. Set the nails and cover the stairs with building paper and wood cleats to protect the nosings and other surfaces.

6. Cut and fit mouldings on top of the stringers at the side walls of the well hole and under the top nosing of the stairs.

**How To Build Housed And Open Stringers**

Often housed stringer stairways are built along a single wall with an open stringer at the open side of the stairs.

1. Select the material for the open stringer. This is generally 1 1/16 inch x 11½ inches by the length of the stairs. Stock 25/32 inch thick is sometimes used but it is hardly strong enough, especially for stringers over 3 feet long.

2. Lay out the open stringer in the same manner as the notched stringer illustrated in figure 14-11.

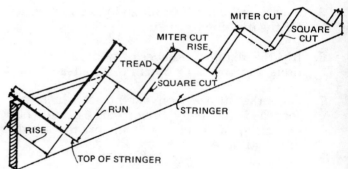

**Layout Of Cut And Mitered Stringer**
**Figure 14-22**

*NOTE:* Figure 14-22 shows how to lay out the stringer and how to miter the riser cuts.

3. Make the tread cuts of the stringer first. These cuts should be square with the face of the stringer.

4. Make the top and bottom cuts of the stringer. These cuts should also be square with the face.

5. Make the miter cuts along the riser marks. Use the riser marks as the long point of the miter.

6. Lay out and cut a carriage to fit behind the mitered stringer (figure 14-23).

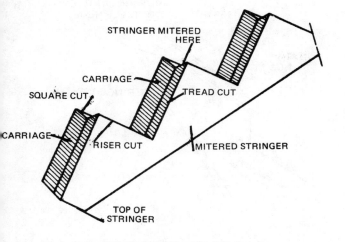

**Assembly Of Carriage And Stringer**
**Figure 14-23**

7. Adjust this carriage to the inside face of the stringer. Keep the tread cuts of the carriage even with the tread cuts of the stringer and the riser cuts of the carriage in line with the short ends of the miter cuts of the stringer. Nail the stringer and the carriage together temporarily.

8. Lay out and house the wall stringers as described previously for housed stringer stairways.

9. Determine the length of the risers.

*NOTE:* To find the length of the risers, lay out on the subfloor the position of the wall stringer and open stringer as shown in figure 14-24. The outside stringer usually projects about 1 inch over the outside wall of the well hole. Measure the length of the riser as shown in figure 14-24. This will give the length to the long point of the miter cut.

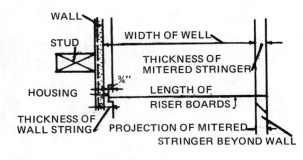

**Length Of Mitered Risers**
**Figure 14-24**

10. Cut a miter on one end of each riser and cut the opposite end square.

*NOTE:* Generally the top and bottom tread boards are assembled in the housings first and the stair frame is then fastened to the saw horses and squared as in assembling the housed stairs. The treads and risers may also be installed into the housed stringer first and then the open stringer assembled to the opposite ends of the treads and risers. This procedure sometimes makes it difficult to square the stairs and should be avoided, especially in long stairs. In short stairs it is satisfactory.

11. Place the square ends of the risers into the riser housings of the wall stringer. Nail, glue and wedge them as in the housed type of stairs.

12. Assemble the mitered ends of the risers to the mitered riser cuts of the open stringer. Keep the top edges of the riser boards even with the tread cuts of the open stringer. Nail the miters with finishing nails to the stair carriage riser cuts and to the miter of the open stringer.

13. Permanently nail the carriage to the open stringer.

14. Find the length of each tread by measuring from the bottom of the tread housing to the outside edge of the open stringer and adding on the amount the end of the tread will project over the open stringer. See A, figure 14-25. This projection should be the same distance as that of the nosing over the riser on the front of the step.

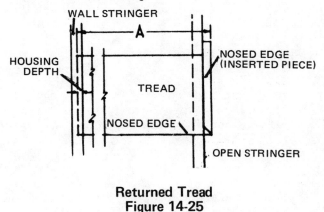

**Returned Tread**
**Figure 14-25**

15. Lay out and make the miter and straight cuts on the ends of the treads as shown in figure 14-25.

16. Cut, glue and nail the mitered pieces to the ends of the treads.

*NOTE:* If balusters are to be tenoned into the treads, leave the end pieces loose until the hand rail has been erected.

17. Insert and fasten the treads the same as in the housed type. Face nail the treads to the tread cuts of the open stringer and to the risers.

18. Cut, fit and nail the moulding under the tread nosing at the face of the risers and under the return of the tread nosing at the stringer. Return the moulding on itself at the back edge of the tread. See figure 14-26.

19. Erect the stairs against the header in the same way as in the housed stairs but be sure the outside stringer is parallel to the wall.

20. Nail the top of the stairs to the header and nail the wall stringer to the studs.

21. Cut and fit a moulding along the bottom edge of the open stringer where it meets the wall. Nail this moulding temporarily until the newel posts have been fitted to the stairs.

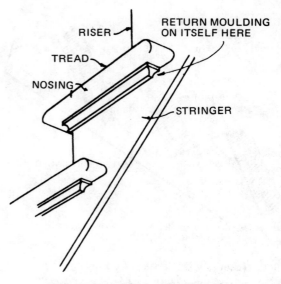

**Moulding At Returned Treads**
**Figure 14-26**

# Chapter 15

# STAIR RAILS

Newel posts and handrails are made in many shapes and sizes. However, there are basic rules for placing them on the stairs. Only square, solid newel posts and straight handrails will be described here becuase the principles involved in layout and fitting newel posts and handrails are the same regardless of the type of posts and rails called for.

Newel posts are built on the stringer, risers and treads of stairs to form a support for the balusters and handrails. In straight run staircases they are generally placed at the starting step and the top step. These are called the starting and landing newels. In "L" shaped stairs there is a third post at the platform. This is called a platform or angle newel. Newel posts may be of the hollow square built-up type or the turned and square solid type. They may be finished plain or capped and paneled depending on their size and the style of the staircase.

Figure 15-1 shows the different lengths of the newels. These are of the solid square type in a colonial style.

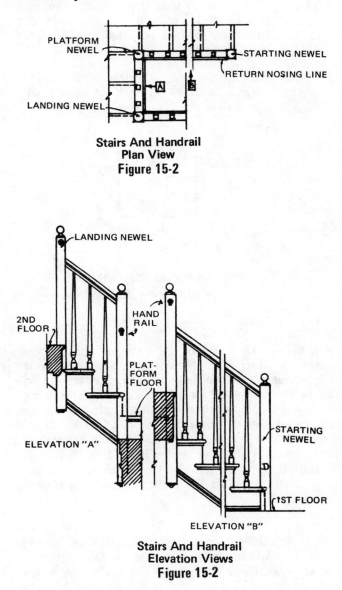

**Stairs And Handrail**
**Plan View**
**Figure 15-2**

**Stairs And Handrail**
**Elevation Views**
**Figure 15-2**

Figure 15-2 shows the plan view and elevation views of an "L" shaped staircase. The locations of the starting, angle and landing newels show how they are fitted to the stringers of the stairs and why the newels are of different lengths.

If the newel posts are 4½ inches or more wide, the side of the post may be cut out to allow the nosing of the tread to enter the post, thus giving

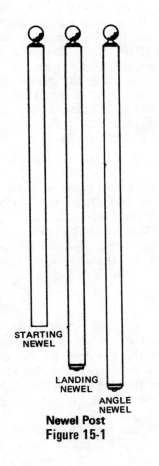

**Newel Post**
**Figure 15-1**

support to the nosing at this point. If the posts are less than 4½ inches wide, it may be necessary to butt the nosing against the side of the newel so that the post will not be weakened by cutting the post for the nosing of the tread. In the drawings, narrow newels are shown and the nosings are butted to the posts as shown by dotted lines. When hollow square posts are used the nosings are generally allowed to enter the post.

### How To Lay Out And Fit The Starting Newel

*NOTE:* It is assumed that the proper newel post is on hand and that the stairs are permanently placed for the fitting of the newels.

1. Lay out the lengths, position of the top of the handrail, and the outlines for the stringer, nosing and riser.

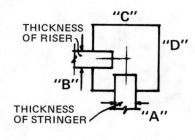

**Starting Newel Diagram**
**Figure 15-3**

Figure 15-3 shows the plan of the starting newel and how it is placed in relation to the outside stringer and the first tread and riser. In locating the exact position of this newel on the stringer and tread, a center line must be drawn on the surface of the newel which is to be fitted to the stringer. See side A, figure 15-4. This center line must line up with the center line of the thickness of the stringer (figure 15-3). Another center line should line up with the center line of the riser B, figure 15-3.

Figure 15-4 shows an elevation of how the surfaces A and B of the newel post are laid out to fit the stringer, tread and riser. The surface A in the plan of figure 15-3 represents the surface A in the elevation of figure 15-4. The sections marked X show the material to be cut out of the post so the stringer will fit into the post and so the post will rest on the top of the first tread. The sides of the post opposite sides A and B will not have to be cut out as they will face the front and the outside of the staircase and extend to the floor. See figure 15-2. The elevation B shows the surface D of the newel shown in figures 15-3 and 15-4. In laying out the starting newel, the height of the handrail above the

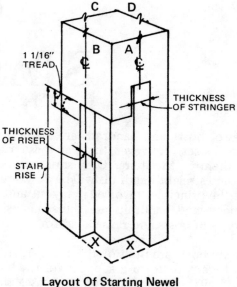

**Layout Of Starting Newel**
**Figure 15-4**

tread must first be considered. This distance is from 2'-6" to 2'-8" from the top member of the handrail to the tread directly below the handrail. After this location has been laid out on the post,

the bottom cut of the post is measured from it. This would be the height of one riser from the top of the finish floor to the top of the tread. The cuts for the stringer, tread and riser are located from the bottom cut of the post. The depth of the cuts into the posts should be only deep enough to allow the post to be centered to the stringer and riser. When laying out the newel it is advisable to check the surfaces of the stair stringer, riser and tread to see that they are perfectly straight so that the straight lines may be used on the layout of the newel.

If narrow newel posts are used, the cuts in the newels may be left square at the riser line and the tread nosings may be butted to the side of the post. If the size of the newels is such as to provide enough projection over the side of the stringer to allow the treads to run into the newels, cut the nosings of the treads into the newels as follows.

2. Use a brace and bit to make the cut for the nosing of the tread. The bit may also be used to start the cut for the stringer by boring a series of overlapping holes along the layout lines on the newel. Power routing equipment will speed and simplify these cuts.

3. Carefully cut out the stock marked X in figure 15-4. Keep ½" inside the layout marks until the surplus stock has been taken out. Then carefully pare to these lines.

4. Cut out the section deep enough to allow the post to fit over the stringer and riser so that the center lines of these members line up with the center lines of the newel.

5. Square and cut the bottom edge of the post and erect it in position on the stairs. Check the fit, and if it is satisfactory, temporarily nail and brace the newel plumb both ways to the floor, tread, stringer, and riser surfaces.

## How To Lay Out And Fit A Platform Or Angle Newel

The angle newel is somewhat longer than the starting or landing newel. This is to allow the handrail of the first flight to meet the angle newel 2'-6" above the top tread of the first flight and also to allow the handrail of the second flight to meet the adjacent side of this newel 2'-6" above the first tread of the second flight. See elevations A and B, figure 15-2. In other words, one rail would be the height of one riser above the other handrail at the angle newel. The center lines of this newel should be in line with the center lines of the stringers of the upper and lower flights. Four side surfaces of this newel will have to be cut to fit the surfaces of the upper and lower flights. See figure 15-2. The only tread nosings that will show on the two sides of the post that face the platform will be the top nosing of the lower flight and the bottom nosing of the upper flight. See figure 15-5.

Figure 15-6 shows a diagram of the angle newel and the surfaces into which the stringers of the first and second flights would enter. It also shows how the top riser of the first flight and the bottom riser of the second flight would enter the sides of this post. In order to start the layout of the surface D as shown in the diagram in figure 15-6 and in the elevation in figure 15-7, it is necessary to know how far the bottom of this newel is to be located below the bottom edge of the stringer of the first flight. See A, figure 15-7. This distance is generally about 4 inches to allow a moulding to fit on the bottom edge of the stringer and to butt against the side of the newel. See figure 15-5. This point may be marked on the wall surface

where the post is to be fitted. From this line measure the vertical distance to the top tread of the lower flight. See Y on figures 15-5 and 15-7. This point locates the top of the tread return shown on side C of the newel in figure 15-5. From this point measure the distance of one riser from the top tread to the platform finish floor line as shown at R, figure 15-7. This point is transferred to the side C of the post and is shown as the floor line in fig-

ure 15-5. From this point measure the height of the first riser of the upper flight and transfer this distance to side D of the newel. This point locates the top of the first tread nosing return of the upper flight.

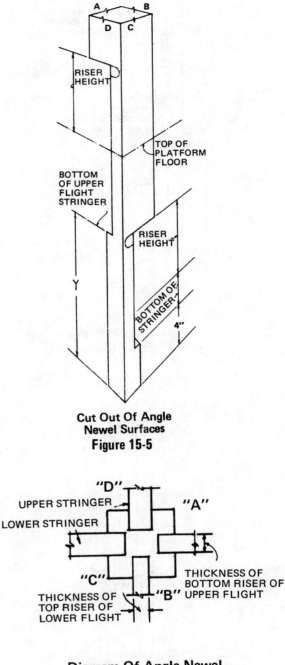

**Cut Out Of Angle Newel Surfaces**
**Figure 15-5**

**Diagram Of Angle Newel**
**Figure 15-6**

The two adjacent faces of this newel would show the tops of the platform front nosing and the tread immediately above the platform floor line. See R, figure 15-8. The center lines of the post should be kept in line with the center lines of the risers.

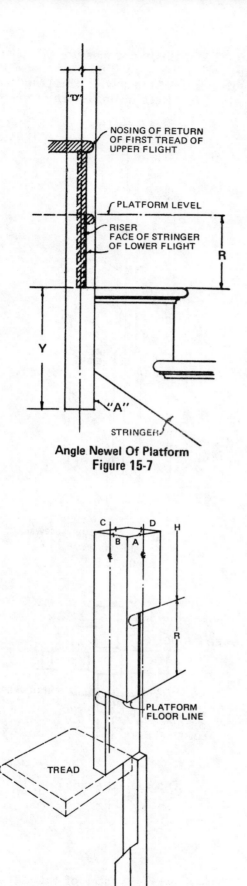

**Angle Newel Of Platform**
**Figure 15-7**

**Cut Out On Newel Surfaces**
**Figure 15-8**

To lay out these sides, transfer the platform floor line of figure 15-5 to side A of figure 15-8. Locate the thickness of the bottom riser of the upper flight on the center line of side A. Also locate A, figure 15-8. Lay out for the tread of the lower flight from the platform floor line and the center line on side B. The height of the handrail is measured from the top of the first tread of the second flight. See H, figure 15-8.

1. When the layout is complete, chisel or cut out the sections in the same general way as in cutting the sections of the starting newel.

2. Cut out the sections so that the newel, when fitted to the stairs, will center with both the stringers and risers.

*NOTE:* It may be necessary to make a trial assembly of the newel to the stairs several times before it fits perfectly.

3. Cut the bottom end square or trim it as desired.

4. When the newel is properly fitted, temporarily nail it to the stair members and wall and brace it in a plumb position.

*NOTE:* This newel generally has to be extensively cut. In some instances where the newel may be weakened by cutting, the return nosings of the treads might better be notched rather than to weaken the post.

**How To Lay Out And Fit The Landing Newel**

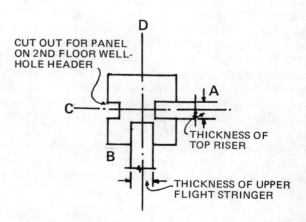

**Landing Newel Diagram**
**Figure 15-9**

Figure 15-9 shows the second floor landing newel layout in relation to the stringer and the riser of the upper flight at the second floor line. To lay out this newel, the bottom of the newel is dropped 4 inches below the bottom edge of the upper flight stringer the same as the bottom end of the newel in figure 15-5. This location is marked on the wall and from this point the vertical distance to the top of the top tread in the upper flight is measured. See figure 15-10. This locates the top edge for the return nosing for this tread. The other lines on this surface are laid out for the thickness of the stringer and the fit of the newel against the wall in a similar manner to side C of the angle newel in figure 15-5.

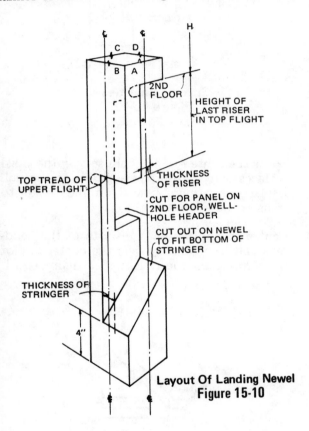

**Layout Of Landing Newel**
**Figure 15-10**

The nosing lines on side A of the newel in figure 15-10 are laid out for the top nosing and riser of the upper flight at the second floor line exactly the same as those on the side A, figure 15-8. The opposite sides C and D are laid out as shown in figure 15-8. On the side C a panel similar in width to the stringer is applied to the wall of the header of the well hole. The slanting cut shows where the newel fits to the bottom of the stringer of this flight. The lines showing how the panel of the well hole fits into the newel are shown as they would be laid out on surface C.

The panel cut in the face C is similar to the cut for the stringers in the other newels. The second floor line as located on the side A, figure 15-10 is transferred to side C of figure 15-11. The drop of 4 inches below the stringer is the same as

the drop below the bottom edge of the stringer in side B, figure 15-10. The other lines on this side are also similar except that the nosing return on side C, figure 15-11 may be omitted where the edge of the second floor projects over the edge of the panel. See figure 15-2. The height of the handrails from the top of the top tread at the second floor is shown at H, figure 15-11.

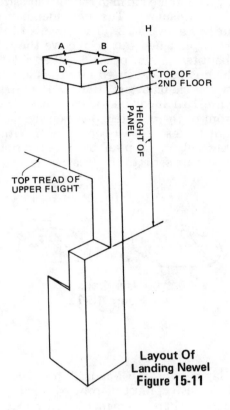

**Layout Of**
**Landing Newel**
**Figure 15-11**

The fitting of this newel to the stair top nosing and floor is similar to that of the landing newel except that one side is fitted around a panel board that is nailed to the face of the stairwell header at the second floor line.

1.  Select a panel board 1 1/16 inch thick and approximately as wide as the stair stringer and as long as the header of the second floor between the newel and end wall of the well hole.

2.  Fit this board to the wall of the header. Keep the top edge in line with the bottom of the finished floor. Nail it in this position and erect the landing newel on the stairs in the same manner as in erecting the angle newel.

3.  Cut and fit the finish floor nosing, allowing it to project over the panel about 1½ inch. Fit moulding below it and to the panel.

*NOTE:*    If the panel is to be butted against the newel, the newel is erected first and the panel and second floor nosing is fitted to the post.

If there are more newel posts in the well hole, they may be fitted and erected in the same general manner as described above for posts.

## How To Fit Handrails

A handrail is the top member of the balustrade. Rails may be obtained in many shapes and sizes from millwork companies. The two member type is shown in B, figure 15-12. The larger of these two members is ploughed out to receive the thickness of the balusters. The other member is a form of fillet which is cut and fitted into the ploughed section between the balusters. Rails of the type shown in B, figure 15-12 may be used at both the top and the bottom of the balusters on open stringers without return treads. The open stringer with return treads uses only the top rail because the bottom of the balusters are set into the tread surfaces.

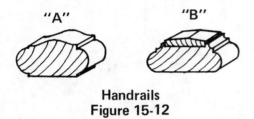

**Handrails**
**Figure 15-12**

In laying out the handrail for this type of stairs, the balusters must be properly spaced. Since there are several arrangements for spacing balusters and placing the newels on the treads, it is difficult to describe a definite method of spacing. However, the spacing of the balusters on the treads in relation to the faces of the risers as shown in figure 15-2 will give a general idea of baluster placement on the tread and handrail.

Balusters are made in many shapes, sizes and lengths and may be round or square. For open stairwork they are generally provided with a dowel on the bottom end for fitting into a hole bored in the tread. The same arrangement is provided at the top end for fitting the balusters into the handrail.

After the centers of the balusters have been located on the treads and the underside of the handrail, small holes are bored into the handrail and the treads to receive the dowels on the top and bottom of the balusters. The handrail is then fitted between the newel post and is fastened with special lag screws or nailed in place with finishing nails. Before fitting the handrail, be sure the newel posts are plumbed both ways and are braced in position.

1. Select the handrail and balusters.

2. Lay the top rail along the tops of the treads and against the sides of the newel posts as shown by dotted lines in figure 15-13. Temporarily nail it in this position.

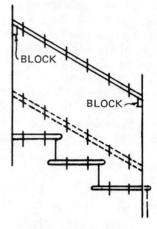

**Spacing Balusters**
**Figure 15-13**

3. Space the centers of the balusters on the tread surfaces and transfer these points to the rail. Use a steel square placed on the treads to transfer these points.

4. Center the points on the width of the handrails and also directly over the center line of the stringer on the treads. See figure 15-14.

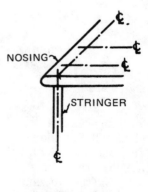

**℄ At Nosing**
**Figure 15-14**

5. Bore holes to fit the dowels of the balusters at the center points on the treads and on the underside of the handrail.

6. Tack blocks of wood to the newels to support the handrail at the correct height from the top and bottom treads. See figure 15-13.

144

7. Lay the handrail on these blocks and against the surfaces of the newel to which it is to be fitted. Mark the length of the handrail and cut it off.

8. Fit the balusters into the treads and mark their lengths where they intersect the handrail. Cut the balusters to length and fit them into the holes in the handrail.

9. Make a trial assembly of the handrail and balusters and mark the handrail centers on the newels. Check the whole assembly to be sure it fits and it is plumb and straight.

10. Remove the top rail and glue the bottom dowels in the holes in the treads. Apply glue to the top dowels of the balusters and replace the top rail, fitting the balusters into their proper holes in the handrails.

11. Nail or bolt the handrail to the newels and toenail the balusters in the underside of the handrail so that they cannot turn.

12. Nail the newel posts permanently to the stairs and fit mouldings along the underside of the open stringers.

13. Sand all rough surfaces and corners and set the nails. Cover the stairs with building paper and cleats to protect the surfaces from injury.

NOTE: In erecting the handrail and balusters on a box stringer, the procedure is similar with the addition of a bottom member of the handrail as shown in B, figure 15-12. This member is nailed to the top edge of the stringer and square balusters are cut at an angle to fit into the top and bottom rail members. Fillet blocks are then fitted between the balusters at the bottom rail. In some cases the member in B, figure 15-12 is also used as a top rail and the balusters are fitted in the same manner as those of the bottom rail.

# Chapter 16

# BASE AND CEILING MOULDING

Base and ceiling moulding should be applied only after the wall covering has been in place some time. This allows the wall coverings to dry out and any defects to show up before the wood trim is placed. The application of the trim differs only slightly from that of casings and stop beads.

### Base Moulding (Baseboard)

Base moulding serves as a finish between the finished wall and floor. It is available in several widths and forms. Two piece base consists of a baseboard topped with a small base cap (figure 16-1, A). When plaster is not straight and true, the small base moulding will conform more closely to the variations than will the wider base alone. A common size for this type of baseboard is 5/8" x 3¼" or wider. One piece base varies in size from 7/16" x 2¼" to ½" x 3¼" and wider (figure 16-1, B and C). Although a wood member is desirable at the junction of the wall and carpeting to serve as a protective "bumper", wood trim is sometimes eliminated entirely.

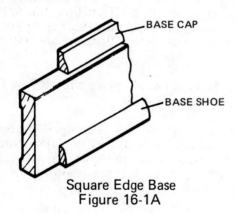

Square Edge Base
Figure 16-1A

Most baseboards are finished with a base shoe, ½" x ¾" in size (figure 16-1, A, B, C). A single base moulding without the shoe is sometimes placed at the wall floor junction, especially where carpeting might be used. The base shoe should be nailed to the base rather than to the floor as it is a part of the base trim. Should any settlement or movement

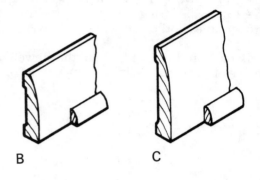

Narrow And Wide Ranch Base
Figure 16-1B And C

of the walls or floor occur, no opening will show between the baseboard and the shoe. If the shoe is nailed to the floor any settling would bring the shoe down with the floor, thus showing an unfinished surface on the base at the top of the shoe.

Square edged baseboard should be installed with a butt joint at inside corners and a mitered joint at outside corners (figure 16-2). It should be nailed to each stud with two eightpenny finishing nails. Moulded single piece base, base mouldings, and base shoe should have a coped joint at inside corners and a mitered joint at outside corners. A coped joint is one in which the first piece is square cut against the plaster or base and the second moulding coped. This is accomplished by sawing a 45 degree miter cut and with a coping saw trimming the moulding along the inner line of the miter (figure 16-2).

Another method of forming internal and external corners is by the use of square blocks to which the base is butted. This method saves installation time and gives a good joint. See figure 16-3. The edges of the blocks project about 3/16 inch beyond the surface of the base and the blocks are chamfered at the corner.

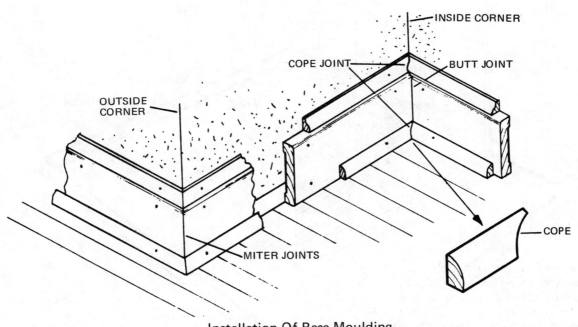

Installation Of Base Moulding
Figure 16-2

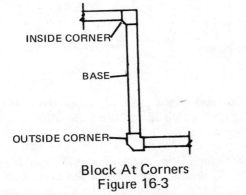

Block At Corners
Figure 16-3

External corners are sometimes butted but this type of joint shows end grain and should be used only in rough work. The mitered joint is the most common method of forming external corners.

## How To Cut And Install Base Moulding

*NOTE:* Baseboards are installed after the door jambs and casings are fitted. They may be installed either before or after the finish floor is laid. The bottom edge of the baseboard is kept about ¼ inch above the location of the top of the finish floor. This space will later be covered up by the base shoe. If no base shoe is to be used, the finish floor is laid before the baseboard which is then scribed to the floor.

1. Select clear baseboard stock free from twists and imperfections. If it is the moulded type, inspect the moulded edges for imperfections such as chipped edges or poorly machined surfaces.

2. Measure the distance from wall to wall along the end of the room marked A, figure 16-4. Use an extension rule for this purpose.

3. Transfer this length to a length of baseboard. Mark these points on the top edge of the baseboard and square from these points. Taper the cut at each end so that the length of the base at the bottom edge will be about ¼ inch shorter than the top edge.

4. Place the baseboard in position, being careful not to injure the wall covering or the baseboard. Use a block of wood to tap the baseboard in place. If the finish floor has not been laid, use a block of finish flooring to keep the baseboard the correct distance above the subfloor.

5. Nail the baseboard in place with two 8d finishing nails in each stud.

6. Measure and cut the baseboard marked B. This measurement should be taken from the face of base A to the opposite wall. Allow enough stock to form a coped joint to fit against base A.

*NOTE:* In most cases, this coped joint will have to be scribed to the surface of base A and there should be an additional ½ inch allowed for this process.

7. Scribe the straight part of the baseboard B, and from the top end of this line, mark a 45 degree line.

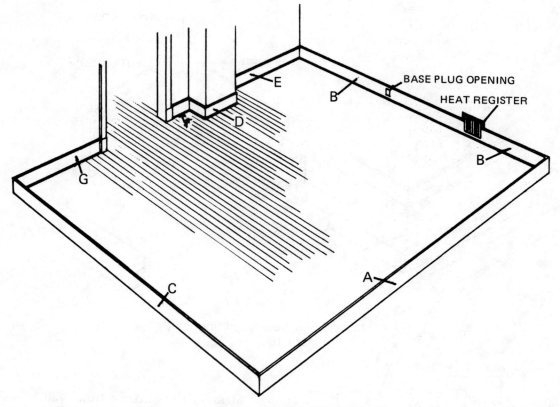

BASE PLUG OPENING

HEAT REGISTER

Method Of Fitting Baseboard
Figure 16-4

8. Cut this miter and cope the moulded section.

9. Cut the straight section to the scribed line.

10. Measure, cut and nail the baseboard around the pilaster (figure 16-4). The measurement is taken from the wall, allowing enough stock for the joint at the outside corner of the pilaster.

*NOTE:* The application of the baseboard around the pilaster before the base E is placed is only necessary when the pieces around the pilaster are short and apt to split when nailed. Applying the baseboard around the pilaster before applying baseboard E permits these short pieces to be longer and to be held in place by the baseboard E which would be coped on both ends. If the pilaster is large, piece E needs to be scribed only to piece B. This same principle holds true in fitting piece F.

12. Cut the piece F to the plinth block or casing and scribe it to the surface of the baseboard on the pilaster.

*NOTE:* Be careful not to cut these pieces so long that they will force the jamb out of line when the pieces are forced and nailed in place. Set the nails in all the baseboards.

13. Cut and place piece C. Cope the end that fits against piece A and butt the other end against the wall.

14. Fit piece G in place. One end should be coped to fit against piece C and the other end should be fitted against the door casing or plinth block.

**How To Cut Base For An Outlet Box**

*NOTE:* Figure 16-4 shows a base plug opening in the baseboard. To locate and cut the opening in the baseboard, proceed as follows:

1. Fit the baseboard in its proper place on the wall. Be sure to put the finish floor blocks under the bottom of the base if the finish floor has not been laid.

2. Mark the outer edges of the outlet box with blue chalk. Replace the baseboard in position and tap it lightly against the edges of the plug box. Remove the baseboard and the outline of the box should show on the back.

3. Bore a hole at each corner of the box outline until the spur of the bit shows through. Remove the bit and complete the hole from the other side.

4. Cut around the chalk lines with a reciprocating saw, allowing about 1/8 inch clearance on all sides. Replace and nail the baseboard.

## How To Fit Base Around A Hot Air Register

*NOTE:* Figure 16-4 shows a hot air register that projects above the top of the baseboard. The baseboard is fitted against and around the top as follows:

1. Cut the baseboard so that it butts against each side of the register. Keep the ends of the baseboard about ½ inch from the register metal lining.

2. Rip pieces about 2 inches wide from the top edge of base stock. These pieces should be long enough to be mitered around the top and sides of the register.

3. Butt the two side pieces onto the top edges of the baseboard and miter them to the piece that extends across the top of the register.

*NOTE:* If moulded baseboard is used, the same procedure is followed, except that the two side pieces may be mitered into the moulded base.

4. Cut the base shoe to length and cope the internal corners.

5. Temporarily nail the shoe in place. It may be permanently nailed after the finish floor is laid.

## How To Install Ceiling Moulding

Ceiling mouldings are sometimes used at the junction of wall and ceiling for an architectural effect or to terminate dry wall paneling of gypsum board or wood (figure 16-5, A). As in the base

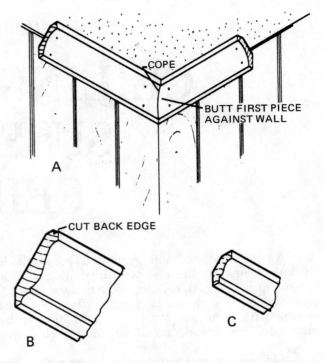

Ceiling Mouldings; A, Installation (Inside Corner);
B, Crown; C, Small Crown
Figure 16-5

mouldings, inside corners should also be cope-jointed. This insures a tight joint and retains a good fit if there are minor moisture changes.

A cutback edge at the outside of the moulding will partially conceal any unevenness of the plaster and make painting easier where there are color changes (figure 16-5, B). For gypsum dry wall construction, a small simple moulding might be desirable (figure 16-5, C). Finish nails should be driven into the upper wall plates and also into the ceiling joints for large mouldings when possible.

# Chapter 17

# CEILING TILE AND SUSPENDED CEILINGS

A wide variety of ceiling materials are available in both acoustical and non-acoustical designs. Tile is usually of a wood, cellulose or a mineral composition material and can be applied directly to the ceiling with adhesive, staples or nails or may be suspended on wood, metal or plastic supports.

Ceiling tile and panels for suspended ceiling systems come in several sizes, but the 12" x 12" size is usually most practical for average size rooms. For best appearance and easier installation, the border tiles or panels are cut if the length or width of the room does not divide evenly by the tile or panel size. Both ends of the room should have tiles or panels cut to the same width when tiles or panels must be cut. Where the length of the room leaves less than full tile at an end, add the length of one full tile to the part tile and divide by two. The result is the width of the border tiles at each end. Using this system each border tile will be at least ½ of the width of a full tile. Applying border tile of 6 inches or less usually causes a noticeable irregularity in the finished ceiling. For example, suppose 12" x 12" tile are being applied to a ceiling 18 feet 2 inches long. Eighteen 12" x 12" tiles will reach to within 2 inches of one end. Rather than cut tiles down to a 2 inch width, use the rule given above. Add 12 inches to the 2 inches (14 inches) and divide by 2. The result, 7 inches, is the width of the border tile at each end of the room. The length of the room will be covered by 17 full tile and one 7 inch tile at each end. Do the same for the width of the room to equalize the border tile at each side.

Tile should be cut with a sharp handsaw or with a power saw. Before cutting, the exposed side should be scored with a sharp utility knife on the finished side. Saw the tile with the finished side up. Because there may be slight variation in color and texture of the tile from one box to the next it is a good practice to take tile alternately from several boxes as the work progresses. The tile may expand or contract slightly as they absorb moisture in the air or give up moisture to the air. Avoid expansion or contraction after application

by exposing the tile to room conditions 24 hours before they are to be applied. Remember that lighter color tiles show smudges or stains and may be difficult to clean after application. Some craftsmen apply talcum powder or corn meal to their hands before handling the tile. When using adhesive, be especially careful to keep the adhesive off the exposed side of the tile. When nailing tile to unexposed ceiling joists you will save time and nails by snapping a chalk line on the plaster or wallboard under each joist once the joists have been located.

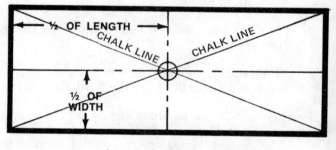

Locating Ceiling Center
Figure 17-1

### How To Apply Tile With Adhesive

When applying tile with adhesive, work is begun from the center of the room. Snap a chalk line between opposite corners. Where the lines cross is the center point of the room (figure 17-1). Placement of the first tile will determine the size of the border tile on all four walls. The size of the border tile will never be less than 6 inches if the following rule is observed. Figure 17-2 represents one 12" x 12" tongue and groove ceiling tile (as seen from below), oriented so that the top edge is parallel to the length of the room and the side edge is parallel to the width of the room. Select the correct center point on the tile that will cover the center point of the room:

1.  When both the width and length of the room in feet are even numbers, the point A should be placed over the room center.

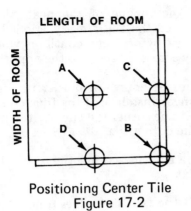

**LENGTH OF ROOM**

**WIDTH OF ROOM**

A    C

D    B

Positioning Center Tile
Figure 17-2

## How To Apply Tile On Wood Furring

If a sound plaster or wallboard ceiling is not present, wood furring strips can serve as a support for the tile. Furring strips can be used even where only exposed joints are present (figure 17-4).

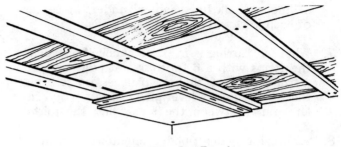

Corner Tile On Furring
Figure 17-4

2. When both the width and length are odd, place point B over the room center.

3. When only the room length is odd, point C is placed over the room center.

4. When only the width is odd, point D is placed over the room center.

5. Apply a thin prime coat of tile adhesive to each corner of the tile about 2 inches from the corner. Then place a walnut-size daub over each prime coat. See figure 17-3. Tile 12" x 24" should have adhesive applied as illustrated in figure 17-3. Each gallon will cover 50 to 60 square feet of tile.

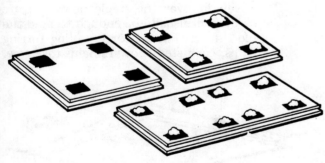

Applying Adhesive
Figure 17-3

6. Press the tile firmly to the ceiling, moving it back and forth slightly.

7. Press succeeding tiles to the ceiling, carefully sliding them into position to engage the tongue and groove.

8. Cut all border tile with a reverse bevel so that the exposed face fits flush against the wall.

9. Clean up excess adhesive with mineral spirits or naphtha.

1. Accurately measure each of the four walls where they join the ceiling. Divide each wall dimension in half and place a mark on the ceiling near the walls. Snap a chalk line between these marks to locate the center point. See figure 17-5.

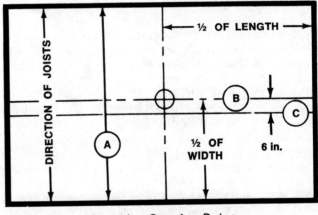

Locating Starting Point
Figure 17-5

2. Determine the number of full tiles that will be required: Subtract the border tile widths to determine if an even or an odd number of full size tiles is required in each direction.

3. If an even number of full size tile is required for ceiling direction A (figure 17-5), the first furring strip will be centered on line B. The furring strip should be at least 1" x 3" softwood.

4. If an odd number of full size tile is required for ceiling direction A, snap a new chalk line C 6 inches from center line B. See figure 17-5. The first furring strip will be centered on line C.

151

5. Working from the first furring strip, install remaining furring strips spaced at 12 inches on centers across the full length of the ceiling. One furring strip should be placed against each side wall.

6. When applying furring strips over an existing ceiling, a chalk line snapped under the center of each joist will save time and nails.

7. When all furring is in place check the level of the strips with a 6 foot straight edge or with a true length of lumber. If necessary to bring the furring into a level plane, insert wood filler shims between the strips and the joists.

8. As previously described, calculate the width of each border tile. Border tile at each end of the room should be the same width and border tile at each side should be the same width.

9. Cut a corner border tile to the size of the two adjacent borders. Cut off only the tongue sides. See figure 17-6.

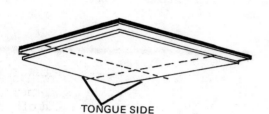

TONGUE SIDE

Cut Corner Board Tile
On Tongue Side
Figure 17-6

10. Face nail or staple the extreme corner tile in place. (Figure 17-4). Use 1 1/8 inch blue nails or 9/16 inch staples at four points on the flanges. When stapling, hold the gun firmly against the tile flange so the staple is driven straight and to the full depth. Staples should be placed as shown in figure 17-7.

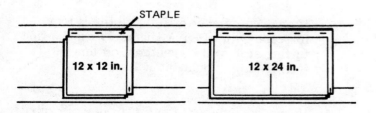

STAPLE

12 x 12 in.     12 x 24 in.

Placing Staples
Figure 17-7

11. Insert the tongue of the next tile into the grooves of the tile already applied. Nail or staple as before and continue working diagonally across the room to the opposite corner.

12. Cut the last course of border tile on the nailing flange. Install all of the final course except the extreme corner tile and the tile next to the extreme corner tile.

13. Cut the extreme corner tile to fit. Install this tile next.

14. Cut off the two side edges (one nailing flange and one tongue) of the final border tile to make insertion possible. Fit the last border tile into place. See figure 17-8. Face nail the last course of border tile.

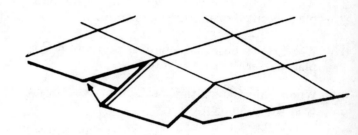

Placing The Final Tile
Figure 17-8

*NOTE:* If a sound gypsum wallboard ceiling exists it may not be necessary to install furring strips. Double action staples, one staple driven in over the staple below (figure 17-9), will usually be enough to hold the tile firmly. Except for installing furring strips, each step above remains the same.

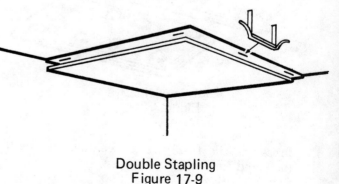

Double Stapling
Figure 17-9

**How To Apply Tile On Metal Furring**

Metal furring strips can be used over an existing ceiling or over exposed joists. Installation begins at one corner but, unlike wood furring work, the entire first border is installed first. Succeeding courses are installed one row at a time. Unlike tile applications over wood furring, the tile are not nailed or stapled. Instead, a moulding strip holds the tile in place at the walls and the metal furring strip interlocks with the other side of the tile to hold each tile in place. See figure 17-10. Using metal furring strips, some unevenness can be allowed in the existing ceiling or the joists without producing a noticeably inferior finished ceiling.

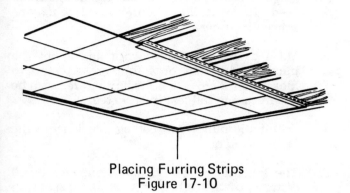

Placing Furring Strips
Figure 17-10

1.  Place the moulding strips on the wall against the existing ceiling or exposed ceiling joists around the perimeter of the room. Nail the moulding at 12 inch intervals.

2.  Determine the size of the border tile and cut the tile to size. Cut the first corner tile on both tongue sides. Figure 17-11, A and B. Cut the remaining tile for the first border on side B only.

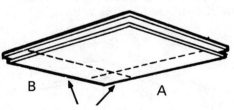

B       A

TONGUE SIDE

Starting Corner Border Tile
Figure 17-11

3.  Snap a chalk line on the ceiling or on the ceiling joists where the first metal furring strip is to be placed. This distance from the wall should be the width of the border tile plus one inch.

4.  Insert the first corner tile and the next three border tile into the moulding.

5.  Nail or staple the furring strip in place so that it supports the first four tile. Use 1 1/8 inch blue nails or 9/16 inch staples. See figure 17-12.

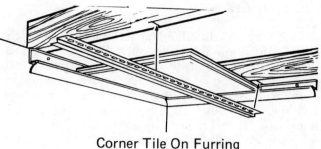

Corner Tile On Furring
Figure 17-12

6.  Install the entire border strip, inserting four border tiles into the moulding and attaching the metal furring strip.

7.  For the next course, install each four tiles by inserting the tongues into the grooves of the preceding course.

8.  For the last course, cut the border tile about ¼ inch short of the space to be filled. Slide the cut edges into the moulding strip. Cut the last corner tile on the two nailing flange sides (figure 17-13). Install the last corner tile before the adjacent border tile. Cut off sides D, figure 17-13 and insert the last border tile. See figure 17-14.

CUT OFF SIDE PROTECTION

A       B

D.

D

NAILING FLANGE

Cutting Last Border Tile On
Nailing Flange Sided
Figure 17-13

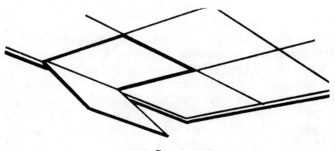

Placing Final Tile
Figure 17-14

*NOTE:* Often 24" x 12" center scored tile are used with metal furring strips. The 24 inch dimension should then be installed parallel to the metal furring strip.

### Suspended Ceilings

A suspended ceiling system consists of a light metal grid hung from the ceiling joists. Tiles, usually either 2' x 2' or 2' x 4' are then dropped into place. This type of system has several advantages. It reduces the sound transfer from the floor above and increases the insulating value of the ceiling. It provides access for ceiling lights, heat supply and return ducts and eliminates the need for any other ceiling finish.

Determine the room size in even number of feet. If the room length or width is not divisible by 2 feet, increase the dimension to the next unit divisible by 2 feet. For example, a room 11 feet 3 inches by 14 feet 2 inches should be considered a 12 foot by 16 foot room. Next, multiply the length times the width to arrive at the material required. In the example, 12 feet times 16 feet equals 192 square feet.

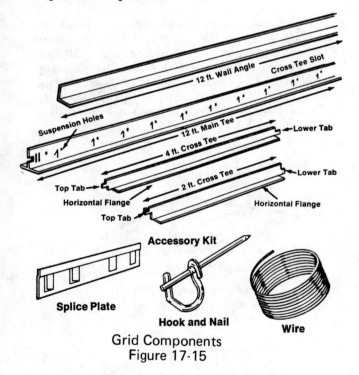

**Grid Components**
Figure 17-15

Figure 17-15 illustrates typical grid components for a suspended ceiling system. Main tees must run perpendicular to joists. For 2' x 2' grid, cross and main tees are 2 feet apart. For 2' x 4' grid, main tees are 4 feet apart and 4 foot cross tees connect the main tees. Then 2 foot cross tees can be used to connect the four foot cross tees. Plan to position the main tees so that border panels at the room edges are as equal and as large as possible. Try several layouts to see which looks best for the main tees. Small rooms should use 2' x 2' panels.

### How To Determine Materials Required

1. Wall angle is installed around the perimeter of the room. Wall angle usually comes in 12 foot sections.

2. Main tees come in 12 foot sections and should run at right angles to the joists across the length of the room. If the room length exceeds 12 feet, two or more main tees may be spliced together.

3. Make a sketch of the layout and count the number of 2 foot or 4 foot cross tees. No more than 2 cross tees for border areas can be cut from one full length cross tee.

4. Count the number of ceiling panels from the layout sketch.

5. The quantity of wire depends on the "drop" distance of the ceiling. Figure one suspension wire and one hook or suspension screw for each four feet of main tee.

### How To Install Suspended Ceiling Grid

1. Determine the new ceiling height and mark a line around the perimeter of the room at this height. The new ceiling should be at least 2 inches below the existing ceiling.

2. Install the wall angle at the marked line. On gypsum wallboard, plaster or paneled walls, install the wall angles with nails or screws. On masonry walls use concrete nails 24 inches apart. Miter the outside corners and overlap the inside corners as shown in figure 17-16. Use a level while installing the wall angle to be sure the finished ceiling is level.

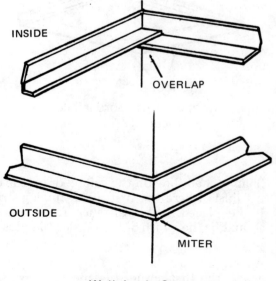

**Wall Angle Corners**
Figure 17-16

3. Suspension wires are required every 4 feet along main tees and on each side of splices. Cut the suspension wires to the proper length - at least 2 inches longer than the distance between the old ceiling and the new ceiling.

4. Before attaching the first suspension wire, extend a length of wire between the wall angles at right angles to the main tees under the point where the first row of suspension wires will be attached to the main tees. This wire serves as a guide for leveling the suspension wires.

5. Position one suspension wire for the first main tee. Measure out from the walls the distance of the two border courses to position the screw eyelet or hook. Pull the wire taught to remove kinks and make a 90 degree bend in the wire at the point where the suspension wire crosses the guide wire. If suspension wires are attached to the ceiling joists, the nail or hook can be attached at either the side or bottom edge of the joist.

6. Position the first suspension wire for the next main tee. Use the same guide wire to find the correct length for the 90 degree bend.

7. Continue placing suspension wires over the guide wire for each main tee. When the first row of suspension wires is complete, move the guide wire four feet toward the other end of the room and continue placing suspension wires. The last row of suspension wires should be no more than 4 feet from the wall. Remember to place suspension wires on both sides of spliced main tees.

8. Determine the length of the main tees and cut all the tees to the correct length. Aluminum tees should be cut with a hacksaw. Steel tees are cut most easily with tin snips.

9. If the length of the room is over 12 feet, two main tees will be spliced together to span the room. If spliced tees are necessary, 6 inches should be cut from one end of each main tee so that cross tees do not end at the splice joints.

10. Install the main tees. For rooms less than 12 feet long, rest both ends of a main tee on the wall angles and attach one suspension wire in the middle. Use a level to adjust the length of the wire. For main tees longer than 12 feet, rest one end on the wall angle and attach the suspension wire closest to the other end. Use a level to adjust the length of the remaining suspension wires. Measure the remaining length of main tee needed, resting one end on the opposite wall angle. Connect the main

tees with a splice plate (figure 17-17). If the main tee splice falls at a cross tee, it may be necessary to cut 12 inches off the first main tee. Start the next main tee with the length cut off the first main tee. Be sure to line up the cross tee slots in the main tees, however.

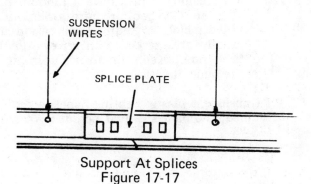

Support At Splices
Figure 17-17

11. Install the cross tees. Simply insert the tab of the cross tee into the slot of the main tee.

NOTE: In some aluminum systems, cross tees have one "high" and one "low" tab. Figure 17-18. Install all the border cross tees on the first main tee by cutting off the "high" tab and resting the cut end in the main slot. On the opposite side of the room, cut off the "low" tab end and rest the cut end on the wall angle. If the border edge is less than half the length of the cross tee, save the balance for use on the opposite side of the room.

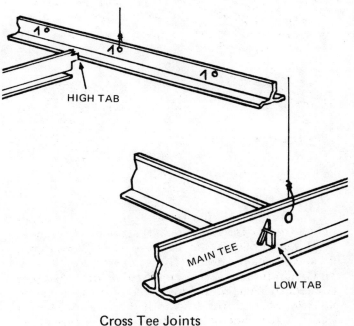

Cross Tee Joints
Figure 17-18

12. Install the ceiling panels. Cut the border panels to size with a sharp knife and a straight edge. Lay the panel on a flat surface with the white side up and cut the panel with the straight edge protecting the panel you intend to use rather than the scrap end.

*NOTE:* Most ceiling panels have a random pattern and do not require orientation. Some panels do require orientation and usually are marked with arrows on the back side. Keep the arrows pointing in the same direction.

13. If translucent plastic lighting panels are to be installed, the panels should be cut by scoring repeatedly with a sharp tool until the panel is completely cut through. Lay in the panel with the glossy side up.

14. If recessed light panels are to be dropped into the grid, each corner of the light fixture must be supported by a suspension wire.

15. If fluorescent lighting fixtures are used above the grid, the light tubes should be centered over the translucent panel. The lighting efficiency will be improved if the sides and ends of the fixtures are enclosed with foil or wood painted a highly reflective white.

# Chapter 18

# CABINETS AND JOINERY

## Prefabricated Kitchen Cabinets

The modern kitchen cabinet is perhaps the most frequently used built-in feature of a house. The planning should be carefully done so the working spaces will be convenient and the right size, and so the storage space will be adequate. There is a tendency to standardize some of the most important dimensions and consequently the planning has become easier. Figure 18-1 shows the front and end views of a typical kitchen cabinet. The front view shows the arrangement of the drawers and doors. The end view shows the heights and depths.

The counter shelf is generally 36 inches high and 25 inches deep. These dimensions provide adequate working space at the most convenient height for the average person. A counter 36 inches high matches the height of most stoves and also brings a built-in sink to the correct height. Drawers are provided directly under the counter shelf for the more frequently used utensils. There are large cupboards underneath with shelves concealed by doors. At the bottom of the cabinet, a 3" x 3" recess is made to provide toe room for a person working at the counter shelf.

The wall cabinet is generally a separate unit fastened to the wall. This cabinet varies from 8 to 14 inches deep and from 30 to 36 inches high. It contains shelves from 8 to 12 inches apart for the storage of dishes. Hinged doors arranged to correspond to the doors of the lower cabinet enclose the shelves. In the section view of figure 18-1, this wall case is shown to contain three shelves. The uppermost shelf should be within seven feet of the floor so it will be within convenient reach. If the ceilings are high, it is necessary to provide a curtain wall to fill the space from the top of the wall cabinet to the ceiling. This wall encloses a space which is sometimes used to house a light over the sink, or electric outlets for a clock or exhaust fan. Many modern kitchens have a drop ceiling which meets the top of the cabinets.

The work space between the top of the counter shelf and the bottom of the wall cabinet should be no less than 14 inches. This is especially true if the wall cabinet is over 12 inches deep and there is a possibility of striking the head against it while working at the counter shelf.

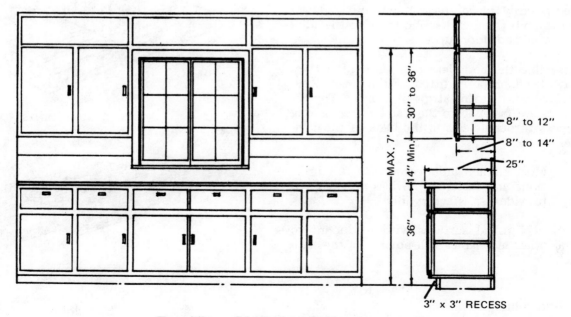

Two Views Of Kitchen Cabinets
Figure 18-1

The framing materials of the cabinet are generally a good grade of soft pine or white wood suitable for painting. The shelves of the upper and lower cabinets are often plywood. The counter shelf, doors, parts of the drawers and the sides of the cabinets are usually made of plywood. The sides, bottom and back of the drawers may also be made of plywood. The drawer front is made of solid stock. If plywood is used for doors. Surface hinges must be used because butt hinges will not hold well on the edges of plywood. Hardware should not be applied until after the cabinets have been painted.

Many types of prefabricated cabinets are obtainable in knocked down or assembled form. They are made in units of standard sizes which may be arranged to fit almost any kitchen layout. It is necessary, however, to decide before the house plans are made whether assembled units are to be obtained from the factory or they are to be built in by the carpenter. Factory built cabinets are often superior to those made by the carpenter.

## How To Install A Prefabricated Kitchen Cabinet

1.  Mark the locations of the studs in the walls where the cabinets are to be fastened.

2.  Inspect the backs of the cabinet units to judge the furring needed or to determine how the manufacturer's directions for installation can be carried out.

3.  Temporarily place the cabinet units. Level and plumb them and scribe them to the adjacent wall and floor surfaces.

4.  Assemble the complete base units after they have been properly fitted. Shim them if necessary with furring strips or braces. The cabinets are fastened to the wall by driving long screws through cleats in the back of the cabinet.

*NOTE:*  Most kitchen units come with full directions and fastening devices necessary to provide a satisfactory job.

5.  Protect finished surfaces with cardboard so that other mechanics will not injure the cabinet.

## Joints And Joining

The basic skill in all cabinetmaking is the art of joining pieces of wood to form tight, strong, well made joints. Simple joints like the butt joint (figure 18-2), the lap joints (figure 18-3), and the miter joints (figure 18-3) are used mostly in rough or finish carpentry, though they may also be used occasionally in millwork and furniture making. More complex joints like the rabbet joints (figure 18-5), the dado and gain joints (figure 18-6), the mortise-and-tenon and slip tenon joints (figure 18-7), the box corner joint (figure 18-8), and the dovetail joints (figure 18-9) are used mostly in furniture, cabinets, and millwork. Of the edge joints shown in figure 18-2A, the dowel and spline are used mainly in furniture and cabinet work, while the plain butt and the tongue-and-groove, are used in practically all types of woodworking.

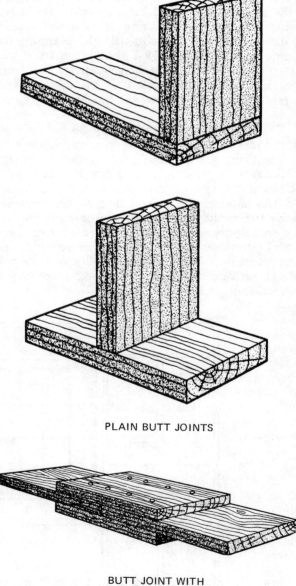

PLAIN BUTT JOINTS

BUTT JOINT WITH
FISH PLATES

Butt Joints
Figure 18-2

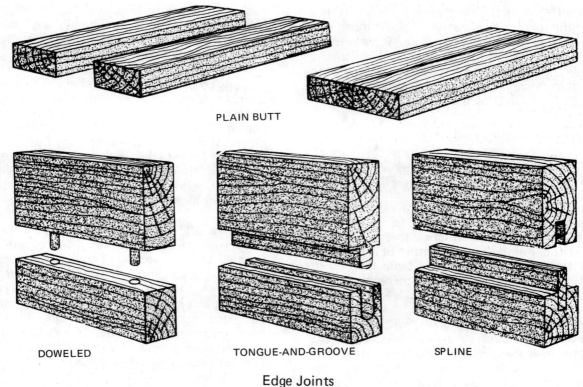

PLAIN BUTT

DOWELED          TONGUE-AND-GROOVE          SPLINE

Edge Joints
Figure 18-2A

The joints used in rough and finish carpentry are for the most part simply nailed together. Nails in a 90 degree plain butt joint may be driven through the member abutted against and into the end of the abutting member, or they may be toe-nailed at an angle through the faces of the abutting member into the face of the member abutted a-gainst.

The more complex furniture and cabinet-making joints are usually fastened with glue, with additional strength provided as necessary by dowels, splines, corrugated fasteners, slip feathers, keys, and other types of joint fasteners. In the dado joint, the gain joint, the mortise-and-tenon joint, the box corner joint, and the dovetail joint the interlocking character of the joint is an additional factor in fastening.

The two pieces which are to be joined to-gether are called members, and the two major steps in joining are the layout of the joint on the ends, edges, or faces of the members, and the cut-ting of the members to the required shapes for joining.

The chief instruments for laying out joints are the try, miter, combination square, sliding T-bevel; the marking or mortising gage; and a scratch awl, sharp pencil or knife for scoring lines. For cutting the more complex joints by hand, the backsaw, dovetail saw, and various chisels are essential, and the rabbet-and-fillister plane (for rabbet joints) and the router plane (for smoothing the bottoms of dados and gains) are very helpful.

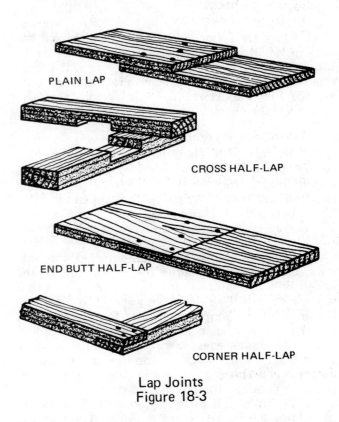

PLAIN LAP

CROSS HALF-LAP

END BUTT HALF-LAP

CORNER HALF-LAP

Lap Joints
Figure 18-3

With the possible exception of the dovetail joint, all the joints which have been mentioned can be cut either by hand or by machine. Whatever the method used and whatever the type of joint, always remember the following important rule: To ensure a tight joint, always cut on the waste side of the line, never on the line itself.

## Half-Lap Joints (Figure 18-3)

For half-lap joints the members to be joined are usually of the same thickness. The method of laying out and cutting an end-butt half-lap or a corner half-lap is as follows: for the end butt half-lap, measure off the desired amount of lap from the end of each member and square a line all the way around at this point. For the corner half-lap, measure off the width of a member from the end of each member and square a line all the way around. These lines are called shoulder lines.

Next, select the best wide surface of each member and place it upward. Call this surface the face of the member, call the opposite surface the back. Set the marking gage to one half the thickness and score a line (called the cheek line) on the edges and end of each member from the shoulder line on one edge to the shoulder line on the opposite edge. Be sure and gage the cheek line from the face of each member. The reason for this is that, if you gage from both faces, the faces will come flush after the joint is cut, regardless of whether or not the gage was set to exactly one half the thickness. Too much waste cut from one member will be offset by less cut from the other. On the other hand, if you gage from the face of one member and the back of the other and the gage happens to be set to more or less than one half the thickness, the faces will be out of flush by the amount of the error. A rule of first importance for half-lap joints is: Always gage the cheek line from the face of the member.

Next make the shoulder cuts by sawing along the shoulder line down to the waste side of the cheek line, sawing from the back of the lapping member and from the face of the lapped member. Use a bench hook if possible; if not, clamp a piece of wood along the starting groove to steady the saw.

The cheek cuts (sometimes called the side cuts) are made next, along the waste side of the cheek line. Clamp the member in the vise so that it leans diagonally away from you. With the member in this position you can see the end and the upper edge, and when the saw reaches the shoulder line on the upper edge, it will still be some distance away from the shoulder line on the edge you can't see. Reverse the member in the vise and saw exactly to the shoulder line on that edge.

Completing the shoulder cut will detach the waste. When both shoulder cuts have been made, the members should fit together with faces, ends, and edges flush, or near enough to it to be brought flush by a little paring with the chisel.

A cross half-lap joint between members of equal cross-section dimensions is laid out and cut as follows: if the members are of the same length and they are to lap each other at the midpoint, place them face-to-face with ends flush, and square a center line all the way around. To test the accuracy of the center calculation, reverse one of the members end-for-end. If the center lines still meet, the center location is correct.

Lay off one half the width of a member on either side of the center lines and square shoulder lines all the way around. Again check for accuracy by reversing a member end-for-end. If the shoulder lines meet, the layout is accurate. Next, gage one half the thickness of a member from the face of each member and score cheek lines on the edges, between the shoulder lines. Next make the shoulder cuts, sawing from the back of the lapping member and from the face of the lapped member.

In this type of joint the waste must be chiseled out rather than sawed out. To make the work of chiseling easier, remove as much stock as possible with the saw first by sawing a series of kerfs between the shoulder cuts. In chiseling, make a roughing cut first, down to just above the cheek line, with a firmer chisel and mallet, holding the chisel bevel down. Then finish off the bottom with a paring chisel, holding the chisel bevel up. For fine work, smooth the bottom with a router plane if you have one.

End butt half-lap and corner half-lap joints are known generally as end half-lap, as distinguished from cross half-lap joints. A third type of half-lap joint is the so called middle half-lap joint, in which the end of one member is half-lapped to the other member at a point other than the end. In this joint the end of the lapping member is recessed as it would be for an end half-lap joint, while the lapped member is recessed as it would be for a cross half-lap joint.

End half-lap joints may be cut with the circular saw by the method described later for cutting tenons. Equipped with the dado head, the circular saw can be used to cut both end half-lap recesses and cross half-lap recesses. For an end half-lap recess, proceed as follows: set the dado head to protrude above the table a distance equal to one half the thickness of a member, and adjust the fence so that when the end of the member bears against it the dado head will cut on the waste side of the shoulder line. Place the member against the universal gage. Set at 90 degrees to the fence, and make the shoulder cut. Then take out the remaining waste by making as many recuts as necessary, each made with the member moved a little less than the thickness of the dado head to the left.

For a cross half-lap recess, proceed as follows: set the dado head so that its height above the table is equal to one half the thickness of a member, and adjust the ripping fence so that when the end of the member is placed against it the dado head will cut on the waste side of the left hand shoulder line. Make the shoulder cut. Then reverse the piece end for end and repeat the same procedure to make the opposite shoulder cut. Take out the remaining waste between the shoulder cuts by making as many recuts as necessary, each made with the member moved a little less than the thickness of the dado head to the left.

Members can be end mitered to 45 degrees in the wooden miter box and to any angle in the steel miter box (by setting the saw to the desired angle) or on the circular saw (by setting the universal gage to the desired angle). Members can be edge mitered to any angle on the circular saw, by tilting the saw to the required angle. Sawed edges are unsuitable for gluing, however, and, if the joint is to be glued, the edges should be mitered on a jointer.

Since abutting surfaces of end-mitered members do not hold well when they are merely glued, they must usually be reinforced. One type of reinforcement is the corrugated fastener, a corrugated strip of metal with one edge sharpened for driving into the joint. The fastener is placed at a right angle to the line between the members, half on one

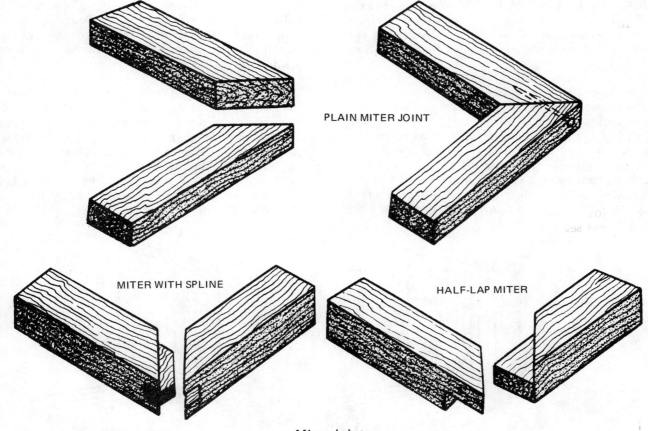

PLAIN MITER JOINT

MITER WITH SPLINE

HALF-LAP MITER

**Miter Joints (Figure 18-4)**

Miter Joints
Figure 18-4

A miter joint is made by mitering (cutting at an angle) the ends or edges of the members which are to be joined together. The angle of the miter cut is one half of the angle which will be formed by the joined members. For members which will form an equal sided figure with other than 4 sides (such as an octagon or a pentagon), the correct mitering angle can be found by dividing the number of sides the figure will have into 180 and subtracting the result from 90. For an octagon (8 sided figure), the mitering angle is 90 minus 180/8, or 67½ degrees. For a pentagon (5 sided figure) the angle is 90 minus 180/5, or 54 degrees.

member and half on the other, and driven down flush with the members.

The corrugated fastener mars the appearance of the surface into which it is driven, and it is therefore used only on the backs of picture frames and the like. A more satisfactory type of fastener for a joint between end-mitered members is the slip feather, a thin piece of wood or veneer which is glued into a kerf cut in the thickness dimension of the joint. Saw about half way through from the outer to the inner corner, apply glue to both sides

Rabbet Joints
Figure 18-5

of the slip feather, and push the slip feather into the kerf. Clamp tight with a clamp and allow the glue to dry. After it has dried, remove the clamp and chisel off the protruding portion of the slip feather.

A joint between edge mitered members may be reinforced with a spline, a thin piece of wood which extends across the joint into grooves cut in the abutting surfaces. A spline for a plain butt edge joint is shown in figure 18-4. The groove for a spline can be cut by hand, by laying out the outline of the groove, removing the major part of the waste by boring a series of holes with a bit of suitable size, and smoothing with a mortising chisel. The best way to cut a groove, however, is on the circular saw.

A two sided recess running along an edge is called a rabbet (figure 18-5). Dados, gains, and rabbets are not, strictly speaking, grooves, but joints which include them are generally called grooved joints.

Grooves on edges and grooves on faces of comparatively narrow stock can be cut by hand with the plow plane. The matching plane will cut a groove on the edge of one piece and a tongue to match it on the edge of another. A dado can be cut by hand with the backsaw and chisel by the same method used to cut a cross half-lap joint by hand. Rabbets on short ends or edges can be sawed out by hand with the backsaw.

DADO JOINT

GAIN JOINT

Dado And Gain Joints
Figure 18-6

### Groove And Rabbet Joints (Figure 18-5)

A groove is a three sided recess running with the grain. A similar recess running across the grain is called a dado. A groove or dado which does not extend all the way across the piece is called a stopped groove or a stopped dado. A stopped dado is also known as a gain (figure 18-6).

A long rabbet can be cut by hand with the rabbet-and-fillister plane as follows: first be sure that the side of the plane iron is exactly in line with the machined side of the plane; then set the width and depth gages to the desired width and depth of rabbet. Be sure to measure the depth from the edge of the plane iron, not from the sole of the plane. If you measure from the sole of the plane, the rabbet will be too deep by the amount that the edge of the iron extends below the sole of the plane. Clamp the pieces in the vise, hold the plane exactly perpendicular, press the width gage against the face of the board, and plane down with even, careful strokes until the depth gage prevents any further planing.

A groove or dado can be cut on the circular saw as follows: lay out the groove or dado on the end wood (for a groove) or edge wood (for a dado) which will first contact the saw. Set the saw to the desired depth of the groove above the table, and set the fence at a distance from the saw which will cause the first cut to run on the waste side of the line that indicates the left side of the groove. Start that saw and bring the piece into light contact with it; then stop the saw and examine the layout to ensure that the cut will be on the waste side of the line. Readjust the fence if necessary. When the position of the fence is right, make the cut. Then reverse the piece and proceed to set and test as before for the cut on the opposite side of the groove. Then make as many recuts as are necessary to remove the waste stock between the side kerfs.

The procedure for grooving or dadoing with the dado head is about the same, except that in many cases the dado head can be built up so as to take out all the waste in a single cut. The two outside cutters alone will cut a groove ¼ inch wide. Inside cutters vary in thickness from 1/16 to ¼ inch.

A stopped groove or stopped dado can be cut on the circular saw, using either a saw blade or a dado head, as follows: if the groove or dado is stopped at only one end, clamp a stop block to the rear of the table in a position that will stop the piece from being fed any further when the saw has reached the place where the groove or dado is supposed to stop. If the groove or dado is stopped at both ends, clamp a stop block to the rear of the table and a starting block to the front. The starting block should be placed so that the saw will contact the place where the groove is supposed to start when the infeed end of the piece is against the block. Start the cut by holding the piece above the saw with the infeed and against the starting block and the edge against the fence. Then lower the piece gradually onto the saw, and feed it through to the stop block.

A rabbet can be cut on the circular saw as follows: the cut into the face of the piece is called the shoulder cut and the cut into the edge or end the cheek cut. To make the shoulder cut (which should be made first), set the saw to extend above the table a distance equal to the desired depth of the shoulder, and set the fence a distance away from the saw equal to the desired depth of the cheek. Be sure to measure this distance from a saw tooth set to the left, or away from the ripping fence. If

you measure it from a tooth set to the right, or toward the fence, the cheek will be too deep by an amount equal to the width of the saw kerf.

Make the shoulder cut first. Then place the face of the piece which was down for the shoulder cut against the fence and make the cheek cut. If the depth of the shoulder and the depth of the cheek are the same, the cheek cut will be made with the saw at the same height as for the shoulder cut. If the depth of the cheek is different, the height of the saw will have to be changed to conform before the cheek cut is made.

By using the dado head you can cut most ordinary rabbets in a single cut. First build up a dado head equal in thickness to the desired width of the cheek. Next set the head to protrude above the table a distance equal to the desired depth of the shoulder. Clamp a 1 inch board to the fence to serve as a guide for the piece, and set the fence so that the edge of the board barely contacts the right side of the dado head. Set the piece against the universal gage (set at 90 degrees, of course), hold the edge or end to be rabbeted against the 1 inch board, and make the cut.

On some jointers a rabbeting strip on the outboard edge of the outfeed table can be depressed for rabbeting. The strip is outboard of the end of the cutterhead. To rabbet on a jointer of this type, you depress the infeed table and the rabbeting strip the depth of the rabbet below the outfeed table, and set the fence the width of the rabbet away from the outboard end of the cutterhead. When the piece is fed through, the unrabbeted part feeds onto the rabbeting strip.

Some jointers are equipped with a rabbeting arm. The rabbeting arm is bolted to the infeed table and moves up and down with it. To rabbet on a jointer of this type, you depress the infeed table the depth of the rabbet below the outfeed table and set the fence the width of the rabbet away from the outboard end of the cutterhead. The rabbeted part of the piece feeds onto the outfeed table, and the unrabbeted part feeds onto the section of the rabbeting arm that extends beyond the cutterhead.

Various combinations of the grooved joints are used in woodworking. The well known tongue-and-groove joint is actually a combination of the groove and the rabbet, the tongued member simply being a member which is rabbeted on both faces. In some types of panel work the tongue is made by rabbeting only one face; a tongue of this kind is called a barefaced tongue. A joint often used in making boxes, drawers, cabinets and the like is the dado and rabbet joint shown in figure 18-11. As you can see, one of the members here is rabbeted on one face to form a barefaced tongue.

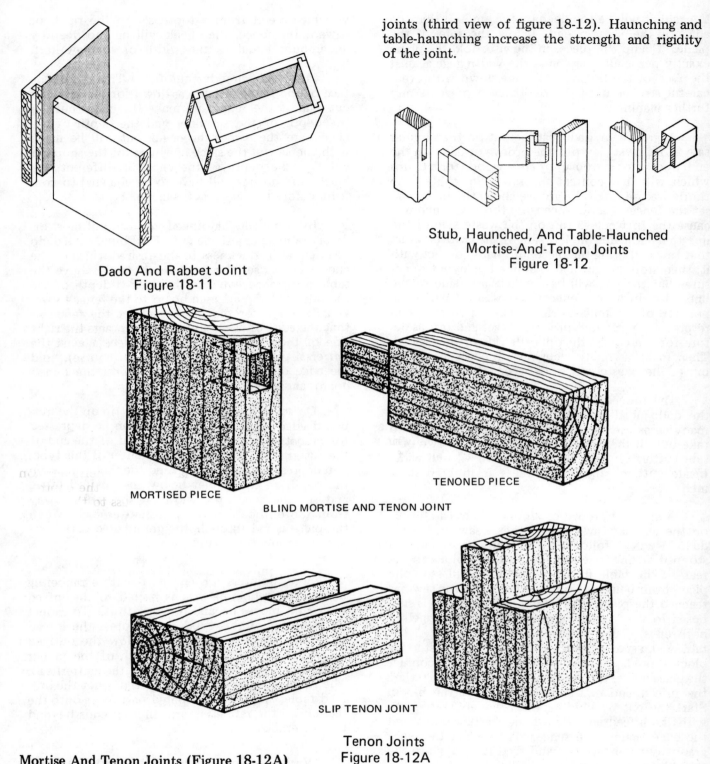

joints (third view of figure 18-12). Haunching and table-haunching increase the strength and rigidity of the joint.

Dado And Rabbet Joint
Figure 18-11

Stub, Haunched, And Table-Haunched
Mortise-And-Tenon Joints
Figure 18-12

MORTISED PIECE

TENONED PIECE

BLIND MORTISE AND TENON JOINT

SLIP TENON JOINT

Tenon Joints
Figure 18-12A

## Mortise And Tenon Joints (Figure 18-12A)

The mortise-and-tenon joint is the most important and most frequently used of the joints used in furniture and cabinet work. In the blind mortise-and-tenon joint, the tenon does not penetrate all the way through the mortised member. A joint in which the tenon does penetrate all the way through is a through mortise-and-tenon joint. Besides the ordinary stub joint (figure 18-12A, top and the first view of figure 18-12), there are haunched joints (second view of figure 18-12) and table-haunched

The layout procedure for an ordinary stub mortise-and-tenon joint is as follows: mark the faces of the members plainly. Lay off from the end of the tenon member the desired length of the tenon, and square the shoulder line all the way around. Then lay off the total width of the tenon member on the mortise member as shown in figure 18-13.

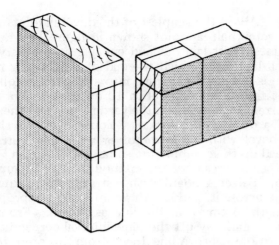

Layout Of Stub Mortise-And-Tenon Joint
Figure 18-13

Determine the thickness of the tenon, which is usually between one-third and one-half of the thickness of the mortise member, and set the points on the mortising gage to this dimension. Adjust the block so that the points will score a double line on the center of the tenon member, as shown in figure 18-13. If the faces of the members are to be flush, use the same gage setting to score a double line on the mortise member, remembering to gage from the face of the member. If the face of the tenon member is to be set back from the face of the mortise member (as is often the case with table rails and the like), the mortising gage setting must be increased by the amount of the set back. Remember, however, that the setting of the points remains the same. Last, lay off from the end of the mortise member and from the appropriate edge of the tenon member the amount of end stock which is to be left above the mortise, as indicated also in figure 18-13, and square lines as shown. For a slip tenon joint like the one shown in figure 18-12A you wouldn't need this last phase of the layout.

Tenons can be cut by hand with the backsaw, by the same method previously described for cutting corner and end half-lap joints. Mortises can be cut by hand with the mortising chisel. As in the case of a spline groove cut by hand, you can remove the major part of the waste by boring a series of holes with a drill of diameter slightly smaller than the width of the mortise. For a blind mortise-and-tenon joint use a depth gage or a wooden block to prevent the drill from boring below the correct depth of the mortise.

Tenons can be cut with the circular saw as follows: to make the shoulder cuts, set the saw the depth of the shoulder above the table and set the ripping fence the length of the tenon away from the saw. Remember to measure from a saw-tooth set to the left.

Set the saw the depth of the cheek above the table, set the fence the width of the shoulder away from the saw, and make the cheek cuts. To maintain the stock upright, use a push board.

Tenons can be cut with the dado head by the same method previously described for cutting end half-lap joints. Mortises are cut mechanically on a hollow-chisel mortising machine. The cutting mechanism on this machine consists of a boring bit encased in a square, hollow steel chisel. As the mechanism is pressed into the wood, the bit takes out most of the waste while the chisel pares the sides of the mortise square. Chisels come in various sizes, with corresponding sizes of bits to match.

The procedure for cutting a mortise on the machine is as follows: install a chisel and bit of the proper size, making sure that the rear edge of the chisel is exactly parallel to the fence on the machine. Place the piece to be mortised against the fence, clamp it to the table, and adjust the position of the table to bring one end of the mortise layout exactly under the chisel. Start the machine, and press down the foot pedal to make a cut to about one-half the depth of the mortise. If you go too deep on the first cut, the cutter may bind in the wood, causing overheating and making extraction difficult. Extract the cutter by releasing the foot pedal, move the table the required distance to the left by operating the large table lateral motion handwheel, and again cut to one-half the depth of the mortise. Continue this process to the end of the mortise; then work the other way, cutting, this time, to the full depth of the mortise.

In some mortise-and-tenon joints, such as those between rails and legs in tables, the tenon member is much thinner than the mortise member. Sometimes a member of this kind is too thin to shape in the customary manner, with shoulder cuts on both faces. When this is the case a barefaced mortise-and-tenon joint may be used. In a bare-faced joint the tenon member is shoulder cut on one side only. The cheek on the opposite side is simply a continuation of the face of the member.

Mortise-and-tenon joints are fastened with glue, and with additional fasteners as required. One or more wood or metal dowels may be driven through the joint. A through mortise-and-tenon joint may be fastened by sawing kerfs in the tenon and driving wedges into the kerfs after the joint is assembled, so as to jam the tenon tightly in the mortise. In a keyed mortise-and-tenon joint the tenon extends some distance beyond the mortised member. The extending part contains a keyway, into which a tapered key is driven. The key jams against the mortised member so as to hold the joint tightly together.

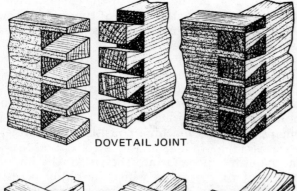

DOVETAIL JOINT

THROUGH SINGLE
DOVETAIL

BLIND SINGLE
DOVETAIL

THROUGH HALF-LAP
SINGLE DOVETAIL

Dovetail Joints
Figure 18-13A

## Dovetail Joints (Figure 18-13A)

The dovetail joint is the strongest of all the woodworking joints. It requires a good bit of labor, however, and is therefore used only for the finer grades of furniture and cabinet work, where it is used principally for joining sides and ends of drawers.

In the dovetail joint one or more pins on the pin member fit tightly into the openings between two or more tails (or, in the case of a single dovetail joint, between two half-tails) on the tail member. A joint containing only a single pin is called a single dovetail joint; a joint containing two or more pins is called a multiple dovetail joint. A joint in which the pins pass all the way through the tail member is a through dovetail joint. A joint in which they pass only part way through is a blind dovetail joint.

About the simplest of the dovetail joints is the dovetail half-lap joint shown in figure 18-14. This joint is first laid out and cut like an ordinary end half-lap, after which the end of the lapping member is laid out for shaping into a dovetail as follows: set the sliding T-bevel to 10 degrees, which is the correct angle between the vertical axis and the sides of a dovetail pin or tail. You can set the sliding T-bevel with a protractor or with the protractor head on the combination square. If you don't have either of these, use the method shown in figure 18-15. Select a board with a straight edge, square a line across it, and lay off an interval of appropriate length, 6 times on the line as shown. From the sixth mark lay off the same interval perpendicularly to the right. A line drawn from this point to the starting point of the first line drawn will form a 10 degree angle with that line.

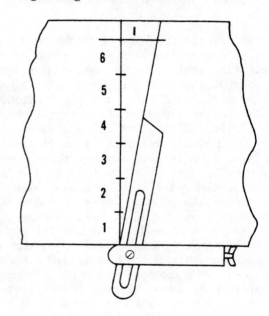

Laying Off 10 Degree Angle For Dovetail Joint
Figure 18-15

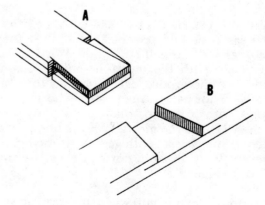

Making A Dovetail Half-Lap Joint
Figure 18-16

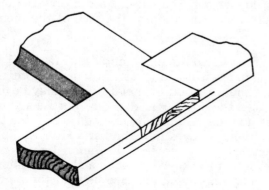

Dovetail Half-Lap Joint
Figure 18-14

Lay off this angle from the end corners of the lapping member to the shoulder line, as shown in figure 18-16, and saw out the waste as indicated. The lapping member now has a dovetail on it. Place this dovetail over the other member, in the position it is supposed to occupy, and score the outline of the recess. Then saw and chisel out the recess, remembering to saw on the waste side of the lines.

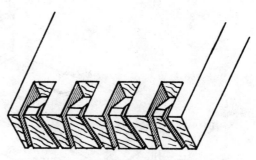

Chiseling Out Waste In A Through-
Multiple-Dovetail Joint
Figure 18-18

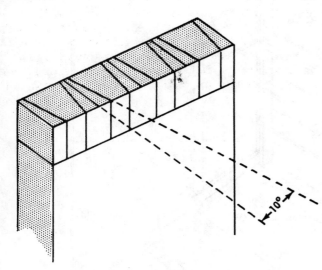

Laying Out Pin Member For Through-
Multiple-Dovetail Joint
Figure 18-17

For a through multiple dovetail joint, the end of the tail member is laid out for cutting as shown in figure 18-17. A joint in which the pins and tails are the same size is the strongest type of dovetail, but for ease in cutting, the pins are usually made somewhat smaller than the tails, as shown. Determine the appropriate number of pins and the size you want to make each pin. Lay off a half-pin from each edge of the member, and then locate the center lines of the other pins at equal intervals across the end of the piece. Lay off the outlines of the pins at 10 degrees to the center lines, as indicated. Then measure back from the end of the member a distance equal to the thickness of the tail member, and square a line all the way around. This line indicates the bottoms of the openings between the pins.

Cut out the pins by sawing on the waste sides of the lines and then chiseling out the waste. Chisel half-way through from one side, as shown in figure 18-18; then turn the member over and chisel through from the other side.

When you have finished cutting out the pins, lay the tail member flat and set the ends of the pins in exactly the position they are to occupy. Score the outlines of the pins, which will, of course, also

be the outlines of the tails. Square lines across the end of the tail member, and saw and chisel out the waste between the tails just as you did the waste between the pins.

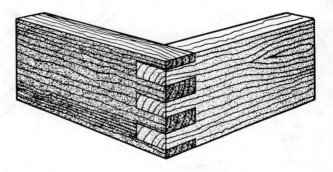

Box Corner Joint
Figure 18-18A

## Box Corner Joints (Figure 18-18A)

With the exception of the obvious difference in the layout, the box corner joint is made in just about the same manner as the through-multiple-dovetail joint.

## How To Build A Base Cabinet (Figure 18-19)

The cabinets should be made of lumber and plywood that will hold its shape, may be cleaned easily, and will endure constant wear. They should be laid out so that the drawers and cupboards are conveniently located for the efficient preparation of food. They should be assembled with care using sound craftsmanship so that all joints are firm and square, drawers slide easily and doors close square and snug.

1.  Lay out a complete floor plan of the cabinet on the floor of the kitchen.

2.  Lay out the back elevation on the back wall and the end elevations on the end walls.

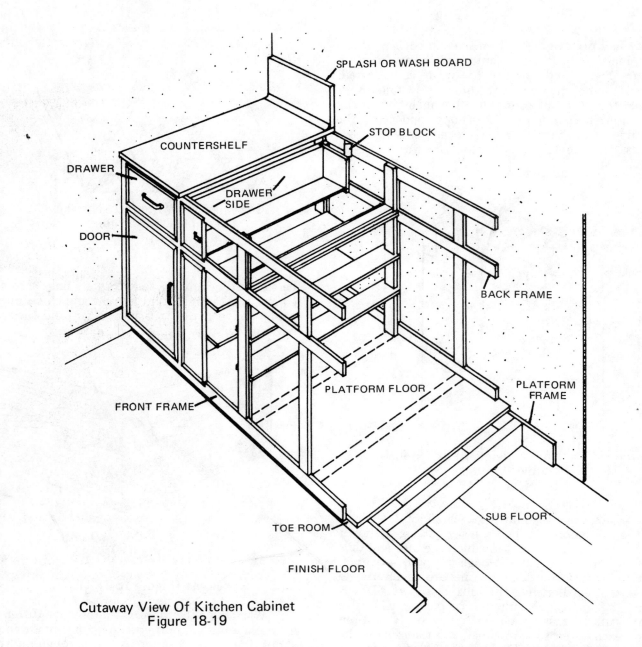

COUNTERSHELF

SPLASH OR WASH BOARD

DRAWER

STOP BLOCK

DRAWER SIDE

DOOR

BACK FRAME

PLATFORM FLOOR

PLATFORM FRAME

FRONT FRAME

SUB FLOOR

TOE ROOM

FINISH FLOOR

Cutaway View Of Kitchen Cabinet
Figure 18-19

*NOTE:* The front stile and rail framework may be laid out from the plan and assembled on the work bench. The stiles and rails may be 25/32 inch thick by about 2¾ inches wide. This width may have to be altered to accommodate standard size cupboard doors. All connecting joints should be put together with half lap or mortise and tenon joints. They should be glued, clamped and screwed together from the back of the frame. Figure 18-20 shows this framework.

The full length of these stiles according to figure 18-1 would be 36 inches minus 1 inch for the counter shelf and 3 inches for the toe space, or 32 inches.

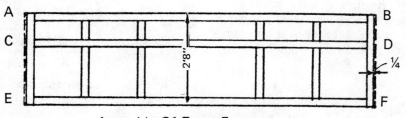

Assembly Of Front Frames
Figure 18-20

3. Lay out the rails AB, CD and EF, figure 18-20, so that they are continuous the full length of the cabinet. Allow ¼ inch on each end so that the stiles and rails may be scribed to the walls. Locate the joints for the stiles on the rails.

4. Lay out the stiles to length AE and locate the position of the rails AB, CD and EF.

5. Half lap or mortise the joints.

6. Assemble and square the front framework.

7. Make a duplicate frame for the back of the cabinet.

## How To Build The Bottom Platform

*NOTE:* The top of the bottom platform is 3 inches above the finished floor. Therefore it will be approximately 4 inches above the subfloor.

1. Lay out and cut seven 2 x 4's to 19½ inches long.

2. Lay out and cut two pieces 25/32" x 3 5/8" by the length of the front frame minus ½ inch. Mark the location of the centers of the stiles of the front framework on these pieces.

3. Center the 2 x 4's on these marks and nail the front and back pieces to the ends of these 2 x 4's with 8d finishing nails. Keep all pieces flush with the top of the 2 x 4's. See figure 18-21.

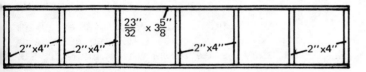

Assembly Of The Platform
Figure 18-21

4. Square the frame and place it on the layout on the floor and against the back and end walls.

5. Level it and toenail it to the floor.

6. Cover the platform with the shelving material. Plywood ½ inch thick is ideal for the purpose. Allow this material to project 2 inches over the front edge of the platform frame.

*NOTE:* Rip the thickness of the platform floor off of the bottom rail of the back frame so that the tops of the front and back frames will be the same height.

7. Place the back framework on top of the platform and against the wall. Level and plumb it and nail it to the walls.

8. Place the front frame in a similar manner but against the front edge and flush with the bottom side of the platform floor. Plumb and brace it to the back frame. See figure 18-22.

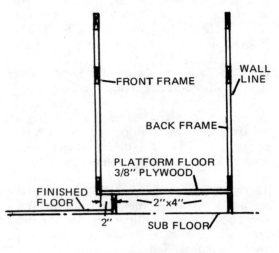

Assembly Of Frames
Figure 18-22

9. Lay out and cut twelve pieces of 25/32 inch stock the same width as the front stiles and long enough to reach from the top of the platform floor to the top of the front framework. In this case, if ½ inch plywood is used for the platform floor, the length will be approximately 31 inches.

10. Place one piece on top of the platform and against the front framework. On this piece mark the location of the top of the rail CD, figure 18-20 and the bottom of the rail AB. Also make a mark 9½ inches below the top of the rail CD. See figure 18-23.

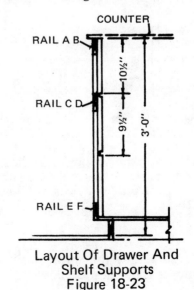

Layout Of Drawer And
Shelf Supports
Figure 18-23

11. Lay out a 25/32 inch dado 3/8 inch deep at these locations and as shown by the dado joints in figure 18-23. Mark the eleven remaining boards in the same way and cut the dado joints.

12. Square and cut twelve pieces of 25/32 inch stock 2 inches wider than the dadoed pieces and long enough to reach from the front to the back frames. Allow for the dado cuts. The length in this case will be approximately 22¾ inches.

*NOTE:* Be sure the front and back frames are plumb before getting this length.

13. Assemble four frames as shown in figure 18-24 by gluing and nailing the pieces A into the dado joints. Let the pieces project 1 inch on each side of the dadoed pieces.

14. Lay out and assemble two more frames in a similar manner. One frame is for the right hand end of the cabinet and one for the left end. Assemble the drawer and shelf supports such as shown in A, figure 18-24. These should be flush with the upright B on the right hand side of the frame for the right end, and flush with the left hand side of the frame for the left end of the cabinet.

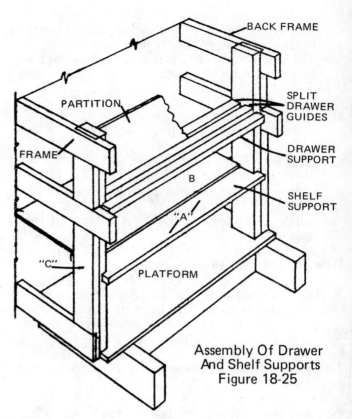

Assembly Of Drawer
And Shelf Supports
Figure 18-25

16. Lay out, cut and fit the lower shelf as at B, figure 18-25. Fasten it to the top of the shelf support A.

*NOTE:* It may be convenient to fit this shelf in the full length of the cabinet in sections and to screw them in place. This method makes it easier to fit and also to remove the shelf for cleaning. Plywood stock is best for shelves.

17. Cut the required number of drawer guides from stock 25/32 inch thick and as wide as the frames stiles as shown in figure 18-26.

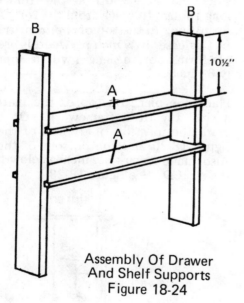

Assembly Of Drawer
And Shelf Supports
Figure 18-24

15. Screw the upright supports (B, figure 18-24) in place from the inside and opposite each upright in the front and back frames. See C, figure 18-25.

*NOTE:* Be sure that the upper surfaces of the drawer slides are square with the face of the front frame and that they are level.

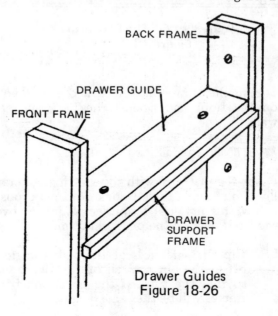

Drawer Guides
Figure 18-26

170

18. Fasten them temporarily with screws to the top of the drawer supports in both sides of the openings where drawers are to be fitted.

## How To Lay Out And Build Drawers

1. Square up either 25/32 inch solid stock or 5/8 inch 5 ply plywood for the drawer sides. Make these sides 1/8 inch narrower than the height of the drawer opening and 2 inches shorter than the length of this opening.

*NOTE:* Drawers may be constructed so that the front will fit flush with the front of the cabinet or they may be lipped. Figure 18-27 shows these two types.

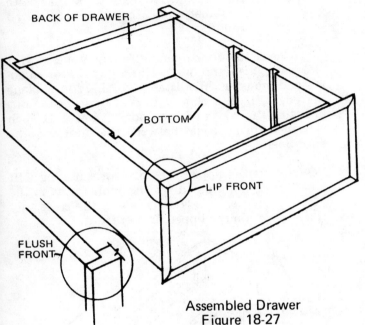

Assembled Drawer
Figure 18-27

2. Lay out two drawer sides as shown in figure 18-28. Be sure to make one right side and one left side.

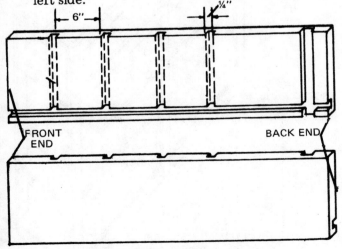

Layout Of Drawer Sides
Figure 18-28

*NOTE:* The groove for the bottom should be about ¼ inch deep and 1 1/16 inches wider than the thickness of the drawer bottom stock. It should be at least ½ inch from the edge.

The dado for the drawer back should also be ¼ inch deep, as wide as the back is thick and at least ¾ inch from the back end. Dadoes may also be cut about 6 inches apart on both sides of the drawers, so that partitions may be temporarily placed to form small compartments in the drawers. See the dotted lines in figure 18-28.

3. Square up the drawer front to the correct size from 25/32 inch or 1 1/16 inch stock.

*NOTE:* The height of the drawer front is the same as the height of the sides plus ¾ inch for the two lips. The length of the drawer front is the same as the width of the opening plus ¾ inch for the two lips.

4. Lay out and cut the rabbets around the four sides of the drawer front as shown in figure 18-29.

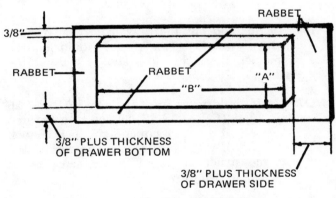

Back Of Drawer Front
Figure 18-29

*NOTE:* The distance A, figure 18-29, should be the same as the distance from the top of the groove in the drawer side to the top edge of this side. Note that the rabbet along the bottom edge of the drawer front is wider than the one along the top edge. The distance B between the two end rabbets of the drawer front should be such that the finishing drawer will be 1/8 inch narrower than the opening.

5. Round the four edges of the drawer front as shown in figure 18-27.

*NOTE:* If an electric table saw is available, the drawer side may be joined to the front as shown in figure 18-30. This forms a strong joint but it must be very accurately made.

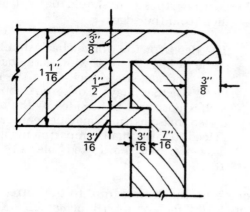

Drawer Lock Joint
Figure 18-30

6. Lay out and cut the drawer back from material the same thickness as the drawer sides.

NOTE: The height of the drawer back should be the same as the distance A, figure 18-29. The length of the drawer back should be the same as the inside width of the drawer (B, figure 18-29) plus the depth of the dado on each drawer side.

7. Lay out and cut the drawer bottom from ¼ inch plywood. This piece should be the same length as the sides and as wide as the back piece is long.

NOTE: If the drawer front is to be of the flush type (figure 18-27), it may be squared and fitted to the opening with 1/16 inch allowance on all sides. The rest of the construction would be the same as for the lipped drawer.

8. Glue the back into the dadoes in the sides. Keep the top edge of the back flush with the top edge of the sides. Drive 1½ inch brads through the sides part way into the back. See figure 18-27.

9. Glue and nail the sides to the front. Keep the top edges of the sides flush with the top rabbet of the drawer front.

10. Slide the bottom into the side grooves. Do not force it as it may spread the joints.

11. Square the drawer and nail the bottom to the lower edge of the back and to the bottom of the front.

12. Finish driving the nails into the back and front from the sides and sand the rough edges of the drawer. Set the nails.

13. Fit the drawer into the opening and adjust the guides so the drawer will slide easily. Be sure the drawer front lips fit squarely against the front of the cabinet.

NOTE: Thumb tacks are sometimes inserted in the wearing surfaces of the drawer supports and guides to make the drawer operate more smoothly.

14. Fit and secure blocks at the back of each drawer opening to stop the drawer front lips from striking the front frame too hard when the drawer is being closed.

### How To Fit Cabinet Doors

NOTE: If the cabinet doors are to be flush with the cabinet front, they should be fitted as follows:

Check the door opening for squareness. If it is square, measure the height of the door opening and transfer this distance to the door. Plane the edges to these lines. Repeat these operations in fitting the width of the door. Allow 1/16 inch clearance on all edges between the door and the door opening.

NOTE: If the lipped type of door is used, the fit is determined by the rabbet cuts in the edges. These are made in the same way as on the lipped drawer fronts.

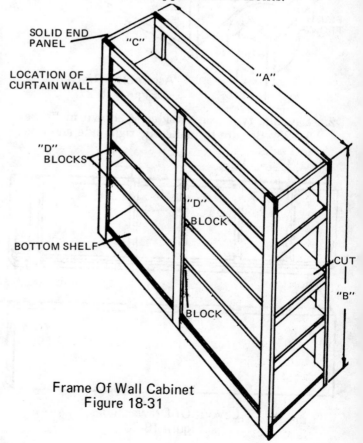

Frame Of Wall Cabinet
Figure 18-31

## How To Build Wall Cabinets

*NOTE:* In figure 18-1 the upper wall cabinet is shown on both sides of the window. The section at each side of the window is built separately and then assembled on the wall as a complete unit.

1. Measure the distance from the edge of the window casing to the end wall. This distance will give the outside length of the right hand cabinet (A, figure 18-31). Measure the distance from the ceiling to within 14 or 16 inches of the counter shelf. This gives the height of the cabinet. See B, figure 18-31.

2. Cut the two end back stiles 25/32" x 2¾" and as long as the cabinet is high. Cut the five back rails to length A, minus the thickness of the end wall of the cabinet. Locate these rails in the frame at the proposed shelf locations to support the back edges of the shelves.

3. Half lap the joints and glue and screw them together.

4. Build a front frame in a similar manner but include only three rails and a middle stile as shown in figure 18-31. This front frame should be as long as the outside dimensions of the cabinet.

5. Build the end C of the cabinet of ½ inch or ¾ inch plywood or solid 25/32 inch stock. It should be as wide as the depth of the wall cabinet minus the thickness of the front frame. The length will be the same as B, figure 18-31.

6. Lay out and cut the stock for the four shelves. They should be the same width as the end C of the cabinet and long enough to extend from one end of the cabinet to the other.

7. Notch out the two back corners of each shelf for the two uprights of the back frame.

8. Nail the end C to the end of the back frame as shown in figure 18-31.

9. Nail the front frame to the edge of the end piece.

10. Square and cut five 25/32" x 2¾" braces as long as the distance between the front and back frames.

11. Nail the braces at the right hand end of the back frame opposite each back rail. Figure 18-31.

12. Nail through the front stile into the ends of these braces. Keep the braces square with the faces of the back and front frames.

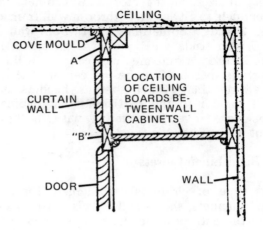

Top Of Wall Cabinet
Figure 18-32

13. Install the shelves and fasten them to the tops of the rails in the back frame and to the braces at the end of the frames. Screw small blocks under the shelves on the middle and left hand stiles of the front frame to support the shelves at these points. See D. Nail or screw the shelves to these blocks.

14. Hang the frame to the ceiling by nailing strips to the inside of the front top rail of the front frame and into the ceiling joists. The strips should be about 1 5/8" x 1 5/8". Nail the back frame to studs in the back wall.

15. Layout, build and hang the left hand wall cabinet in the same manner. Connect the cabinets with rails 25/32" x 2¾". See A and B, figure 18-32.

16. Fit the doors in the same manner as those of the lower cabinet.

17. Measure the length and width of the front curtain wall board. This board should be the same thickness as the lip on the doors. Round the edges and nail the board to the faces of the two erected cabinets and rails A and B as shown in figure 18-32.

18. Measure, cut and fit the ceiling board between the top ends of the two wall cabinets above the sink as shown in figure 18-31.

19. Install curtain walls in the upper sections of the two wall cabinets in the same manner.

20. Cut and nail mouldings to the ceiling board and at the front curtain wall as shown in figure 18-32.

### Medicine Cabinets

These cabinets are made either of aluminum, wood, or enameled steel, and come ready to install in a variety of sizes. Most factory built cabinets are shallow enough to fit into a bathroom wall framed with 2 x 4 studs. Sometimes a bathroom wall is built of 6 inch studs which would allow a deeper cabinet to be used. Some medicine cabinets will fit between studs spaced 16 inches on center. Others which are wider than 14 inches require headers and uprights framed into the partition. The cabinet should be placed over the lavatory with the bottom about 4 feet from the floor.

## How To Build Linen Closets

This type of closet is used largely for the storage of blankets, sheets and towels. It may be located in the bathroom, in the hall between bedrooms, or in a bedroom as a combination clothes closet and linen closet. It usually has drawers in the lower part and shelves in the upper part. If the closet is to be used for storage of woolens which might be damaged by moths, it may be lined with 3/8 inch cedar.

Sometimes the bottom part of a linen closet has a space for a hamper for soiled clothes or a chute to the basement for the same purpose. Figure 18-33 shows a typical linen closet for a small home.

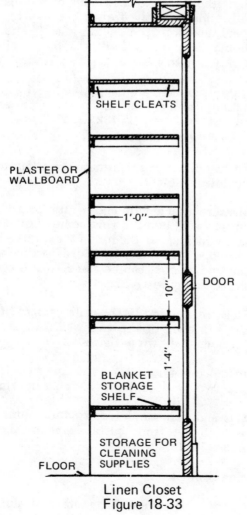

PLASTER OR WALLBOARD

SHELF CLEATS

1'-0"

10"

DOOR

1'-4"

BLANKET STORAGE SHELF

STORAGE FOR CLEANING SUPPLIES

FLOOR

Linen Closet
Figure 18-33

1. Mark the locations of the shelf cleats on one end wall of the closet. Use a spirit level to get these marks on the opposite end wall at the same height. Nail the shelf cleats to these marks on the walls.

2. Cut, fit and nail the shelves on the cleats.

3. Fit the doors, allowing ¾ inch clearance between the floor and the bottom of the lower door.

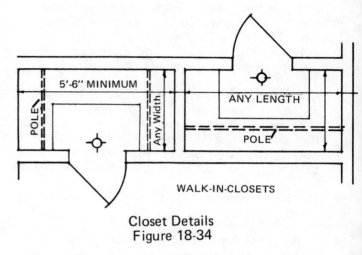

5'-6" MINIMUM

POLE

Any Width

ANY LENGTH

POLE

WALK-IN-CLOSETS

Closet Details
Figure 18-34

## Clothes Closets

Walk-in clothes closets are used frequently in larger custom built homes. Figure 18-34 shows a plan view of two walk-in closets. They should be provided with the necessary drawers, shelves, hanging rods and hook strips for the storage of wearing apparel.

Figure 18-35 shows a section of a series of trays and shelves that may be used in a large or small clothes closet or in a linen closet. The dimensions of the trays are such that they are convenient for towels, bed linen and wearing apparel.

## How To Build Recessed Niches

Some architectural styles call for the construction of recessed niches in walls. These openings can serve as a small shelf or for holding ornaments. Larger shelves require a framed cabinet permanently built on the wall. The width of these openings is generally the distance between two studs. If the opening must be wider, the proper headers should be installed in the framework of the building. A frame is used when the opening is cased. If casings are omitted and the opening is arched, the framework of the opening is made of thin plywood bent to form the arch. Figure 18-36 shows a typical wall niche.

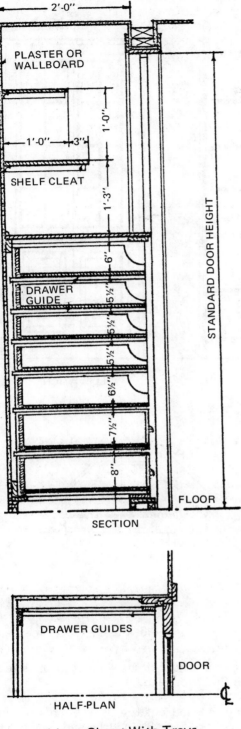

SECTION

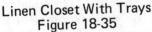

HALF-PLAN

Linen Closet With Trays
Figure 18-35

1. Measure the width, height and depth of the opening in the wall.

2. Lay out and cut 25/32 inch material 1½ inches wider than the depth of the opening and about 4 inches longer than the width of the cabinet opening.

3. Lay out this piece like a window stool as shown in figure 18-36.

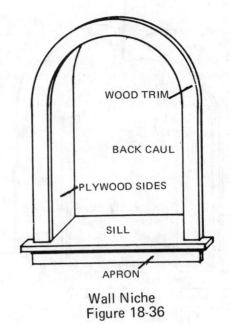

Wall Niche
Figure 18-36

*NOTE:* Allow ¾ inch for the back of the niche, and 1½ inches for the overhang over the wall line. Assuming the niche is to be placed in a 3 5/8 inch partition, the measurements of the stool would be as shown in figure 18-37.

4. Cut two cauls of ¾ inch stock to form the arched jamb piece. The front caul should be as high as the opening and 13 3/8 inches wide (figure 18-38). The back caul should be ¾ inch higher so it can be nailed against the back of the stool.

5. Temporarily nail the front caul to the stool as shown by the dotted lines in figure 18-38. Nail the back caul flush with the bottom of the back edge of the stool.

6. Measure with a flexible rule the length of the plywood that will make up the sides and arch of the niche.

7. Cut a piece of thin plywood to this length and to the width B in figure 18-37.

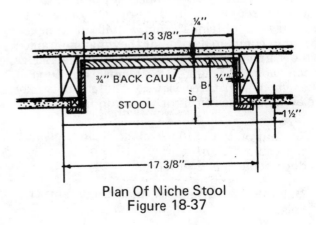

Plan Of Niche Stool
Figure 18-37

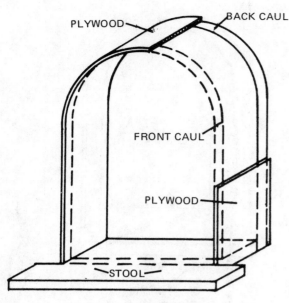

Framework Of Niche
Figure 18-38

8. Nail one end of the plywood to one end of the stool and bend it around the cauls. Nail it to the other end with 1¼ inch flat head nails.

9. Nail the back edge of the plywood to the back caul and remove the front caul.

10. Lay out and cut a casing from ½ inch or 25/32 inch stock about 2¼ inches wide.

*NOTE:* Use a radius ¼ inch less than when laying out the cauls. This will allow the casing to overlap the edge of the plywood at the front of the niche.

11. Fit and nail the casing to the stool, arched jamb and wall.

12. Fit, nail and return a small moulding underneath the stool.

## How To Build Corner Cabinets

Corner cabinets are sometimes built into the corners of rooms to hold dishes or ornaments. They may be obtained from a mill in knocked down or in completed form, or they may be framed by the carpenter in the same general manner as kitchen cabinets. Figure 18-39 shows one type of corner cabinet in three views. The cabinets may have either an open front or glazed doors.

1. Lay out on the subfloor an exact floor plan of the cabinet showing the outline of the stiles, door opening and shelves.

2. Make the front frame to these dimensions and heights.

SECTION          ELEVATION

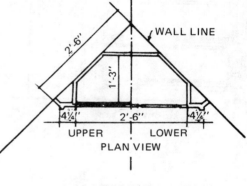

Corner Cabinet
Figure 18-39

3. Lay out and cut the shelves to the size shown on the floor plan.

4. Lay out and cut the back boards of the cabinet. The lengths, widths and bevel cuts may be found by temporarily nailing the top, middle and bottom shelves to the front frame and fitting the back board around the back contour of the shelves as shown. The back may be 25/32 inch stock or ½ inch plywood.

5. Square the assembled frame, shelves and back boards.

*NOTE:* If these shelves are to be adjustable, metal shelf support strips such as shown in figure 18-40 may be used.

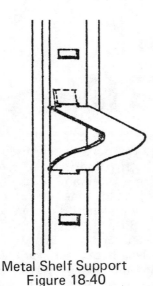

Metal Shelf Support
Figure 18-40

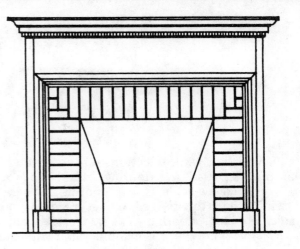

Flush Mantel
Figure 18-41

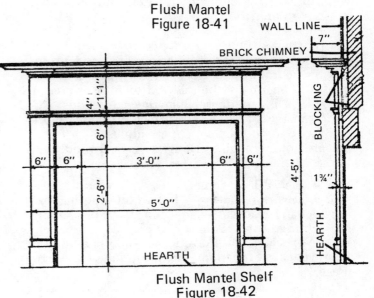

Flush Mantel Shelf
Figure 18-42

6. Cut out and place the required shelf supports on the back boards.

7. Notch the adjustable shelves around the supports so they may be easily removed.

8. Fit and nail the side casings of the front frame to the wall surface.

9. Lay out and cut the ornamental head casing from 25/32" x 8" stock similar in design to the one shown in figure 18-39. Nail it in place.

10. Fit the glazed and paneled doors by the same method used in fitting kitchen cabinet doors.

## Mantel Shelves

The fireplace is usually decorated by placing a mantel shelf above the opening. This shelf may be almost any height and size depending upon the shape and size of the chimney. When the brickwork of the fireplace is built flush with the wall line, a casing, frieze and cap is built around the brickwork. The cap forms a shelf as shown in figure 18-41. Mantels and fireplace trim may be built by the carpenter or may be obtained in standard sizes and styles from the mills and assembled on the job.

## How To Build A Mantel Shelf On A Flush Chimney

*NOTE:* Assume that the brickwork is flush with the face of the wall and that the mantel shelf is supported by pilasters as shown in figure 18-41.

1. Lay out the length and width of the pilasters and frieze according to the size of the chimney. Cut them accordingly.

2. Lay out and build the shelf according to the width of the chimney and similar to that shown in figure 18-41.

3. Assemble the frieze and pilasters by nailing them in a plumb position on the wall and overlapping the sides of the chimney about 1 inch.

4. Place wooden plugs in the masonry joints so that the mantel shelf may be securely attached to the masonry surface.

5. Place the assembled mantel shelf on top of the pilasters across the face of the chimney. Nail it in a level position to the wooden plugs in the joints of the masonry.

*NOTE:* It is sometimes necessary to scribe the shelf to the wall surface. A small moulding may be used to cover an unscribed joint.

The surfaces of the pilasters and frieze may be decorated by fluting, by forming miniature columns and bases, or by mitering mouldings in various designs.

6. Finish the pilaster and frieze surfaces similar to the one shown in figure 18-41. Set all nails and sand the surfaces.

# Chapter 19
# WOOD FLOORING

There is a wide selection of wood materials that may be used for flooring. Hardwoods and softwoods are available as strip flooring in a variety of widths and thicknesses and as random width planks and block flooring. Tile flooring is available in a particleboard which is manufactured with small wood particles combined with resin and fabricated under high pressure.

Softwood finish flooring costs less than most hardwood species and is often used to good advantage in bedroom and closet areas where traffic is light. It might also be selected to fit the interior decor. It is less dense than the hardwoods, less wear resistant, and shows surface abrasions more readily. Softwoods most commonly used for flooring are southern pine, Douglas fir, redwood, and western hemlock.

Table 19-1 lists the grades and description of softwood strip flooring. Softwood flooring has tongued-and-grooved edges and may be hollow backed or grooved. Some types are also end matched. Vertical grain flooring generally has better wearing qualities than flat grain flooring under hard usage.

Hardwoods most commonly used for flooring are red and white oak, beech, birch, maple, and pecan. Table 19-1 lists grades, types, and sizes. Manufacturers supply both prefinished and unfinished flooring.

Perhaps the most widely used pattern is a 25/32" x 2¼" strip flooring. These strips are laid length wise in a room and normally at right angles to the floor joists. Some type of a subfloor of diagonal boards or plywood is normally used under the finish floor. Strip flooring of this type is tongued-and-grooved and end-matched (figure 19-2). Strips are random length and may vary from 2 to 16 feet or more. End-matched strip flooring in 25/32 inch thickness is generally hollow backed (figure 19-2, A). The face is slightly wider than the bottom so that tight joints result when flooring is laid. The tongue fits tightly into the groove to prevent movement and floor "squeaks." All of these details are designed to provide beautiful finished floors that require a minimum of maintenance.

Another matched pattern may be obtained in 3/8" x 2" size (figure 19-2, B). This is commonly used for remodeling work or when subfloor is edge-blocked or thick enough to provide very little deflection under loads.

Square edged strip flooring (figure 19-2, C) might also be used occasionally. It is usually 3/8" x 2" in size and is laid up over a substantial subfloor. Face nailing is required for this type.

Flooring should be laid after plastering or other interior wall and ceiling finish is completed

| Species | Grain orientation | Size | | First grade | Second grade | Third grade |
| | | Thickness | Width | | | |
| --- | --- | --- | --- | --- | --- | --- |
| | | | SOFTWOODS | | | |
| Douglas-fir and hemlock | Edge grain | $\frac{25}{32}$ | 2⅜–5³⁄₁₆ | B and Better | C | D |
| | Flat grain | $\frac{25}{32}$ | 2⅜–5³⁄₁₆ | C and Better | D | -------------- |
| Southern pine | Edge grain and Flat grain | ⁵⁄₁₆–1⁵⁄₁₆ | 1¾–5⁷⁄₁₆ | B and Better | C and Better | D (and No. 2) |
| | | | HARDWOODS | | | |
| Oak | Edge grain | $\frac{25}{32}$ | 1½–3¼ | Clear | Select | -------------- |
| | Flat grain | ⅜ | 1½, 2 | Clear | Select | No. 1 Common |
| | | ½ | 1½, 2 | | | |
| Beech, birch, maple, and pecan | | $\frac{25}{32}$ | 1½–3¼ | First grade | Second grade | -------------- |
| | | ⅜ | 1½, 2 | | | |
| | | ½ | 1½, 2 | | | |

Grades And Description Of Strip Flooring
Table 19-1

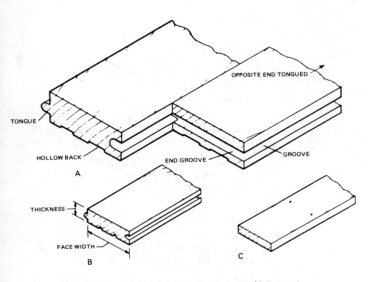

A Side And End-Matched = 25/32 Inch
B Thin Flooring Strips - matched
C Thin Flooring Strips - Square-Edged

Types Of Strip Flooring
Figure 19-2

and dried out, windows and exterior doors are in place, and most of the interior trim, except base, casing, and jambs, are supplied, so that it may not be damaged by wetting or by construction activity.

Board subfloors should be clean and level and covered with a deadening felt or heavy building paper. This felt or paper will stop a certain amount of dust, will somewhat deaden sound, and, where a crawl space is used, will increase the warmth of the floor by preventing air infiltration. To provide nailing into the joists wherever possible, location of the joists should be chalklined on the paper as a guide. Plywood subfloor does not normally require building paper.

Strip flooring should normally be laid crosswise to the floor joists (figure 19-3). In conventionally designed houses, the floor joists span the width of the building over a center supporting beam or wall. Thus, the finish flooring of the entire floor area of a rectangular house will be laid in the same direction. Flooring with "I" or "T" shaped plans will usually have a direction change at the wings, depending on joist direction. As joists usually span the short way in a living room, the flooring will be laid lengthwise to the room. This is desirable appearance wise and also will reduce shrinkage and swelling effects on the flooring during seasonal changes.

Flooring should be delivered only during dry weather and stored in the warmest and driest place available in the house. Moisture absorbed after delivery to the house site is one of the most common causes of open joints between flooring strips that appear after several months of the heating season.

Floor squeaks are usually caused by movement of one board against another. Such movement may occur because: (a) Floor joists are too light, causing excessive deflection, (b) sleepers over concrete slabs are not held down tightly, (c) tongues are loose fitting, or (d) nailing is poor. Adequate nailing is an important means of minimizing squeaks, and another is to apply the finish floors only after the joists have dried to 12 percent moisture content or less. A much better job results when it is possible to nail the finish floor through the subfloor into the joists than if the finish floor is nailed only to the subfloor.

Various types of nails are used in nailing different thicknesses of flooring. For 25/32 inch flooring, it is best to use 8d flooring nails; for ½

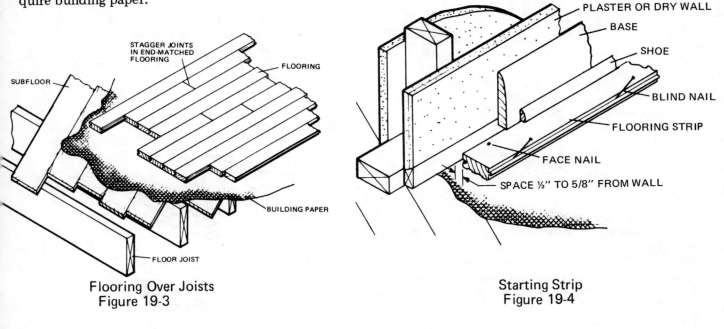

Flooring Over Joists
Figure 19-3

Starting Strip
Figure 19-4

inch, 6d; and for 3/8 inch 4d casing nails. (All the foregoing are blind nailed.) For thinner square-edge flooring, it is best to use a 1½ inch flooring brad and face nail every 7 inches with two nails, one near each edge of the strip, into the subfloor.

Other types of nails, such as the ring shank and screw shank type, have been developed in recent years for nailing of flooring. In using them, it is well to check with the floor manufacturer's recommendations as to size and diameter for specific uses. Flooring brads are also available with blunted points to prevent splitting of the tongue.

Figure 19-4 shows the method of nailing the first strip of flooring placed ½ to 5/8 inch away from the wall. The space is to allow for expansion of the flooring when moisture content increases. The nail is driven straight down through the board at the groove edge. The nails should be driven into the joist and near enough to the edge so that they will be covered by the base or shoe moulding. The first strip of flooring can also be nailed through the tongue. Figure 19-5 shows in detail how nails should be driven into the tongue of the flooring at an angle of 45 to 50 degrees. The nail should not be driven quite flush so as to prevent damaging the edge by the hammerhead (figure 19-6). The nail can be set with the end of a large size nail set or by laying the nail set flatwise against the flooring (figure 19-6). Nailing devices using standard flooring or special nails are often used by flooring contractors. One blow of the hammer on the plunger drives and sets the nail.

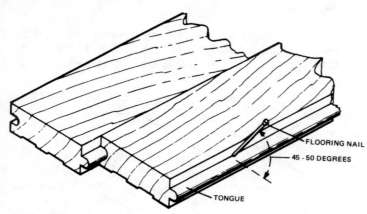

Nailing Strip Flooring
Figure 19-5

To prevent splitting the flooring, it is sometimes desirable to predrill through the tongue, especially at the ends of the strip. For the second course of flooring from the wall, select pieces so that the butt joints will be well separated from those in the first course. Under normal conditions, each board should be driven up tightly. Crooked pieces may require wedging to force them into

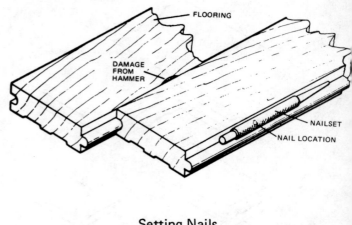

Setting Nails
Figure 19-6

alignment or may be cut and used at the ends of the course or in closets. In completing the flooring, a ½ to 5/8 inch space is provided between the wall and the last flooring strip. Because of the closeness of the wall, this strip is usually face-nailed so that the base or shoe covers the set nailheads.

## How To Lay Strip Flooring

1. Sweep all particles from the subfloor. Inspect the surface for loose boards and imperfections. Be sure that each board is fully face nailed to the joists.

2. Lay a strip of building paper or felt on the floor where the flooring is to be started.

3. Select long pieces of flooring and cut the first course of boards to length so that they extend about ½ inch under the baseboards on each end.

*NOTE:* If it is necessary to make butt joints of the ends of the pieces, use a try square to mark the cut. Make the cut on a slant of 1/32 inch on 1 inch. See figure 19-7.

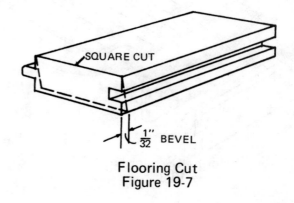

Flooring Cut
Figure 19-7

4. Allow the groove edge of the flooring to extend under the baseboard and to within 5/8 inch of the wall. Straighten the tongue edge and face nail the flooring near the groove so that the base shoe will later cover the nail. Space these nails about 16 inches apart and nail into joists if possible.

*NOTE:* If the room is large, use a chalked line as a guide for the first flooring strips.

5. Select pieces for the second course of flooring. Use lengths that will locate the butt joints of this course as far away from the first course joints as possible.

6. Toenail these boards as shown in figure 19-8.

*NOTE:* Often 13/16 inch and 1 1/16 inch hardwood flooring is drilled at 16 inch intervals for nailing.

7. Use a short piece of flooring and a hammer to drive the second course of flooring up tight to the first course.

*NOTE:* Do not depend entirely upon the toenailing to draw the boards together. Use a chisel or pinch bar and a short piece of flooring to pry the boards up tightly. See figure 19-8. When the joint is tight, drive the nail home. Be careful not to injure the top edge of the tongued flooring. Do not use the pinch bar or chisel unless it is necessary. Use the bar with even pressure in each case. When undue pressure is necessary, there is generally something wrong besides the normal fitting of the joint, and the board should be loosened and examined to find the cause.

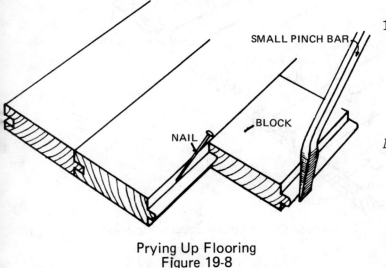

Prying Up Flooring
Figure 19-8

Good tongue-and-groove flooring is perfectly machined for a tight fit and unless the flooring has become damp, it will draw up tight. A common reason for a poor flooring job is that the carpenter may injure the tongue edge of the flooring with his hammer. This causes difficulty in drawing up the next board. If the tongue is injured, this part should be carefully cut away so as not to interfere with the next board.

8. Lay the succeeding courses of flooring in the same manner as the second course. Distribute the butt joints over the surface as evenly as possible.

9. When the opposite side of the room is reached, rip a flooring board to fit under the baseboard if necessary so that the base shoe will cover the joint between the last flooring board and the baseboard.

*NOTE:* If the direction of the flooring changes at the doors or if it is to be butted against a door threshold, temporarily nail a straightedge on the subfloor so the square ends of the finish floor may be butted to it to form a straight joint at this point. See figure 19-9.

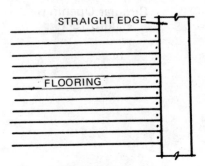

Forming Straight Butt Joints
Figure 19-9

10. Face nail the butts of the flooring boards at doorways and thresholds. Plane the groove off the flooring board that is to be used against the ends of the flooring when the straightedge is removed. Face nail and toenail this board and continue laying the flooring.

*NOTE:* If the flooring is to be fitted around irregular openings, use dividers, sliding T bevel or cardboard and scribers to lay out the opening on the flooring boards. See figure 19-10. Lay several pieces of flooring boards together tightly. Measure the diameter of the opening if it is circular, and outline the opening with the dividers on several assembled floor boards. See figure 19-11.

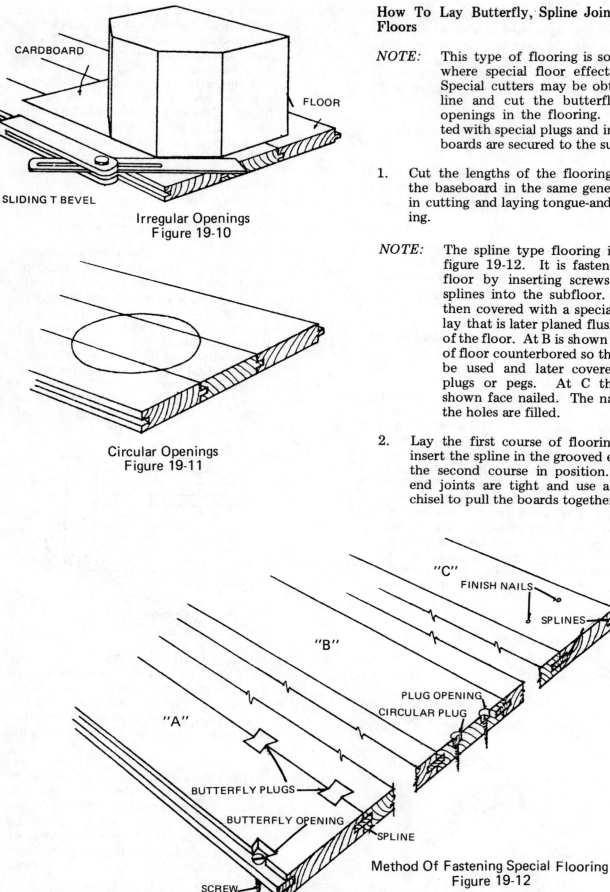

CARDBOARD

FLOOR

SLIDING T BEVEL

Irregular Openings
Figure 19-10

Circular Openings
Figure 19-11

**How To Lay Butterfly, Spline Joints And Plank Floors**

*NOTE:* This type of flooring is sometimes used where special floor effects are desired. Special cutters may be obtained to outline and cut the butterfly and dowel openings in the flooring. These are fitted with special plugs and inlays after the boards are secured to the subfloor.

1. Cut the lengths of the flooring to fit under the baseboard in the same general manner as in cutting and laying tongue-and-groove flooring.

*NOTE:* The spline type flooring is shown at A, figure 19-12. It is fastened to the subfloor by inserting screws through the splines into the subfloor. The screw is then covered with a special butterfly inlay that is later planed flush with the top of the floor. At B is shown the same type of floor counterbored so that screws may be used and later covered with wood plugs or pegs. At C the boards are shown face nailed. The nails are set and the holes are filled.

2. Lay the first course of flooring in position, insert the spline in the grooved edge and place the second course in position. Be sure the end joints are tight and use a pinch bar or chisel to pull the boards together.

"C"
FINISH NAILS
SPLINES

"B"
PLUG OPENING
CIRCULAR PLUG

"A"
BUTTERFLY PLUGS
BUTTERFLY OPENING
SPLINE

SCREW
SPLINE

Method Of Fastening Special Flooring
Figure 19-12

3. Nail blocks of wood on the subfloor to hold the finish floor courses tightly together.

4. Cut the butterfly opening at the joint by using a special cutter for this purpose or by using a router and butterfly guide.

5. Drill and countersink a hole through the spline at the bottom of the opening and fasten the flooring to the subfloor with a 1¼ inch flat head screw as shown at A.

6. Cover the screws by gluing and inserting the inlays. Finish them flush with the surface of the floor.

*NOTE:* The location of the inlays may be staggered at random over the surface of the floor so as to give a pleasing appearance.

7. Use a Forstner bit to drill the holes for the plugs as shown at B. Insert the screws and plugs in the same general manner as when fitting the butterfly inlays.

8. Facenail the flooring as shown at C. Be sure that the hammer does not injure the surface of the flooring and that the nails are long enough to go through the subfloor into the joists.

*NOTE:* Finishing, casing or cut nails may be used. The finishing nail holes should be filled with filler to match the floor whereas the casing or cut nail holes should be filled with a darker filler to give a pegged effect to the floor surface.

## Strip Flooring Installed Over Concrete

The most important factor in installing wood strip flooring over concrete is the use of a good vapor barrier under the slab to resist the movement of ground moisture and vapor. The vapor barrier is placed under the slab during construction. However, an alternate method must be used when the concrete is already in place.

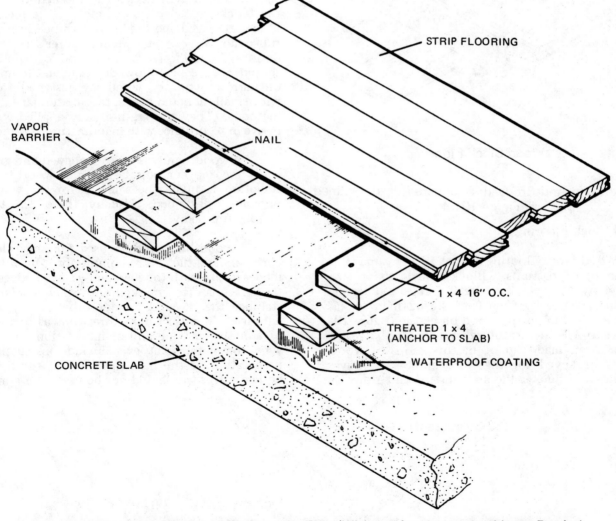

Base For Wood Flooring On Concrete Slab (Without An Underlying Vapor Barrier)
Figure 19-13

One system of preparing a base for wood flooring when there is no vapor barrier under the slab is shown in figure 19-13. To resist decay, treated 1" x 4" furring strips are anchored to the existing slab, shimming when necessary to provide a level base. Strips should be spaced no more than 16 inches on center. A good waterproof or water-vapor resistant coating on the concrete before the treated strips are applied is usually recommended to aid in reducing moisture movement. A vapor barrier, such as a 4-mil polyethylene or similar membrane, is then laid over the anchored 1" x 4" wood strips and a second set of 1 by 4's nailed to the first. Use 1½ inch long nails spaced 12 to 16 inches apart in a staggered pattern. The moisture content of these second members should be about the same as that of the strip flooring to be applied. Strip flooring can then be installed as previously described.

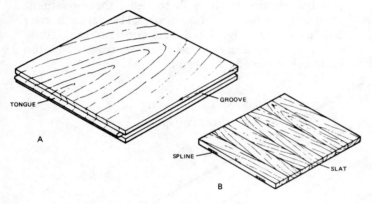

Wood Block Flooring:

A, Tongued-And-Grooved; B, Square-Edged - Splined
Figure 19-14

## Wood Block Flooring

Wood block flooring (figure 19-14) is made in a number of patterns. Blocks may vary in size from 4 by 4 inches to 9 by 9 inches and larger. Thickness varies by type from 25/32 inch for laminated blocking or plywood block tile (figure 19-14, A) to 1/8 inch stabilized veneer. Solid wood tile is often made up of narrow strips of wood splined or keyed together in a number of ways. Edges of the thicker tile are tongued and grooved,

but thinner sections of wood are usually square edged (figure 19-14, B). Plywood blocks may be 3/8 inch and thicker and are usually tongued-and-grooved. Many block floors are factory finished and require only waxing after installation.

Wood and particleboard blocks are, for the most part, applied with adhesive on a plywood or similar base. The exception is 25/32 inch wood block floor, which has tongues on two edges and grooves on the other two edges. If the base is wood, these tiles are commonly nailed through the tongue into the subfloor. However, wood block may be applied on concrete slabs with an adhesive. Wood block flooring is installed by changing the grain direction of alternate blocks. This minimizes the effects of shrinking and swelling of the wood.

One type of wood floor tile is made up of a number of narrow slats to form 4" x 4" and larger squares. Four or more of these squares, with alternating grain direction, form a block. Slats, squares, and blocks are held together with an easily removed membrane. Adhesive is spread on the concrete slab or underlayment with a notched trowel and the blocks installed immediately. The membrane is then removed and the blocks tamped in place for full adhesive contact. Manufacturer's recommendations for adhesive and method of application should always be followed. Similar tile made up of narrow strips of wood are fastened together with small rabbeted cleats, tape or similar fastening methods. They too are normally applied with adhesive in accordance with manufacturer's directions.

Plywood squares with tongued-and-grooved edges are another popular form of wood tile. Installation is much the same as for the wood tile previously described. Usually, tile of this type is factory finished.

A wood base product used for finish floors is particleboard tile. It is commonly 9 by 9 by 3/8 inches in size with tongued-and-grooved edges. The back face is often marked with small saw kerfs to stabilize the tile and provide a better key for the adhesive. Manufacturer's directions as to the type of adhesive and method of installation are usually very complete; some even include instruction on preparation of the base upon which the tile is to be laid. This tile should not be used over concrete.

# Chapter 20

# ESTIMATING FINISH CARPENTRY

The figures in this chapter will be useful when developing labor estimates for finish carpentry work. These figures are based on a large number of jobs but may not apply in cases where inexperienced labor, lack of easy access, inadequate tools or equipment, small size or inadequate supervision influence production. No allowance is made for supervision or other unproductive labor. Where unproductive labor is used, it should be figured separately.

Judgement must be used in estimating any job. These figures are included as an aid to good judgement rather than a replacement for it. Many types of work can be done in either a careless or a craftsman - like manner and the time required may vary greatly depending on the class of work required. The figures here are based on good quality work, but exceptionally fine work may take longer. Jobs such as cabinet making and stair construction are very difficult to estimate and only reasonable standards can be given. The times given in all cases are the total man hours and include both skilled and unskilled labor where unskilled labor is used.

## Cornice

A simple cornice consisting of two members (frieze and crown moulding) can be placed at a rate of about 7 to 8 man hours per 100 linear feet. A single member fascia up to 6" wide can be installed at a rate of about 3½ to 4 man hours per 100 linear feet. A closed cornice consisting of a fascia, precut and ventilated soffit, moulding and frieze will take about 12 man hours to install 100 linear feet. A wide box cornice will take about 15 hours per 100 linear feet including cutting and installing lookouts and fitting the soffit. Prefabricated metal soffit 12" to 18" wide will be installed at 3 to 3½ man hours per 100 linear feet.

## Gutters And Downspouts

Ten to twelve man hours are required to cut, fit, caulk and install 100 linear feet of wood gutter. Each downspout will add about ¾ man hours to the job. One hundred linear feet of formed metal gutter can be installed in 7½ to 8 hours. Add ½ man hour for each downspout.

## Wood Shingle Roofing

At standard 5" exposure an experienced shingler can cover about 100 square feet of roof in 2½ hours. This includes the time required to move materials to the roof and cover hips and valleys. Less experienced craftsmen may require 3 to 3½ hours to cover 100 square feet including placing ridge and valley shingles. At 6" or 8" exposure, about ½ hour to 1 hour less will be required per 100 square feet. Pitches over 9 in 12 will require more time: figure 1 hour additional for scaffolding on any pitch over 9 in 12. Roll or preformed valley flashing can be placed at 4 to 4½ man hours per 100 linear feet. Figure about ¾ hour to flash and caulk around a chimney and about 10 man hours per 100 linear feet for flashing against a masonry wall. Installing shingles over an existing asphalt or shingle roof will take no more time than new construction. However allow ½ man hour per 100 square feet for preparing the roof for reshingling and one man hour per 100 square feet extra if the old roof covering must be removed.

## Composition Roofing

Roll roofing can be installed at nearly 100 square feet per man hour including valley strip where required. Individual asphalt shingles require about 3½ man hours per 100 square feet and strip shingles can be laid at about 2½ man hours per 100 square feet. On pitch roofs over 9 in 12 or roofs that are small or cut up allow an additional one man hour per 100 square feet. Where a felt underlay is required, add ¾ hour per 100 square feet. Asbestos shingles can be applied at between 4 and 7 man hours per 100 square feet. The larger 14" x 30" shingles require considerably less labor than the smaller sizes, 9" x 16", especially on larger roofs. Built-up felt and asphalt roofing can be figured using the rates given in table 20-1.

| | |
|---|---|
| 2 ply, 2 coat | 2.0 |
| 3 ply, 3 coat | 3.0 |
| 4 ply, 4 coat | 4.5 |
| 5 ply, 4 coat | 5.0 |
| Typical rock or slag surface | 1.0 |

Built-Up Roofing, Man Hours Per 100 S.F.
Table 20-1

## Windows

A window frame takes about one man hour to set. Double or triple frames may take up to two hours for the unit. Add about one hour to 1½ hours to cut, fit and install sash in each frame and about one hour to install trim. A factory built, unassembled double hung or casement window should take less than 2½ hours including frame, sash, trim and hardware. Storm windows may add up to 1 hour to this figure. A fully prefabricated and assembled wood or metal window can be set in a prepared opening in less than 1½ man hours. Larger sizes over 5½ feet wide will require up to 2 hours per opening.

## Doors

Door installations can be figured using table 20-2.

Fully assembled, prehung doors can be installed in about ½ hour. Highly experienced craftsmen using modern power equipment can reduce installation times for doors by 50% or more. Weatherstripping can be installed in about 1½ hours.

| Exterior Doors | Single | Double |
|---|---|---|
| Make and set frame | 2 | 3 |
| Hang door | 1¼ | 2½ |
| Install lockset | ¾ | 1 |
| Install trim | 1 | 1½ |
| | 5 | 8 |

| Interior Doors | Single |
|---|---|
| Install head and jambs | 1 |
| Hang door (3 hinges) | 1¼ |
| Install lockset | 1 |
| Install trim | ¾ |
| | 4 |

Door Installation Man Hours
Table 20-2

## Siding

Use Table 20-3 to figure installation man-hours for siding. Table 20-3 is based on good quality work with mitered corners. Use of factory-made corners will eliminate miter cuts and reduce installation times up to 25%.

| | |
|---|---|
| Most patterns,   6″ | 21 |
| Most patterns,   8″ | 19 |
| Most patterns, 10″ or 12″ | 17 |
| Bevel or lap,   6″ | 22 |
| Bevel or lap,   8″ | 20 |
| Bevel or lap, 10″ to 12″ | 18 |
| Vertical patterns,   6″ or 8″ | 30 |
| Vertical patterns, 10″ or 12″ | 26 |
| Sheet siding, 4′ x 8′ panels | 14 |

Siding Installation Man-Hours Per 1000 S.F.
Table 20-3

| | | Nominal Size | WIDTH | | AREA FACTOR* | LBS. NAILS PER 1000 B.F. BACKING SPACING | | | |
|---|---|---|---|---|---|---|---|---|---|
| | | | Dress | Face | | 12″ | 16″ | 20″ | 24″ |
| SHIPLAP | | 1 x 6 | 5 7/16 | 4 15/16 | 1.22 | 44 | 34 | 29 | 24 |
| | | 1 x 8 | 7 1/8 | 6 5/8 | 1.21 | 32 | 25 | 21 | 17 |
| | | 1 x 10 | 9 1/8 | 8 5/8 | 1.16 | 37 | 29 | 25 | 20 |
| | | 1 x 12 | 11 1/8 | 10 5/8 | 1.13 | 35 | 28 | 24 | 20 |
| TONGUE AND GROOVE | | 1 x 4 | 3 7/16 | 3 3/16 | 1.26 | 66 | 52 | 44 | 36 |
| | | 1 x 6 | 5 7/16 | 5 3/16 | 1.16 | 43 | 33 | 28 | 23 |
| | | 1 x 8 | 7 1/8 | 6 7/8 | 1.16 | 32 | 24 | 21 | 17 |
| | | 1 x 10 | 9 1/8 | 8 7/8 | 1.13 | 37 | 29 | 24 | 20 |
| | | 1 x 12 | 11 1/8 | 10 7/8 | 1.10 | 34 | 25 | 23 | 20 |
| S4S | | 1 x 4 | 3 1/2 | 3 1/2 | 1.14 | 60 | 47 | 40 | 33 |
| | | 1 x 6 | 5 1/2 | 5 1/2 | 1.09 | 40 | 31 | 26 | 22 |
| | | 1 x 8 | 7 1/4 | 7 1/4 | 1.10 | 30 | 23 | 20 | 17 |
| | | 1 x 10 | 9 1/4 | 9 1/4 | 1.08 | 36 | 28 | 24 | 19 |
| | | 1 x 12 | 11 1/4 | 11 1/4 | 1.07 | 32 | 25 | 22 | 19 |
| PANELING PATTERNS | | 1 x 6 | 5 7/16 | 5 1/16 | 1.19 | 44 | 34 | 29 | 24 |
| | | 1 x 8 | 7 1/8 | 6 3/4 | 1.19 | 32 | 25 | 21 | 17 |
| | | 1 x 10 | 9 1/8 | 8 3/4 | 1.14 | 37 | 29 | 25 | 20 |
| | | 1 x 12 | 11 1/8 | 10 3/4 | 1.12 | 35 | 28 | 24 | 20 |
| BEVEL SIDING | | 1 x 4 | 3 1/2 | 3 1/2 | 1.60 | 25 | 17 | 13 | 11 |
| | | 1 x 6 | 5 1/2 | 5 1/2 | 1.33 | 16 | 11 | 9 | 7 |
| | | 1 x 8 | 7 1/4 | 7 1/4 | 1.28 | 10 | 8 | 7 | 6 |
| | | 1 x 10 | 9 1/4 | 9 1/4 | 1.21 | 21 | 16 | 13 | 11 |
| | | 1 x 12 | 11 1/4 | 11 1/4 | 1.17 | 18 | 14 | 11 | 9 |

*   Add 5 B.F. per 100 S.F. for waste and 4 B.F. per 100 S.F. for diagonal patterns.

Materials For Board Siding
Table 20-4

Table 20-4 lists the nominal sizes, actual sizes, board footage required to cover each square foot of wall at maximum design exposure and nails required.

Where less than maximum exposures are used for bevel siding the quantity of materials must be increased. See Table 20-5.

| Size | Exposure | Bd. Ft. Per Sq. Ft. Of Wall Area | LBS. NAILS PER MBM OF SIDING Stud Spacing | | |
|---|---|---|---|---|---|
| | | | 16" | 20" | 24" |
| 4" | 2½" | 1.75 | 17 | 13 | 11 |
| | 2¾" | 1.60 | | | |
| 6" | 4½" | 1.40 | 11 | 9 | 7 |
| | 4¾" | 1.33 | | | |
| 8" | 6" | 1.32 | 8 | 7 | 6 |
| | 6½" | 1.23 | | | |
| 10" | 8" | 1.25 | 16 | 13 | 11 |
| | 8½" | 1.18 | | | |
| 12" | 10" | 1.19 | 14 | 11 | 9 |
| | 10½" | 1.14 | | | |

Bevel Siding Coverage
Table 20-5

Wood and asbestos shingles can be installed on sidewalls in from 4 to 5 hours per 100 square feet depending on the exposure used and shingle size. Water table and belt courses can be installed at 100 linear feet per 5 man hours. For corner board, figure 4 man hours per 100 linear feet.

## Porch Trim

Most sizes of porch flooring can be laid at 3½ hours per 100 square feet. Factory built columns up to 12 feet high can be installed in about 2 hours including the cap and base. A built-up structural porch column can be assembled and installed in about 2½ hours. Smaller decorative posts take between ½ and 1 hour per post to install. Figure 8 to 10 man hours to lay out, cut, fit and install a flight of 4 or 5 porch steps. Building porch handrail may take as much as 35 hours per 100 linear feet including balustrade and posts. A simple railing will take about 25 hours per 100 linear feet, especially where there are few or no corner posts. Wrought iron railing can be installed at a rate of 20 to 25 man hours per 100 linear feet including setting posts. Long straight runs will require even less time.

## Interior Wall Cover

Lath and plaster can be applied at rates listed in Table 20-6.

| | |
|---|---|
| Wood grounds, per 100 L.F. | 3 |
| Metal corner bead, per 100 L.F. | 4 |
| Cornerite, per 100 L.F. | 2 |
| Gypsum lath, wall, per 100 S.Y. | 9 |
| Metal lath, wall, per 100 S.Y. | 9½ |
| Gypsum lath, ceiling, per 100 S.Y. | 10 |
| Metal lath, ceiling, per 100 S.Y. | 10½ |
| Two coat plaster, per 100 S.Y. | 23 |
| Three coat plaster, per 100 S.Y. | 28 |
| Two coat with Keene's Cement Finish, per 100 S.Y. | 30 |
| Three coat with Keene's Cement Finish, per 100 S.Y. | 37 |

Lath And Plaster Man Hours
Table 20-6

Gypsum lath comes in bundles with 6 lath to the bundle. Lath 32 inches wide will cover 23 square feet to the bundle and lath 48 inches wide will cover 32 square feet to the bundle. The following number of 100 pound sacks of sanded plaster are required per 100 square yards of surface at ½ inch coverage: Metal lath-50, gypsum lath-26, masonry-40. For each 1/8 inch more or less in thickness add or deduct for metal lath 12½ sacks, for gypsum lath 6½ sacks, for masonry 10 sacks. One hundred square yards of plaster finish require 7½ sacks for a sand float finish, 6 sacks for a trowel float finish and 4½ sacks of Keene's Cement Finish.

Gypsum wallboard can be applied to walls at a rate of about 1½ to 2 man hours per 100 square feet. Ceilings take about 3 man hours per 100 square feet. Figure joint finishing at one man hour per 100 square feet of wall or ceiling. Two layer jobs will nearly double application time. Approximately ½ pound of filler and 38 feet of tape are required for each 100 square feet of wallboard.

Most sheet paneling can be applied at a rate of 3½ hours per 100 square feet including fitting mouldings where required. Board paneling can be done at about the same rate but exceptionally fine work may take 5 to 6 hours per 100 square feet.

## Stairs And Handrails

The labor required to frame stairways and install treads and risers will vary widely from one job to the next. Highly repetitive jobs done by specialized crews will require less time than indicated below. All figures are for straight runs with only the landings indicated. For a 9 foot rise basement stairway with open risers, no landing, one simple handrail, and cleat or dado treads only, about 8 man hours will be required. For the same stairway with one landing add about three hours to the job. It takes about 7 hours to lay out, cut and install the carriage for a main stairway and about 13 hours additional to cut, fit, install and finish the treads and risers and install a finished simple handrail. Where a landing is included, add about 3 hours. Where materials are precut to size, about 3 hours less will be required. A well-made newel and baluster handrail will take nearly ½ hour per linear foot to complete. An elaborate housed main stairway up to 48 inches wide made from job cut materials and with newels and handrails may take up to 60 hours to complete. A rough plank 12 foot high stairway suitable for exterior use will take about 12 hours including all the basic framing required.

## Moulding

Base moulding can be installed at these rates per 100 linear feet: Single member-3½ man hours, two member-5 man hours, three member-7 man hours. Ceiling crown moulding can be installed at about 6 to 7 man hours per 100 linear feet.

## Ceiling Tile

Tile can be applied to ceilings with staples or metal furring at between 2¼ and 3 hours per 100 square feet. In a large room the larger sizes (12" x 24") will take less time than the smaller tile (12" x 12"). Adhesive jobs take ¼ to ½ hour per 100 square feet longer. Wood furring can be applied over an existing ceiling at about one man hour per 100 square feet. A 2' x 2' suspended ceiling grid can be installed at a rate of 3½ man hours per 100 square feet. Allow extra time for heights over 12 feet. Cutting and laying in the tile or plastic panels and making the grid adjustments that may be necessary seldom take more than one hour for an entire room.

## Cabinets And Closets

Fully factory assembled base or wall cabinets can be installed in between 1 and 2½ hours per unit. Larger units, especially wall units, require more time than smaller cabinets. Completely job built base cabinets require about one hour per square foot of face not including doors or drawers. A well made drawer will take about 1 hour and a door can be cut, fit and prepared for finishing in ½ hour. Taller broom closets take about 5 hours including the door. A clothes closet will take about 2½ hours to complete including doors, hooks, a shelf and pole. Closets over 6 feet long may take somewhat longer. A well-made linen closet takes between 4 and 6 hours to complete.

## Wood Flooring

Softwood finished flooring can be installed at about 2½ man hours per 100 square feet. Narrow 2¼ inch hardwood flooring takes 4½ to 5 hours per 100 square feet and wider strips take about 4 hours per 100 square feet. Floors can be machine sanded using power equipment at a rate of 1½ hours per 100 square feet. Figure about 2 hours per 100 square feet to remove an existing hardwood floor including surface preparation for the new floor.